EARLY
HISTORY OF THE DEKKAN
Down to the Mahomedan Conquest

EARLY HISTORY OF THE DEKKAN

Down to the Mahomedan Conquest

BY

RAMKRISHNA GOPAL BHANDARKAR

GYAN

Published by

GYAN

Gyan Publishing House
5, Ansari Road
Daryaganj, New Delhi-110002
Phone: 011-47034999, 9811692060
E-mail: books@gyanbooks.com

Distribution Network
gyanbooks.com
India, USA, Canada, UK, Australia

ISBN: 978-93-6280-764-9 (PB)
First Published, 1884

2nd Impression 2024

Printed at: Gyan Press, Delhi.

EARLY HISTORY OF THE DEKKAN DOWN TO THE MAHOMEDAN CONQUEST

Author: RAMKRISHNA GOPAL BHANDARKAR

EARLY
HISTORY OF THE DEKKAN

Down to the Mahomedan Conquest

BY

RAMKRISHNA GOPAL BHANDARKAR,
M.A., PH.D., C.I.E.,

HONORARY MEMBER OF THE ROYAL ASIATIC SOCIETY OF GREAT BRITAIN AND IRELAND, OF THE AMERICAN ORIENTAL SOCIETY, AND OF THE ITALIAN ASIATIC SOCIETY; CORRESPONDING MEMBER OF THE GERMAN ORIENTAL SOCIETY AND OF THE IMPERIAL ACADEMY OF SCIENCES, ST. PETERSBURG; FELLOW OF THE UNIVERSITIES OF BOMBAY AND CALCUTTA; LATE PROFESSOR OF ORIENTAL LANGUAGES, DEKKAN COLLEGE.

THIRD EDITION

CHUCKERVERTTY, CHATTERJEE & CO., LTD.
15, COLLEGE SQUARE, CALCUTTA
1928

PREFACE TO THE SECOND EDITION

In this second edition of the "Early History of the Dekkan," I have embodied the results of fresh researches published by others and myself within the last ten years. Some of my own have, however, been laid before the public now for the first time in this book.

R. G. B.

Poona, 10th January, 1895.

PREFACE TO THE THIRD EDITION

After finishing his book on "Vaiṣṇavism, Śaivism and minor religious systems" in the Encyclopaedia of Indo-Aryan Research, my revered father very much wanted to bring out a revised edition of his "Early History of the Dekkan". But multifarious engagements and continued ill-health prevented him from carrying it out. He asked me in his last wishes to bring out a third edition with notes and indicated what important records had been published since the last edition. I do not know how long I would have been unable to carry out this sacred task. But Chuckervertty, Chatterjee & Co., who are to India what Trübner & Co. are to Europe, of their own motion made proposals to me for the publication of the book ; and the result is that this new edition with Notes is now before the scholarly public long before I expected it. It is true that much new material has been available since the publication of the second edition. But the main conclusions of the book from the period of the Early Chālukyas onwards have remained unshaken, and whatever changes are now required in reconstructing the history of the earlier period have been pointed out in the Notes.

The additional notes of the present (third) edition have been given at the end, and the text and notes of the second edition have been kept intact in the body of the book. It has not, however, been found possible to adhere to the pagination of the second edition. To facilitate reference, the paging of the second edition is given in bold type in square brackets in the body of the book.

D. R. BHANDARKAR.

CONTENTS

CORRECTIONS

Page 38, *line*	7	from bottom,	*for* Vasishṭîputra	*read*	Vâsishṭîputra
„ 67 „	5	„ „	„ Guṇâdhya	„	Guṇâḍhya
„ 95 „	9	„ „	„ Traikûtaka	„	Traikûṭaka
„ 96 „	9	„ top	„ Gurjara	„	Gûjara
„ 99 „	19	„ „	„ Âshaḍha	„	Âshâḍha
„ 100 „	23	„ „	„ Paṭṭaḍakal, *here as elsewhere.*	„	Paṭṭadakal
„ 104 *ls.* 6 & 2		„ „	„ Brahmaṇism	„	Brâhmaṇism
„ „ *line*	7	„ „	„ in the Southern	„	in Southern
„ 106 „	4	„ „	„ Yadû	„	Yadu
„ 111 „	18	„ „	„ Paiṭhan, *here as elsewhere.*	„	Paiṭhaṇ
„ 117 „	13	„ „	„ Śîlâhâra	„	Śilâhâra
„ 130 „	12	„ „	„ Kâlanjara	„	Kâlañjara
„ 150 „	13	„ „	„ Gaddaka, *here as elsewhere.*	„	Gadag
„ 180 „	13	„ bottom	„ Singhaṅa	„	Siṅghaṇa
„ 184 „	15	„ „	„ Sûktimuktavali	„	Sûktimuktâvali
„ 185 „	14	„ „	„ Sukt-, *here as elsewhere.*	„	Sûkt-

EARLY HISTORY OF THE DEKKAN.

ADDITIONS AND FURTHER CORRECTIONS.

P. 62, *footnote* 1, *add at the end,* Karhâḍ plates recently put into my possession and not yet published.

P. 63, *line* 35, *after* Wardhâ, *here as well as everywhere henceforward except in l.* 14, *p.* 75, *add* and Karhâḍ *and make the necessary grammatical changes.*

P. 67, *line* 30, *after* death, *add* The Karhâḍ charter represents the fire of his prowess to have burnt the Châlukya race.

P. 73, *line* 23, *after* months, *add* In the Bhadan grant[1] the latter is represented to have reigned for a year.

P. 75, *lines* 6 *and* 7, *for the sentence ending with* dominions, *substitute* He expelled the prince Rachchhyâmalla from the throne of the Gaṅga country and placed on it a person of the name of Bûtuga, or Bûtayya which name has been Sanskritized into Bhûtârya ; and destroyed the Pallavas to whose race the Dantiga killed by him probably belonged.

P. 75, *line* 20, *at the end add* The Karhâḍ charter was issued in 880 Śaka, *i.e.*, 18 years after the Wardhâ grant. It contains two stanzas more about Kṛishṇa III. than the latter ; and these must in consequence be regarded as alluding to events which occurred between Śaka 862 and 880. As stated therein, to consolidate his power Kṛishṇa deprived some of his feudatories of their principalities, and granted them to others who were meritorious ; some were separated from each other and others joined together. "With the idea of conquering the south, he uprooted the Chola race, placed the territory ruled over by it under his own dependents, made the kings of the Chera, Pâṇḍya, and other countries along with Siṁhala or Ceylon his tributaries, and erected a triumphal column at Re(â)meśvara." In an inscription at Âtakûr in the Maisur territory, dated 872 Śaka, Kṛishṇarâja is represented to have

1 Published by Prof. Kielhorn, Epigraphia Indica, Vol. III., p. 271.

fought with the Chola prince Râjâditya and killed him. In this last act he was assisted by Bûtuga, his Gaṅga feudatory mentioned above, and Gûtuga was rewarded for his services by being granted additional territory.[2] In a village in the Chingleput district of the Madras Presidency, which must have formed a part of the ancient kingdom of the Pallavas, there are two inscriptions dated in the seventeenth and nineteenth years of the reign of Kannaradeva, *i.e.* Kṛishṇadeva, in which he is spoken of as the conqueror of Kachchi or Kâñchîpura the capital of the Pallavas and Tañjai identified with Tanjor (Tañjâvûr or Tañjâpura) which was the capital of the Chola princes. Another inscription at Vellore is dated in the twenty-sixth year of his reign ; and there are two more containing his name in South Arcot[3] which was probably included in the Chola kingdom. These facts bear out the statement in the Karhâḍ grant of his having uprooted the Chola race and held the country by placing it under his dependents, and another in this and the Wardhâ grant that the Pallavas were destroyed by him. This latter event, however, took place before Śaka 862 the date of the Wardhâ grant, while the conquest of the Chola prince came on later. By the Karhâḍ charter which was issued on Wednesday the 13th of the dark half of Phâlguna when 880 years had elapsed since the time of the Śaka king, the cyclic year being *Kâlayukta,* Kṛishṇa granted,—while encamped at Melpâṭî with his victorious army for the purpose of apportioning the southern provinces among his dependents, taking charge of all the possessions of Areleśvara, and constructing temples to be dedicated to certain gods,—the village of Kaṅkiṁ in the district of Karahâṭaka to the great Śaiva ascetic Gaganaśiva, who was the pupil of Îśânaśiva and was conversant with the Śivasiddhântas or sacred books of the Śaiva sect, for the benefit of the whole group of ascetics. It would appear from this that Saivism flourished about the district of Karhâḍ at this period.

P. 78, *to the dates under Kṛishṇa III. add* 872, 880.

---

2 Epigraphia Indica, Vol. II., pp. 172-74.

3 *Ib.* Vol. III., pp. 282-85.

Page 10, *line* 5 from bottom,	*for* Brâhmana	*read*	Brâhmaṇa
,, 23 ,, 24 ,, top	,, Mysore	,,	Maisur
,, 23 ,, 27 from ,,	,, Saliyaputta	,,	Satiyaputta
,, 43 ,, 9 ,, ,,	,, Dakshiṇapatha	,,	Dakshiṇâpatha
,, 49 ,, 5 ,, ,,	,, Dakshinâpatha	,,	Dakshiṇâpatha
,, 73 ,, 23 from bottom,	,, Kânara	,,	Kânarâ
,, 79 ,, 9 ,, top	,, Râshṭrakûta	,,	Râshṭrakûṭa
,, 80 ,, 4 ,, bottom,	,, Lâṭ *here as elsewhere*	,,	Lâṭa
,, 96 ,, 21 from top	*for* Tajika	,,	Tâjika
,, 98 ,, 5 ,, ,,	*insert* date *after latest*		
,, 111, *footnote* 18	,, IV	,,	III
,, 120 ,, 11 from top	,, Lâta	,,	Lâṭa
,, 126 ,, 21 ,, ,,	,, Sâhâsaṅka	,,	Sâhasâṅka
,, 157 ,, 3 ,, ,,	,, Kâkateya	,,	Kâkatîya
,, 163 ,, 3 ,, ,,	,, Liṇgâyata *here as elsewhere.*	,,	Liṅgâyata
,, 184 ,, 15 ,, ,,	,, Jahlâṇ's	,,	Jahlaṇa's
,, 187 ,, 1 ,, bottom	,, यजार्जुनं	,,	ययार्जुनं

EARLY
HISTORY OF THE DEKKAN

INTRODUCTORY

INDIA has no written history. Nothing was known till within recent times of the political condition of the country, the dynasties that ruled over the different provinces which composed it, and the great religious and social revolutions that it went through. The historical curiosity of the people was satisfied by legends. What we find of a historical nature in the literature of the country before the arrival of the Mahomedans comes to very little. **Introductory.**

I. We have a chronicle of Kaśmir called the Râjataraṅgiṇî, in which, however, there is a good deal which is not supported by contemporary evidence. Now and then, a bountiful prince or minister found a poet to sing his glories ; and the works thus composed, contain a good deal of historical information, though, of course, an undue praise of the patron and his ancestors is to be expected. But a few such works only have hitherto been discovered ; and the oldest of them gives an account of a prince who lived in the first half of the seventh century. The literature of the Jainas of the Śvetâmbara sect contains accounts mostly of the later princes of Gujarât and other noted personages. There are also similar accounts of the princes of Râjaputâna. In the beginning or at the end of some Sanskrit works the names of the princes under whose patronage or in whose reign they were composed, are given ; and

Introductory. sometimes we find a long genealogy of the family to which the particular prince belonged, with some short observation with reference to each of his ancestors. Lastly, the Purâṇas contain genealogies of the most powerful royal families which ascend to a higher antiquity than the works noticed hitherto.

II. But the information to be gathered from all these sources is extremely meagre ; and there are many provinces on the history of which they do not throw any light. And the facts mentioned in them cannot be systematically arranged, or even chronologically connected, except with the assistance of other sources of information to which we shall now proceed. The invasion of Alexander the Great brought the Greeks in contact with the Hindus ; and his successors in Syria kept up an intercourse with the Indian emperors for a long time. The notices of Indian persons and events contained in the writings of the Greeks, when compared with the statements occurring in the Purâṇas, admit, in some cases, of an easy identification ; and from the known dates of the corresponding Greek persons or events, we are able to determine those of the Indian persons or events. In this manner the date of the foundation of the Maurya dynasty by Chandragupta has been determined to be about 322 B.C., and a good many other dates in Indian history have been ascertained. The writings of Chinese authors also throw a great deal of light on some periods of Indian history. Buddhism was introduced into China in the first century of the Christian era ; and from time to time men from that country came to India as pilgrims ; and some Indian Buddhists also must have found their way to China. The Chinese pilgrims wrote accounts of what they saw and did in India, and these works, which have come down to us, are

Introductory.

very valuable for the elucidation of Indian history. The Chinese possessed a perfect system of chronology, and the dates of the pilgrimages are useful for the purposes of the Indian antiquarian. Valuable accounts of India written by the Arabic visitors to the country in the Middle Ages have also become available.

III. Another very important source, and fuller than any hitherto noticed, consists of inscriptions. Some of these are cut on stones or rocks, and others engraved on copperplates. These last are in all cases charters conveying grants of land made mostly by princes or chiefs to religious persons or to temples and monasteries. A great many of these are dated in one of the current eras. It is usual in these charters to give the pedigree of the grantor. The names of his ancestors together with some of their famous deeds are mentioned. As the authors who composed the grants cannot be expected to be impartial in their account of the reigning monarch, much of what they say about him cannot be accepted as historically true. And even in the case of his ancestors, the vague praise that we often find, must be regarded simply as meaningless. But when they are represented to have done a specific deed, such as the conquest of Harshavardhana by Pulakeśi II. of the early Châlukya dynasty, it must be accepted as historical; and when we have other sources available, we find the account confirmed, as Hwhan Thsang does that of Pulakeśi's exploit. Even in the case of the reigning monarch, the specific deeds such as wars with neighbouring princes, which are mentioned, may be accepted as historical; though, however, legitimate doubts may be entertained as regards the reported results.

The stone-inscriptions are intended to commemorate the dedication of a temple or monastery or any part thereof, and of works of public utility such as tanks and wells, and sometimes grants of land also. A good many of these benefactions are by private individuals ; but not seldom the name of the king, in whose reign the dedication was made, is given together with the year of his reign, as well as the date in the current era. When it is a royal benefaction that is commemorated, we have a longer account of the reigning prince, and sometimes of his ancestors.

The great pioneer in the deciphering and interpretation of inscriptions was James Prinsep ; but no great progress was made after him, in this branch of antiquarian work, till the establishment of the "Indian Antiquary" and the institution of the Archæological Survey. These gave a strong impetus to it, and many scholars entered into the field with zeal. Twenty years ago, it would have been impossible to write the following pages.

IV. I must not omit to mention old coins as a valuable source of information as to the names of the successive monarchs of a dynasty, and sometimes their dates. A study of these too has led to very important results.

The materials for the history of the development of Indian thought and of changes in the social condition are the whole literature itself. But this is an independent inquiry with which we are not here directly concerned ; and the conclusions arrived at are applicable to the whole Hindu race, and not to any particular province. I have consulted general literature only in discussing points concerning the Âryan settlement of the Dekkan. The materials used in the preparation of the other sections, which fall under each of the four classes noticed above, are as follows :

I.—Bilhaṇa's Vikramâṅkacharita, Introduction to the Vratakhaṇḍa, Introduction to Jahlaṇa's anthology, the Purаṇic genealogies; and scattered notices in the Kathâsaritsâgara, Hâla's Saptaśatî, Vâtsyâyaṇa's Kâmasûtra, Kavirahasya, Digambara Jaina works—such as the Harivaṁśa, the Uttara Purâṇa, the Yaśastilaka, the Praśnottararatnamâlikâ &c.—Vijñâneśvara's Mitâksharâ, the Abhilashitârthachintâmaṇi, the Basava Purâṇa, the Lekhapañchâśikâ, the Śabdârṇavachandrikâ, the Jñâneśvarî, and a few others.

II.—Ptolemy's geography, the Periplus, Hwhan Thsang's Itinerary.

III.—Inscriptions in the cave-temples of Western India; Rudradâman's inscription at Junâgaḍ; stone inscriptions in the Southern Maratha Country; copper-plate charters of the early Châlukyas, the Râshṭrakûṭas, and other dynasties, of which we have now a large number.

IV.—Coins of the Śâtavâhanas found at Kolhâpur and in the lower Godâvarî district.

Since the political history of the Dekkan before the advent of Mahomedans was entirely unknown before, and the difficulty of ascertaining facts is very great, my object has been to collect as many of them as possible. The absence of proportion in the space allotted to important and unimportant events due to this circumstance, will, it is hoped, be excused. This does not pretend to be a literary production, but merely a congeries of facts.

SECTION I.

ETYMOLOGY OF THE WORD "DEKKAN" AND ITS DENOTATION.

Section I.

Etymology of the word "Dekkan."

[1] THE word "Dakkhan" represents the vernacular pronunciation of the Sanskrit word Dakshiṇa, meaning "southern," used to designate the portion of the Indian Peninsula lying to the south of the Narmadâ. The name more usually met with in Sanskrit works and elsewhere is Dakshiṇâpatha or "the Southern Region." That this name was in ordinary use in ancient times is shown by the fact that the author of the Periplus calls that portion of the country Dakhinabades.[1] In the vernacular or Prâkṛit speech of the time, the Sanskrit Dakshiṇâpatha must have become Dakkhiṇâbadha or Dakkhiṇâvadha by the usual rules, and the Greek writer must have derived his name from this popular pronunciation. The shorter form of the name also must have been in use, since in the beginning of the fifth century of the Christian era, Fah-Hian,[2] the Chinese traveller, was told at Benares that there was a country to the south called Ta-Thsin, which word corresponds to the Sanskrit Dakshiṇa.

Denotation of the word Dekkan.

Dakshiṇâpatha or Dakshiṇa was the name of the whole peninsula to the south of the Narmadâ. Among the countries enumerated in the Mârkaṇḍeya,[3] Vâyu,[4] and Mâtsya[5] Purâṇas as comprised in Dakshiṇâpatha

[1] Indicates page 1 of the original edition.

1 Indian Antiquary, VIII. 143.

2 Travels of Fah-Hian by S. Beal, 139.

3 Chap. 57 Verse 45, Edition Bibliotheca Indica. The reading of the second line, however, is wrong. It ought to be, Pâṇḍyâś cha Keralâś chaiva Cholâḥ Kulyâs tathaiva cha, as it is in the manuscript I have consulted.

4 Chap. 45 Verse 124, Edition Bibliotheca Indica.

5 Chap. 112 Verse 46, Poona Lithographed Edition

Section I.

are those of the Cholas, Pâṇḍyas, and Keralas, which were situated in the extreme south of the peninsula, and correspond to the modern provinces of Tanjor, Madura, and Malabâr. In the Mahâbhârata, however, Sahadeva, the youngest of the Pâṇḍu princes, is represented in his career of conquest to have gone to Dakshiṇâpatha after having conquered the king of the Pâṇḍyas.[6] This would show that the country of the Pâṇḍyas was not included in Dakshiṇâpatha. Again, the rivers Godâvarî and others springing from the Sahyâdri are spoken of in the Vâyu Purâṇa as rivers of Dakshiṇâpatha,[7] while the Narmadâ and the Tâpî are not so styled ; whence it would seem that the valleys of those rivers were not included in Dakshiṇâpatha. The word thus appears not to have been always used in the same sense. In modern times it is the name of the country between the Narmadâ on the north and a variable line along the course of the Kṛishṇâ to the south, exclusive of the provinces lying to the extreme east. It is thus almost identical [2] with the country called Mahârâshṭra or the region in which the Marâṭhî language is spoken, the narrow strip of land between the Western Ghâṭs and the sea being excluded. A still narrower definition is that which excludes from this tract the valleys of the Normadâ and the Tâpî ; and to this extent we have seen that there is authority for it in the Vâyu Purâṇa. Thus the word Dekkan expresses the country watered by the upper Godâvarî and that lying between that river and the Kṛishṇâ. The name Mahârâshṭra also seems at one time to have been restricted to this tract. For that country is, in the Purâṇas[8] and other works,

---

6 Sabhâparvan, Chap. 31 Verse 17, Bombay Edition.

7 Chap. 45 Verse 104, Ed. Bib. Ind.

8 See the chapters of the three Purâṇas referred to in the notes on page 1.

distinguished on the one hand from Aparânta or Northern Konkan, and from the regions on either side of the Narmadâ and the Tâpî inhabited by the Pulindas and Śabaras, as well as from Vidarbha on the other. In a comparatively modern work entitled Ratnakośa,[9] Mahârâshṭra, Vaidarbha, Tâpî-taṭa-deśa and Narmadâ-taṭa-deśa (*i.e.*, the countries on either side of those rivers), and the Koṇkan are spoken of as distinct from each other. The Dekkan or Mahârâshṭra in this the narrowest sense of the word forms the subject of the present notice.

---

9 Prof. Aufrecht's Catalogue of Manuscripts in the Bodleian Library, 352.

SECTION II.

Settlement of the Âryas in the Dekkan.

Section II.

Settlement of the Âryas in the Dekkan.

[3] It is now a recognised fact that the Âryas who came to India were at first confined to eastern Afghanistan and the Panjâb. Thence they emigrated to the east and for a time the easternmost province occupied by them was Bramhâvarta or their holy land, lying between the rivers Sarasvatî the modern Sarasuti, and Dṛishadvatî,[1] a stream in the vicinity, that is, the country about Thanesar. There the system of castes and orders and the sacrificial religion seem to have been fully developed. Thence they spread to the east and the south, and gradually occupied the whole country between the Himâlaya and the Vindhya. This last mountain range must for a long time have formed the southern boundary of their settlements. For the name Âryâvarta or the region occupied by the Âryas, as explained by Manu[2] and even by Patañjali,[3] the author of the Mahâbhâshya on Pâṇini's grammar, signified exclusively the part of the country situated between those mountain ranges. The Vindhya, which by its height seemed to obstruct the passage of the sun, was impassable to them. The name Pâriyâtra was given to the more northern and western portion of the range from which the rivers Chambal and Betvâ take their rise, probably because it was situated on the boundary of their Yâtrâ or range of communication. After a while, however, the sage Agastya, in poetical

---

[1] Manu, II. 17.

[2] Manu, II, 23.

[3] Patañjali's Mahâbhâshya under Pâṇini, II. 4, 10.

Section II.

language, bade the mountain not to grow high, that is, crossed it and established an Âśrama or hermitage to the south and thus led the way to other settlements. The first or oldest Âryan province in the southern country must have been the Vidarbhas or the Berârs. For in the Râmâyaṇa when Sugrîva the monkey-king sends his followers to the different quarters in search of Râma's wife Sîtâ and Râvaṇa her ravisher, he directs them to go among other southern countries to Vidarbhas, Ṛichîkas, and Mahishakas, and also to Daṇḍakâraṇya (the forest of Daṇḍakâ) and the river Godâvarî.[4] This shows that while the country about the Godâvarî, that is, the Dekkan or Mahârâshṭra in the narrowest sense of the terms, was a forest, Vidarbha was an inhabited country. In the Mahâbhârata also Agastya is represented to have given a girl that he produced by his miraculous powers to the king of Vidarbha, and after she had grown to be a woman demanded her of the king in marriage.[5] In the Râmâyaṇa, Râma is represented to have lived for a long time in Daṇḍakâraṇya, at a place called Pañchavaṭî situated on the banks [4] of the Godâvarî about two yojanas from the hermitage of Agastya.[6] That this Daṇḍakâraṇya was the modern Mahârâshṭra is shown by the fact stated above, that it was watered by the river Godâvarî, and by several others. According to the Hindu ritual it is necessary when beginning any religious ceremony to pronounce the name of the country in which it is performed. The Brâhmaṇs in Mahârâshṭra do not utter the name Mahârâshṭra but Daṇḍakâraṇya with the word *deśa* or "country" attached to it. In the introduction to

Vidarbha, the first Âryan province in the South.

Daṇḍakâraṇya, the same as Mahârâshṭra.

4 Râmâyana, IV. Chap. 41, Bombay Edition.

5 Mahâbhârata, Bombay Edition, III. Chap. 96, 97.

6 Râmâyana, III. 13, 13 Bom. Ed.

Section II.

Pañchavaṭî.

Hemâdri's Vratakhaṇḍa, a work written more than six hundred years ago, Devagiri, the modern Daulatâbâd, is spoken of as situated in a district on the confines of Daṇḍakâraṇya. Nâsik claims to be the Pañchavaṭî where Râma lived. But the poet could hardly be expected to have brought his hero from the Vindhya to such a remote westerly place as Nâsik. The river Godâvarî must, from the description occurring in the Râmâyaṇa as well as in Bhavabhûti's Uttara Râmacharita, have been wide at Râma's Pañchavaṭî. It could hardly have been so at Nâsik, which is very near its source. On the other hand, "the region about the northern part of the Sahyâdri through which flowed the river Godâvarî and in which Govardhana was situated" is in the Purâṇas represented as "the most charming on earth ; and there, to please Râma, the sage Bhâradvâja caused heavenly trees and herbs to spring up for his wife's enjoyment, and thus a lovely garden came into existence."[7] In the Mârkaṇḍeya, Govardhana is spoken of as a town ; but the Vâyu and the Mâtsya seem to mean it to be a mountain. This Govardhana must, from the given position, be the same as the village of that name near Nâsik ; and thus the three Purâṇas must be understood as supporting the identification of Pañchavaṭî with Nâsik.

The complete subjugation of Mahâ-

But though Mahârâshṭra was the last country occupied by the Indian Âryas, their subjugation of it was no less thorough than that of all the northern

---

7 Mârkaṇḍeya, Chap. 57 Verses 34-35; Vâyu, Chap. 45 Verses 112-114; and Mâtsya, Chap. 112 Verses 37-39. The passage, however, is corrupt. The three Purâṇas evidently derive their reading from the same original, but the text has been greatly corrupted. The most ancient version of it seems to be that in the Vâyu.

Section II. rāshṭra by the Âryas, proved by the prevalent dialect of the country.

countries. Here, as there, they drove some of the aborigines to the fastnesses of mountains and jungles, and incorporated the rest into their own society. The present Marâṭhî language is as much an offshoot of the Sanskrit as the other languages of Northern India. The ancient representatives of these dialects —the Mahârâshṭrî, the Śaurasenî, and the Mâgadhî, as well as an earlier form of speech, the Pâli—show extensive corruptions of Sanskrit sounds, reducible however to a few general laws. These cannot be accounted for by the natural operation of the causes which bring about the decay of a language spoken throughout its history by the same race. For, this operation is slow and must be in continuance for a very long time in order to produce the wide-going phonetic changes which we observe in those Prâkṛit dialects, as they are called. This long-continued process must at the same time give rise to a great many changes in other respects. Such, [5] however, we do not find in those dialects, and they do not in those respects show a very wide departure from the Sanskrit. The extensive corruptions of Sanskrit sounds, therefore, must be accounted for by the supposition that the language had to be spoken by races whose original tongue it was not. Those alien races could not properly pronounce the Sanskrit words used by the conquering Âryas ; and thus the Prâkṛit forms of Sanskrit words represent their pronunciation of them. A few sounds unknown to Sanskrit as well as some words not traceable to that language are also found in the Prâkṛits, and these point to the same conclusion. It thus appears that the Indian Âryas in their progress through the country came in contact with alien races, which were incorporated with their society and learnt their language, at the same time that they preserved some of their original words and

Prâkṛit Dialects.

Section II.

The subjugation of the country farther South, partial.

phonetic peculiarities.[8] This was the state of things in the north down to the Marâṭhâ country. But farther south and on the eastern coast, though they penetrated there and communicated their own civilization to the aboriginal races inhabiting those parts, they were not able to incorporate them thoroughly into their own society and to root out their languages and their peculiar civilization. On the contrary, the Âryas had to learn the languages of those races and to adopt a portion at least of their civilization. Thus the Kanarese, the Telugu, the Tamil, and the other languages now spoken in Southern India are not derived from the Sanskrit but belong altogether to a different stock, and hence it is also that southern art is so different from the northern. The reason why the result of the Âryan irruption was so different in Southern India from what it was in the north appears to be that when the Âryas penetrated to the south there existed already well-organized communities and kingdoms. In the passage in the Râmâyaṇa, referred to above, the monkey-soldiers are directed to go to the countries of the Andhras (Telugu people), the Pâṇḍyas, the Cholas, and the Keralas, in the south ; and are told that they will there see the gate of the city of the Pâṇḍyas adorned with gold and jewels. And these races, their country, and their kings are alluded to in other Sanskrit works, as will be noticed hereafter. In the north, however, at the time of the Âryan invasion, the condition of the country must have been similar to that of Daṇḍakâraṇya, which is represented in the Râmâyaṇa as a forest infested by Râkshasas or wild tribes who disturbed the religious rites of the Brâhmaṇ sages. And

---

[8] These points I have developed in my Lectures on Sanskrit and the Prâkṛit languages derived from it; Jour. Bom. B. R. A. S. Vol. XVI. pp. 290-91.

throughout the older portion of Sanskrit literature, which is to be referred to the times when the Âryas were gradually progressing from the Panjâb, the wild tribes they met with are spoken of under the name of Dasyus, Râkshasas, and others. **Section II.**

[6] SECTION III.

Approximate Date of the Âryan Settlement in the Dekkan and Notices of Southern India in Ancient Indian Literature and Inscriptions.

Section III.

The Âryas acquainted with Northern India in the time of the Aitareya Brâhmaṇa.

We will now endeavour to determine approximately the period when the Âryas settled in Daṇḍakâraṇya, and trace the relations between the civilized Âryan community of the north and the southern country at different periods of Sanskrit literature and at well-known dates in Indian history. In the Aitareya Brâhmaṇa, which is anterior to the whole of the so-called classical Sanskrit literature, the sage Viśvâmitra is represented to have condemned by a curse the progeny of fifty of his sons to "live on the borders" of the Âryan settlements, and these, it is said, "were the Andhras, Puṇḍras, Śabaras, Pulindas, and Mûtibas, and the descendants of Viśvâmitra formed a large portion of the Dasyus."[1] Of these the first four are spoken of as people living in the south, the Puṇḍras in the Râmâyaṇa, and the other three in the Purâṇas.[2] From the later literature, the Pulindas and Śabaras appear to have been wild tribes living about the Vindhyas.[3] Ptolemy places the former along the Narmadâ. The Andhras, who in these days are identified with the Telugu people, lived about the mouth of the Godâvarî or perhaps farther to the north. If these were the posi-

1 Aitareya Brâhmana, VII. 18. Pulindas are omitted in the corresponding passage in the Śâṅkhâyana Sûtra.

2 See the passages above referred to.

3 In his Kâdambarî Bâṇa places the Śabaras in the forest on the Vindhya range.

Section III.

tions of the tribes in the time of the Aitareya Brâhmaṇa, the Indian Âryas must at that time have been acquainted with the whole country to the north of the Vindhya and a portion to the south-east of that range.

Also in Pâṇini's time.

Pâṇini in his Sûtras or grammatical rules shows an extensive knowledge of the geography of India. Of the places and rivers mentioned by him a good many exist in the Panjâb and Afghanistan ; but the names of countries situated in the eastern portion of Northern India also occur in the Sûtras. The countries farthest to the south mentioned by him are Kachchha (IV. 2, 133), Avantî (IV. 1, 176), Kosala (IV. 1, 171), Karûśa (IV. 1, 178)[4] [7] and Kaliṅga (IV. 1, 178).[5] The first is the same as the modern country

4 This name does not occur in the Sûtra, but is the second in the list or Gaṇa beginning with Bharga. As regards the words occurring in these Gaṇas, I have on a previous occasion expressed my opinion that though it is not safe to attribute a whole Gaṇa to Pâṇini (and in several cases we have clear indications that some of the words were inserted in later times), still the first three words might without mistake be taken to be his. This was objected to by Professor Weber. But as my reasons were, as I thought, obvious, I did not think it necessary to defend my view. I may, however, here state that since Pâṇini refers to these Gaṇas in his Sûtras by using the first word in the list with *âdi*, equivalent to "and others," added to it, and since he uses the plural of the noun so formed, and the plural of a noun cannot be used unless three individuals at least of the class are meant, it is proper that we should understand him to be thinking of the first and two words at least more. This observation is meant to be applicable generally. In the present case, however, the expression *Bhargâdi* forms a part of the compound, and the plural is not actually used, though it is clearly implied.

5 In the so-called Pâṇinîya Śikshâ the expression Saurâshṭrikâ nârî or "a woman of Surâshṭra" occurs. But this should by no means be regarded as showing that Pâṇini

Section III. of that name, Avantî is the district about Ujjayinî, and Kaliṅga corresponds to the modern Northern Circars. Kosala, Karûśa, and Avantî are mentioned in the Purâṇas as countries situated on the back of the Vindhya.[6] In the Ratnâvalî, a dramatic play, Kosala is also placed near that mountain range. Supposing that the non-occurrence of the name of any country farther south in Pâṇini's work is due to his not having known it, a circumstance which, looking to the many names of places in the north that he gives, appears very probable, the conclusion follows that in his time the Âryas were confined to the north of the Vindhya, but did proceed or communicate with the northernmost portion of the eastern coast, not by crossing that range, but avoiding it by taking an easterly course.

Southern India unknown in all likelihood in Pâṇini's time.

Southern India known to Kâtyâyana but unknown to Pâṇini

Kâtyâyana, however, the object of whose aphorisms called Vârtikas is to explain and supplement Pâṇini, shows an acquaintance with southern nations. Pâṇini gives rules for the formation of derivatives for the names of tribes of warriors which are at the same time the names of the countries inhabited by them, in the sense of "one sprung from an individual belonging to that tribe," and also, it must be understood, in the sense of "king of the country." Thus a man sprung from an individual of the tribe of the

---

was acquainted with Surâshṭra. The Pâṇinîya Śikshâ cannot be the work of Pâṇini; for the author of that treatise begins by stating that he is going to explain Śikshâ according to the views of Pâṇini and ends with a few verses in praise of the great grammarian. Besides, the author notices the Prâkṛit dialects to which there is no allusion whatever in Pâṇini's great work and writes in verse. Grammatical treatises in verse are later than those in the form of Sûtras. The Pâṇinîya Śikshâ therefore must have been composed long after Pâṇini.

6 See the passages cited above.

Pañchâlas, or the king of the country Pañchâlas, is to be called Pâñchâla ; a descendant of a Sâlva, or the king of the country of the Sâlvas, is to be called Sâlveya, &c. Kâtyâyana notices here an omission ; the name Pâṇḍya is not explained by Pâṇini. Kâtyâyana therefore adds, "one sprung from an individual of the tribe of the Pâṇḍus or the king of their country, should be called a Pâṇḍya."[7] Similarly, Pâṇini tells us that in either of these senses no termination should be appended to the word *Kambojas,* which was the name of a non-Âryan people in the north-west, nor should any of its vowels be changed ; but that the word *Kamboja* itself means "one sprung from an individual of the Kamboja tribe, or the king of the country of the Kambojas."[8] Kâtyâyana says that in this rule, the expression "and others" should be added to the word *Kambojas ;* for the rule applies also to the names "Cholas and others," that is, persons sprung from an individual of the Chola and other tribes, and the kings of the Chola and other countries should be called by the names "Chola and others." Similarly, Pâṇini tells us that the countries Kumudvat, Naḍvat, and Vetasvat are so called because they contain Kumudas or water-lilies, [8] Naḍas or reeds, and Vetas or canes, respectively.[9] Kâtyâyana adds, "Mahishmat is so called because it contains Mahishas or buffaloes."

Section III.

Now Mahishmat appears to be the same southern country which in the Purâṇas is associated with Mahârâshṭra and is called Mahishakas. Mâhishmatî on the banks of the Narmadâ was probably its capital. Here we may, I think, argue, as Professor Goldstucker has done in many similar cases, that had

7 Pâṇḍor ḍyaṇ, which is a Vârtika on Páṇ. IV. 1, 168.

8 Pâṇ. IV. 1, 175.

9 Pâṇ. IV. 2, 87.

Section III.

Pâṇini known the Pâṇḍyas, Cholas, and Mahishmat, he would not have omitted the names from his rules, considering how careful a grammarian he was. Very likely, then, he did not know them, and this supposition is strengthened by the fact alluded to above that the name of no other southern country occurs in his Sûtras. Thus then the Âryas of the north were not familiar with the southern countries and tribes in the time of Pâṇini, but were so in the time of Kâtyâyana. The latter author also mentions a town of the name of Nâsikya,[10] which is very likely the same as our modern Nâsik.

Patañjali intimately acquainted with Southern India.

Patañjali shows an intimate acquaintance with the south. As a grammarian he thinks it his duty to notice the lingual usages in the south, and tells us that in Dakshiṇâpatha the word *Sarasî* is used to denote large lakes.[11] He mentions Mâhishmatî,[12] Vaidarbha,[13] Kâñchîpura,[14] the modern Conjeveram, and Kerala[15] or Malabâr. Patañjali's date, B.C. 150, may now be relied upon. That author notices variant readings of Kâtyâyana's Vârtikas as found in the texts used by the schools of the Bhâradvâjîyas, Saunâgas, and others. Some of these might be considered as emendations of the Vârtikas, though Patañjali's introduction of them by the verb *paṭhanti*, "they read," is an indication that he regarded them as different readings. A sufficiently long time therefore must have elapsed between Kâtyâyana and Patañjali to give rise to these variants or emendations. I am therefore inclined to accept the popular

Chronological Relations between Kâtyâyana and Patañjali.

10 In a Vârtika on Pâṇ. VI. 1, 63.

11 Mahâbhâshya on Pâṇ. I. 1, 19.

12 On Pâṇ. III. 1, 26.

13 IV. 1, fourth Âhnika.

14 IV. 2, second Âhnika.

15 IV. 1, fourth Âhnika.

Section III.

tradition which refers Kâtyâyana to the time of the Nandas who preceded the Mauryas, and to assign to him the first half of the fourth century before Christ. In this manner the interval between Kâtyâyana and Patañjali was about two hundred years. Now, Professor Goldstucker has shown from an examination of the Vârtikas that certain grammatical forms are not noticed by Pâṇini but are taught by Kâtyâyana, and concludes that they did not exist in the language in Pâṇini's time. I have followed up the argument in my lectures "On the Sanskrit and Prâkṛit languages,"[16] and given from the Vârtikas several ordinary instances of such forms. From these one of two conclusions only is possible, *viz.*, either that Pâṇini was a very careless and ignorant grammarian, or that the forms did not exist in the language in his time. The first is of course inadmissible ; wherefore the second must be accepted. I have also [9] shown from a passage in the introduction to Patañjali's Mahâbhâshya, that verbal forms such as those of the perfect which are taught by Pâṇini as found in the Bhâshâ or current language, not the Chhândasa or obsolete language, had gone out of use in the time of Kâtyâyana and Patañjali, and participles had come to be used instead.[17] Professor Goldstucker has also given a list of words used by Pâṇini in his Sûtras in a sense which became obsolete in the time of Kâtyâyana, and shown what portion of Sanskrit literature did not probably exist in Pâṇini's time but was known to Kâtyâyana, and in one case comes to the not unjustifiable conclusion that the time that elapsed between Pâṇini and Kâtyâyana was so great that certain literary works which either did not exist in Pâṇini's time or were not old to him came to be

Between Kâtyâyana and Pâṇini.

16 Jour. Bom. B. R. A. S. Vol. XVI. p. 273.

17 Jour. Bom. B. R. A. S. Vol. XVI., pp. 269-71.

Section III. — considered by Kâtyâyana to be as old as those which were old to Pâṇini. No less an interval of time than about three centuries can account for all these circumstances. Pâṇini, therefore, must have flourished in the beginning of the seventh century before the Christian era, if not earlier still ; and against this conclusion I believe no argument has been or can be brought, except a vague prejudice. And now to our point, the Indian Âryas had thus no knowledge of Southern India previous to the seventh century before Christ ; they had gone as far as the Northern Circars by the eastern route, but no farther ; and the countries directly to the south of the Vindhya they were not familiar with. About that time, however, they must have begun to penetrate still further, since they had already settled in or had communication with the countries on the northern skirts of the Vindhya and Kaliṅga, and first settled in Vidarbha or Berâr, approaching it still, it would appear, by the eastern route ; but in the course of some time more they crossed the Vindhya and settled in Daṇḍakâraṇya along the banks of the Godâvarî, that is, in Mahârâshṭra or the Dekkan. Before B.C. 350 they had become familiar with the whole country down to Tanjor and Madura.

The Âryas penetrated to the Dekkan after the beginning of about the seventh century B.C.

Chronological value of the Epics.

A chronological conclusion based on the occurrence of certain words or names in the great epics is not likely to be so safe. Though a Mahâbhârata existed before Pâṇini and Âśvalâyana, it is highly questionable whether our present text is the same as that which existed in their times. On the contrary, the probability is that the work has been added to from time to time ; and the text itself has undergone such corruption that no one can be positively certain that a particular word was not foisted into it in comparatively modern times. The text of the

Section III.

Râmâyaṇa also has become corrupt, though additions do not seem to have been made to it. Still the Bengali rescension of the poem like the Bengali rescensions of more recent works does contain additions. The text prevalent in this part of the country and in the south is more reliable ; and though innumerable differences of reading exist in the different manuscripts even on this side still there is hardly any material difference. But [10] the date of the Râmâyaṇa is uncertain ; the present Hindu belief based on the Purâṇas is that Râma's incarnation is older than Kṛishṇa's, and consequently the Râmâyaṇa older than the Mahâbhârata ; but it is not a little curious that while there is an allusion to Vâsudeva and Arjuna and to Yudhishṭhira in Pâṇini, and Patañjali frequently brings in Mahâbhârata characters in his illustrations and examples, there is not one allusion to Râma or his brothers or their father Daśaratha in the works of those grammarians. Even a much later author, Amarasiṁha the lexicographer, in his list of the synonyms of Vishṇu, gives a good many names derived from the Kṛishṇa incarnation ; but the name of Râma, the son of Daśaratha, does not occur, though Râma or Balabhadra, the brother of Kṛishṇa, is mentioned. Still, whatever chronological value may be attached to the circumstance, the occurrence of the names of places in the Dekkan contained in those epics I have already to some extent noticed. Sahadeva is represented to have subdued the Pâṇḍyas, Draviḍas, Uḍras, Keralas, and Andhras,[18] and also to have visited Kishkindhâ, which was probably situated somewhere near Hampi, the site of the Pampâ lake or river, where Râma met Sugrîva the monkey chief, though the country Kaishkindha is

Places in the Dekkan alluded to in the poems.

[18] Sâbhap, Chap. 31.

Section III. placed by the Purâṇas among those near the Vindhyas. He went also to Śûrparaka, the modern Supârâ near Bassein, Daṇḍaka, the same as Daṇḍakâraṇya but not mentioned as a forest, Karahâṭaka the modern Karhâḍa on the confluence of the Kṛishṇâ and the Koinâ, and to others. The countries mentioned in the passage in the Râmâyaṇa, alluded to above, as lying to the south are Utkala, probably the modern Ganjam, Kaliṅga, Daśârṇa, Avantî, Vidarbha, and others. The district near Bhilsâ must have been called Daśârṇa in ancient times ; for its capital was Vidiśâ, which was situated, as stated by Kâlidâsa in the Meghadûta, on the Vetravatî or Betvâ, and is thus to be identified with the modern Bhilsâ. All these are thus in the vicinity of the Vindhya or nearly in the same line with it farther east. But between these and the southernmost countries of the Cholas, Pâṇḍyas, and Keralas, the Râmâyaṇa mentions no other place or country but Daṇḍakâraṇya. This condition of the country, as observed before, is to be considered as previous to the Âryan settlements in the Dekkan, while that represented by the Mahâbhârata in the place indicated seems subsequent ; and herein we may see a reason for believing that the Râmâyaṇa is the older of the two epics. The name Mahârâshṭra does not occur in either of them.

Names of peoples in the Dekkan in the inscriptions of Aśoka.

In the middle of the third century before Christ, Aśoka, the great king of the Maurya dynasty reigning at Pâṭaliputra in Magadha, speaks in the fifth Edict of his rock-inscriptions, which are found at Girnâr in Kâṭhiâvâḍ on the west, Dhauli in Katak and Jaugaḍ in Ganjam on the eastern coast, at Khalsi in the Himâlaya, Shahbaz-garhi in Afghanistan, and Mansehra on the northern frontier of the Panjab, of his having sent ministers of religion [11] to the Râsṭikas

and the Petenikas and to the Aparântas.[19] The last Section III.
which we know best is Northern Konkan, the capital of which was Sûrpâraka. Petenikas is not unlikely the same as Paiṭhaṇakas, *i.e.*, the people or country about Paiṭhaṇa on the Godâvarî. The vernacular pronunciation of the name of the city, which in Sanskrit is Pratishṭhâna, was in those days, as it now is, Peṭhaṇa or Paiṭhaṇa, for both the author of the Periplus and Ptolemy call it Paithana or Baithana. The Râsṭikas, or, according to the Mansehra version, Raṭrakas, corresponding to the Sanskrit Râshṭrikas, were very likely the people of Mahârâshṭra, for a tribe of the name of Raṭṭas has from the remotest times held political supremacy in the Dekkan. One branch of it assumed the name of Râshṭrakûṭas and governed the country before the Châlukyas acquired power. It re-established itself after about three centuries, but had to yield to the Châlukyas again after some time. In later times, chieftains of the name of Raṭṭas governed Sugandhavarti or Saundatti in the Belgaum district. In the thirteenth Edict in which the countries where Aśoka's moral edicts were respected are enumerated, the Petenikas are associated with Bhojas instead of Râsṭikas. Bhojas,

---

19 ये वाप्यन्येऽपरान्ताः is the Sanskrit of the original Prâkṛit. It might be translated as "and also those other called Aparântas," *i.e.* also that other country called Aparânta. If we take it in this way, Aparânta is clearly Northern Konkan; for that is the name of that part of the country found in Sanskrit and Pâli Literature from the remotest times. In the Mahâvaṁśa and Dîpavaṁśa quoted below, Mahârâshṭra is associated with Aparântaka. It is possible to translate it as "and also other western countries" as M. Senart does. But the word "other" certainly refers to *Rastika-Petenikânâm* and not to the preceding Yonam Kambojam &c., as he takes it so as to make these last also western countries. (Inscriptions of Aśoka, Vol. II., p. 84.)

Section III.

we know, ruled over the country of Vidarbha or Berâr[20] and also in other parts of the Dekkan. In the inscriptions in the caves at Kuḍâ[21] the name "Mahâbhoja" or Great Bhoja occurs several times, and once in an inscription at Beḍsâ. Just as the Bhojas called themselves Mahâbhojas, the Râshṭrikas, Raṭṭis, Raṭṭhis, or Raṭṭhas called themselves Mahâraṭṭhis or Mahâraṭṭhas, as will be shown below, and thus the country in which they lived came to be called Mahâraṭṭha, the Sanskrit of which is Mahârâshṭra. In the second and the thirteenth edicts, the countries of the Cholas, Pâṇḍyas, Ketalaputras (Chera or Kerala), and the Andhras and Pulindas are mentioned. Thus about a hundred years before Patānjali, the whole of the southern peninsula up to Cape Comorin was in direct communication with the north, and the Dekkan or Mahârâshṭra had regular kingdoms governed by Raṭṭas and Bhojas.

Etymology of the name "Mahârâshṭra."

The occurrence of the names "Mahâraṭṭhi," "Mahâraṭṭha" and "Mahârâshṭra" in books and inscriptions.

In the Mahâvaṁso, a Ceylonese chronicle which was written in the third quarter of the fifth century of the Christian era, and in the Dîpavaṁso, which is much older, the Buddhist saint Moggaliputto, who conducted the proceedings of the third convocation said to [12] have been held in the time of Aśoka, is represented to have sent missionaries to Mahâraṭṭha, Aparântaka, and Vanavâsî.[22] Whether the name Mahâraṭṭha or Mahârâshṭra had come into use in the

---

20 In the Daśakumâracharita, the family of Bhojas has been represented as having held sway over the Vidarbha country for a long time.

21 Kuḍâ inscriptions Nos. 1, 9, 17, 19, 23, and Beḍsâ No. 2; Arch. Surv. of West. Ind., No. 10.

22 Mahâvaṁso, Turnour's Ed., pp. 71 and 72, and Dîpavaṁso, Oldenberg's Ed., p. 54. The latter however omits Vanavâsî.

time of Aśoka does not appear clear from this, but that it was used in the early centuries of the Christian era admits of little doubt. In some inscriptions in the cave-temples at Bhâjâ, Beḍsâ and Kârli which are to be referred to the second century, the male donors are called Mahârathi and the female Mahârathinî, which names, as observed before, correspond to Mahâbhoja and Mahâbhojî and signify the great Rathi (man and woman).[23] Similarly, in the large cave at Nânâghâṭ a Mahârathi hero is mentioned. Of the old Prâkṛits the principal one was called Mahârâshṭrî, because we are told it was the language of Mahârâshṭra. We have a poem in this dialect entitled Setubandha attributed to Kâlidâsa and mentioned by Daṇḍin, and a collection of amorous verses attributed to Śâlivâhana. It is the language of Prâkṛit verses put into the mouths of women in Sanskrit dramatic plays. Its grammar we have in Vararuchi's Prâkṛit Prakâśa ; but the date of this author is uncertain, though there is reason to believe that he was one of the nine gems of the court of Vikramâditya and was thus a contemporary of Varâhamihira and Kâlidâsa. Though the date of

Section III.

---

23 Arch. Surv. of West. Ind. No. 10; Bhâjâ No. 2; Beḍsâ No. 2; Kârli Nos. 2 and 14. Paṇḍit Bhagavânlâl appears to me clearly wrong here in taking Mahârathi to be equal to the Sk. Mahârathi and translating it as "a great warrior," for in Beḍsâ No. 2, a woman is called Mahârathinî where the word certainly cannot mean a great warrior, and to interpret it as "the wife or daughter of a great warrior" is simply begging the question. Mahârathi appears clearly to be the name of a tribe and is the same as our modern Marâṭhâ. It will appear from this inscription that there were intermarriages between the Mahâbhojas and the Mahârathis, for the lady mentioned in this inscription was the daughter of a Mahâbhoja and a Mahârathinî or the wife of a Mahârathî.

Section III. Kâlidâsa has not yet been satisfactorily determined, still he is mentioned as a poet of great merit in the first half of the seventh century by Bâṇa in his Harshacharita in the north,[24] and in an inscription at Aihole[25] dated 556 Śaka in the south. A hundred years is not too long a period to allow for the spread of his fame throughout the country, perhaps it is too short. Kâlidâsa may therefore be referred to that period of Sanskrit literature in which the nine gems flourished, and which has been placed by Dr. Kern in the first half of the sixth century.[26] The Mahârâshṭrî dialect, therefore, in which Kâlidâsa wrote the Setubandha and the Prâkṛit verses in his plays, must have undergone a course of cultivation for about two or three centuries earlier and been called by that name, since it has been known by no other in the whole literature. Varâhamihira also, who lived in the beginning of the sixth century, speaks of Mahârâshṭra as a southern country; and in the Aihole inscription alluded to above Mahârâshṭra is mentioned as comprising three [13] countries and ninety-nine thousand villages. Hwan Thsang, the Chinese traveller, calls the country ruled over by the Châlukyas in the second quarter of the seventh century, Moholocha, which has been properly identified with Mahârâshṭra. The occurrence of the name of Mahârâshṭra in the Purâṇas has already been noticed.

---

24 Dr. Hall's Vâsavadattâ, Preface, p. 14.
25 Ind. Ant. Vol. VIII., p. 243.
26 Ed. of Vârâhamihira, Preface, p. 20.

[14] SECTION IV.

POLITICAL HISTORY OF THE DEKKAN OR MAHÂRÂSHṬRA —ANALYSIS OF THE HISTORICAL INSCRIPTIONS IN THE CAVE-TEMPLES OF WESTERN INDIA.

Section IV.

No clue to the political history of Mahârâshṭra in the centuries immediately preceding the Christian era is now available. The Purâṇas contain lists of kings and dynasties whose chronology has been to some extent determined by their known connection with the successors of Alexander the Great ; but clear traces of their occupation of the south have not yet been found. Chandragupta, who founded the Maurya dynasty in about B.C. 320, ruled over Northern India as far as Kâṭhiâvâḍ, and his grandson Aśoka, who reigned from B.C. 263 to B.C. 229, retained possession of the province.[1] The rock-inscriptions of the latter, which were evidently planted in the countries which owned his sway, show that his empire extended to Kaliṅga or the Northern Circars in the east and Kâṭhiâvâḍ in the west. But stray edicts have been discovered farther south ; a fragment of the eighth being found at Supârâ and three minor ones on the northern frontier of Mysore. In the second rock-edict he speaks of his own dominions as "the conquered countries" and mentions Chola, Pâṇḍya, Ketalaputta, and Saliyaputta down to Tambapanni or Ceylon as outlying provinces. These therefore did not own his sway. But in the fifth edict he mentions the Râsṭikas, Petenikas and Aparântas and a few more provinces as those for the benefit of which he appointed religious ministers.

Extent of the dominions of Chandragupta and Aśoka.

1 See inscription of Rudradâman ; Ind. Ant., Vol. VII., p. 260, line 8.

Section IV.

If these were as much a part of his dominions as the many others which are not named, there is no reason why they should be named. Again he includes most of these in the thirteenth edict among countries which received his moral teaching, along with Chola, Pâṇḍya and others, and the territories ruled over by Antiochus and four other Greek princes. It would thus appear that though the countries of the Râsṭikas, Bhojas, Petenikas, and Aparântas were not outlying provinces like those of the Cholas, the Pâṇḍyas, and Ketalaputtas, they enjoyed a sort of semi-independence ; and only owned allegiance to him as suzerain. The appearance of fragments of his inscriptions at Supârâ and on the confines of Mysor is to be accounted for by this fact, or by the supposition that his dominions extended up to Supârâ on the western coast and along a strip in the centre of the peninsula to Mysor, leaving the western countries of the Râsṭikas, the Bhojas, and Petenikas, and the southern coast in a state of semi-independence. And there is some positive evidence to that effect. Vidarbha, the country of the Bhojas, must have existed as a separate kingdom about that time. For in the dramatic play of Mâlavikâgnimitra, the political events narrated in which may be accepted as historical, Agnimitra the son of Pushyamitra, the first king of the Śuṅga dynasty, who reigned in [15] the second and third quarters of the second century before Christ, is represented to have reigned at Vidiśâ, which I have before identified with Bhilsâ, probably as his father's viceroy. He had made proposals of marriage with Mâlavikâ to her brother Mâdhavasena, the cousin of Yajñasena, king of Vidarbha. Between these cousins there was a quarrel as regards the succession to the throne. When Mâdhavasena was

Vidarbha, a separate kingdom in the time of Śuṅgas.

secretly on his way to Vidiśâ, the general of Yajña-sena, posted on the frontier of the kingdom, captured him. His counsellor Sumati and Mâlavikâ escaped, but Mâdhavasena was kept in custody. Thereupon Agnimitra demanded of Yajñasena the surrender of Mâdhavasena. Yajñasena promised to give him up on condition that his wife's brother, who was the counsellor of the last Maurya king and had been imprisoned by Agnimitra or his father Pushya-mitra, should be released. This enraged Agnimitra, who thereupon sent an army against Yajñasena and vanquished him. Mâdhavasena was released, and the country of Vidarbha was divided between the two cousins, each ruling over each side of the river Varadâ.

Paiṭhaṇ, the capital of a kingdom.

Paiṭhaṇ also must have been the capital of a kingdom about the time. In the inscriptions in the caves at Pitalkhorâ near Châlisgâṁv, which from the forms of the characters in which they are engraved must be referred to the second century before Christ, the religious benefactions of merchants from Pratish-ṭhâna are recorded, as well as those of the physician to the king and of his son and daughter.[2] The king referred to must be the ruler of Pratishṭhâna or Paiṭhaṇ. No more particular information is available. On the history of the early centuries of the Christian era and the first century previous, however, the in-scriptions in the cave-temples on the top of the Sahyâdri throw a good deal of light. I will here bring together the information deducible from them, noticing the inscriptions in the chronological order clearly determined by the forms of the characters.

An inscription[3] in a small cave at Nâsik mentions

---

2 Inscriptions, pp. 39, 41. Arch. Surv. West. Ind., No. 10.

3 No. 6, Nâsik Inscriptions, Vol. VII., Jour. B. B. R. A. S., and p. 338, Trans. Oriental Congress, 1874.

Section IV.

Inscriptions of king Kṛishṇa and others of the Sâtavâhana race at Nâsik and Nânâghâṭ.

that the cave was scooped out by the lieutenant at Nâsik of King Kṛishṇa of the Śâtavâhana race. In a cave at Nânâghâṭ there is another, which is much mutilated and the purport of which consequently is not quite clear. In that same cave figures of persons are carved on the front wall, and the following names are inscribed over them: 1, Râyâ Simuka Sâtavâhano, *i. e.*, king Simuka Śâtavâhana; 2, Devî Nâyanikâyâ raññо cha Siri Sâtakanino, *i. e.*, of queen Nâyanikâ and king Srî Śâtakarṇi; 3, Kumâro Bhâyâ, *i. e.*, prince Bhâyâ; 4, Mahâraṭhiganakayiro, *i. e.*, the heroic Marâṭhâ leader or the hero of the Marâṭhâ tribe; 5, Kumâro Haku Siri, *i.e.*, prince Haku Śrî; 6, Kumâro Sâtavâhano, *i.e.*, prince Śâtavâhana. Of these the second who has been mentioned along with his queen must have been the reigning prince, the first was an earlier king of the same [16] dynasty, the fourth was a local Marâṭhâ warrior, and the rest were young princes of the Sâtavâhana dynasty.

Ushavadâta's principal inscription at Nâsik.

In another Nâsik cave there are four inscriptions. In the first we are told that the cave was caused to be constructed on mount Triraśmi in Govardhana or the Nâsik District by the benevolent Ushavadâta, the son-in-law of king Kshaharâta Nahapâna and son of Dînîka. Ushavadâta gave away three hundred thousand cows; constructed flights of steps on the river Bârṇâsâyâ; assigned sixteen villages to gods and Brâhmaṇs; fed a hundred thousand Brâhmaṇs every year; got eight Brâhmaṇs at Prabhâsa or Somanâth Paṭṭaṇ married at his own expense; constructed quadrangles, houses, and halting places at Bharukachchha or Bharoch, Daśapura in Mâlvâ, Govardhana, and Śorpâraga, the modern Supârâ near Bassein; made gardens and sank wells and tanks; placed ferry boats over the

Section IV.

Ibâ, Pârâdâ, Damaṇâ, Tâpî, Karabeṇâ, and Dâhanukâ, which were rivers along the coast between Ṭhâṇâ and Surat ; constructed rest-houses and endowed places for the distribution of water to travellers on both sides of these rivers ; and founded certain benefactions in the village of Nânaṁgola, for the Charaṇas and Parishads (Vedic schools of Brâhmaṇs) in Pîṇḍitakâvaḍa, Govardhana, Suvarṇamukha, Śorpâraga, and Râmatîrtha. One year in the rainy season he marched at the command of his lord to the relief of the chief of a tribe of Kshatriyas called Uttamabhadras, who had been attacked and besieged by the Mâlayaś. At the sound of his martial music the Mâlayas fled away, and they were made the subjects of the Uttamabhadras. Thence he went to Poshkarâṇi and there performed ablutions and gave three thousand cows and a village.[4]

Ushavadâta's other inscriptions.

In the second inscription Ushavadâta is spoken of as having, in the year 42, dedicated the cave monastery for the use of the Buddhist mendicant priests coming to it from the four quarters. He deposited with a guild of weavers residing in Govardhana a sum of two thousand Kârshâpaṇas at an annual interest of one hundred Kârshâpaṇas. Out of this interest he directed that a garment should annually be given to each of the twenty priests residing during the rains in his cave monastery. With another guild he deposited one thousand Kârshâpaṇas, the interest on which was seventy-five Kârshâpaṇas. Out of this other things (Kuśaṇa) were to be provided for the priests. The carrying out of these directions was secured by their being declared in the corporation of the town of Govardhana and

4 No. 17. Nâsik Inscriptions, Vol. VII., Jour. B. B. R. A. S. and Trans. Oriental Congress, 1874, p. 326.

Section IV.

inscribed on the door of the monastery. In the years 41 and 40 he gave away a large sum of money[5] for gods and Brâhmaṇs. The third inscription, which is a short one, mentions that the apartment on which it is engraved was the religious benefaction of Ushavadâta's wife Dakhamitrâ.[6] The fourth is greatly mutilated but sufficient remains to show that that also records similar gifts of Ushavadâta's.[7] In the cave-temple of Kârli there is an inscription [17] in which Ushavadâta is represented to have granted the village of Karajika for the support of the mendicant priests in the cave monastery of Valûraka, as the hill or the country about it seems to have been called at the time.[8] There also is given an account of his charities similar to that in the first of his Nâsik inscriptions. In an inscription at Junnar, Ayama, the minister of the lord Nahapâna the great Kshatrapa, is mentioned as having caused a tank to be dug and a hall to be constructed.[9] The minister appears to have been a Brâhmaṇ, since he is spoken of as belonging to the Vatsa Gotra.

Inscriptions of Gotamîputra Śâtakarṇi and Puḷumâyi at Nâsik.

Next in order come the inscriptions in which certain kings of the names of Gotamîputra Śâtakarṇi and Puḷumâyi are mentioned. In the longest of the four occurring in the cave-temple at one extremity of the hill at Nâsik, we are told that in the nineteenth year of the reign of king Puḷumâyi, the son of Vâsishṭhî, the cave was caused to be constructed and dedicated for the use of Buddhist mendicants of the

[5] Nos. 18 and 16, *Ibid*, which together form one inscription.

[6] First part of No. 16, *Ibid*.

[7] No. 14 *Ibid*.

[8] No. 13, Kârli Inscriptions—Arch. Surv., W. Ind., No. 10.

[9] No. 25, Junnar Inscriptions, *Ibid*.

Bhadrâyanîya sect by Gotamî, the mother of king Sâtakarṇi Gotamîputra. She is there called "the mother of the great king and the grandmother of the great king." Gotamîputra is spoken of as king of kings and ruler of Aśika, Aśmaka, Mûḷaka,[10] Surâshṭra, Kukura, Aparânta, Anûpa, Vidarbha and Âkarâvantî.[11] He was the lord of the mountains Vindhyâvat, Pâriyâtra, Sahya, Kṛishṇagiri, Malaya, Mahendra, Śreshṭhagiri, and Chakora. His orders were obeyed by a large circle of kings, and his feet were adored by them. His beasts of burden drank the waters of the three seas. He protected all who sought an asylum with him, and regarded the happiness and misery of his subjects as his own. He paid equal attention to the three objects of human pursuit, *viz.*, duty, worldly prosperity, and the satisfaction of desires, appointing certain times and places for each. He was the abode of learning, the support of good men, the home of glory, the source of good manners, the only person of skill, the only archer, the only hero, the only protector of Brâhmaṇs. He conferred upon Brâhmaṇs the means of increasing their race, and stemmed the progress of the confusion of castes. His exploits rivalled those of Râma, Keśava, Arjuna, and Bhîmasena, and his prowess was equal to that of Nabhâga, Nahusha, Janamejaya, Sagara, Yayâti, Râma, and Ambarîsha. He was

Section IV.

---

10 Aśmaka and Maulika are mentioned among the southern countries in the Purâṇas.

11 Surâshṭra is Southern Kâṭhiâvâḍ, Kukura, a portion of Râjputânâ, and Aparânta, Northern Konkan. Anûpa is mentioned in tne Purâṇas as a country situated in the vicinity of the Vindhyas. It was the country on the upper Narmadâ with Mâhishmatî for its capital, according to the Raghuvaṁśa. Âkarâvanti must be the eastern portion of Mâlvâ.

Section IV. descended from a long line of kings. He vanquished the host of his enemies in innumerable battles, quelled the boast and pride of Kshatriyas, destroyed the Śakas, Yavanas, and Pahlavas, left no trace or remnant of the race of Khagârâta, and re-established the glory of the Śâtavâhana family. In the last line of the inscription mention [18] is made of the grant of a village for the support of the establishment in the cave-temple.[12]

Charter of Puḷumâyi

In a later inscription engraved in smaller characters below this, Vâsishṭhîputra Śrî Puḷumavi, the lord of Navanara, issues orders to his lieutenant in Govardhana, Sarvâkshadalana. He calls his attention to the fact that the village granted by the "lord of Dhanakaṭa"[13] (Gotamîputra) in accordance with the above, was not liked by the Bhadrâyanîyas, and therefore assigns another to them by this charter.

Charter of Gotamîputra.

On the wall to the left of the verandah of the cave is another inscription. It purports to be an order or notice issued from the camp of the victorious

---

12 Inscription No. 26, Vol. VII. Jour. B. B. R. A. S. and Trans. Or. Congr. 1874, p. 307.

13 Paṇḍit Bhagvânlâl and Dr. Bühler, whose transcripts and translations of the Nâsik inscriptions were published about ten years after mine, read the expression thus understood by me as धनकटसमनेहि for the Sanskrit धनकटश्रमणैः. But what the Śramaṇas or Buddhist priests of Dhanakaṭa, which was situated hundreds of miles away on the lower Kṛishṇâ, could have to do with the matter of the granting of a village near Nâsik to the Bhadrâyanîya mendicants of the place it is impossible to conceive. The expression must, I think, be taken as धनकटसामिनेहि for the Sanskrit धनकटस्वामिभिः or धनकटसामियेहि corresponding to महासामियेहि in the first part of No. 25, the Sanskrit of which is महास्वामिकैः. The form सामिनेहि must have come into use on the analogy of such forms as अत्तनेहि for आत्मभिः and राजानेहि for राजभिः.

Section IV.

army of Govardhana, by Gotamîputra Sâtakarṇi, lord of Dhanakaṭaka, to Vishṇupâlita, his lieutenant in Govardhana, informing him that the king has granted a field measuring 200 Nivartanas, which was up to that time in the possession of one Ushabhadâta, for the benefit of recluses. The charter here engraved is represented to have been originally issued in the year 18, that is, in the year preceding that in which the cave-temple was completed and dedicated. Below this is inscribed another charter issued in the form of an order to Śramaka, the governor of Govardhana, by the queen of Gotamîputra Sâtakarṇi, who is also called the royal mother. She therein speaks of a field granted before, probably the one conveyed by the above charter, and says that it measures one hundred Nivartanas, and she assigns another hundred by this charter out of a field belonging to the crown which was her patrimony. It appears that two hundred Nivartanas were granted by the first charter, but probably it turned out that the field measured one hundred only ; hence she now makes it up by granting another hundred out of another field. The date of this grant is 24, *i.e.*, it was made six years after the first.[14]

Of the wife of Gotamîputra.

Besides these, there are two inscriptions at Nâsik recording the benefactions of private individuals, dated in the second and seventh years of the reign of Siri (Śrî) Puḷumâyi, and two in the cave at Kârli,[16] dated in the seventh and twenty-fourth years of his reign.

Private inscriptions containing Puḷumâyi's name.

Since Gotamî is spoken of as the mother of a king and the grandmother of a king, and the wife of

Relations between the kings

14 No. 25, *Ibid.*

15 Nos. 3 and 27, *Ibid.*

16 Nos. 14 and 20, Arch. Surv. West. Ind., No. 10.

Section IV.

and queens mentioned in the inscriptions in Gotamî's cave.

her son Gotamîputra Śâtakarṇi is [19] represented as the mother of a king, and since the only other king besides Śâtakarṇi mentioned in these inscriptions is Puḷumâyi, it appears that this last was the grandson and son respectively of these two ladies. He was therefore the son and his mother Vâsishṭhî the wife of Gotamîputra Śâtakarṇi. Śâtakarṇi issued the charter contained in the second inscription in the year 18, which must be the eighteenth year of Puḷumâyi's reign, since dates referring to his reign only are found at Nâsik and Kârli and not to that of Gotamîputra. Even the date of the large inscription noticed above in which Gotamîputra's great deeds are recorded is referred to Puḷumâyi's reign. And the grant of the village alluded to in that inscription and the one below appears to have been made by Gotamîputra, since he is spoken of as "the lord of Dhanakaṭaka," though the portion of the rock containing the words that would have rendered the sense clear has been cut away. Gotamî is spoken of as dedicating the cave in the present tense, wherefore it must be understood she was alive at the time. The father and the son appear thus to have reigned at the same time, the son on this side of the country since the inscriptions are dated in his reign, and the father at Dhanakaṭaka, which has been identified with Dharaṇikoṭ in the Guntur district of the Madras Presidency. And this is confirmed by the fact, mentioned above, of Gotamî's having been called the mother of the great king and the grandmother of the great king. This statement would be pointless if she were not both at one and the same time.[17]

---

[17] Dr. Bühler (Arch. Surv. of West. Ind., Vol. IV., p. 110,) supposes me to have rested my conclusion as regards this point on this statement alone, and calls it a mistake.

Section IV.

Since the charter of the year 24, intended as supplementary to that of 18, was issued by Vâsishṭhî, while the first was issued by her husband, it appears probable that Gotamîputra had died in the interval and Vâsishṭhî reigned as regent at the capital, while Puḷumâyi continued to govern the Dekkan or Mahârâshṭra. The years given in the charter must be those of Puḷumâyi, since even the large inscription is dated in the nineteenth year of his reign. These kings belonged to the Sâtavâhana dynasty.

Maḍharîputra. Yajña Srî.

The names of other kings, apparently of the same dynasty, are found in other inscriptions. In one of the caves at Kânheri near [20] Ṭhânâ, a grant is recorded in the eighth year of the reign of Maḍharî-

---

But he will find my other reasons also stated in the remarks at the end of my article in the Transactions of the Oriental Congress of 1874. And even this statement has a very high corroborative value. For, if the object of the writer was to represent Gotami's "special claim" to honour, that is better served by supposing that her son and grandson were great kings at one and the same time. Every queen belonging to a dynasty in power is the mother of a king and grandmother of a king; and there is nothing special in the fact if the son and the grandson bore the title at different times. If the son was dead, no object is gained as regards this point by saying she was the mother of that son that is not gained by saying she was the grandmother of a *living* great king. And if it was a fact that Gotamîputra was dead when the cave-temple was dedicated and Puḷumâyi alone was reigning, we should expect to find the exploits of the latter also celebrated in the inscription, but there is not a word in praise of him. If Puḷumâyi became king only after Gotamîputra, the latter must have died nineteen years before the dedication of the temple, and it certainly is not what one acquainted with the manner and motive of Hindu inscription-writers would expect that a king who had been dead for nineteen years should be highly extolled in the inscription and the reigning king altogether passed over in silence.

Section IV. — putra Śakasena.[18] In two other inscriptions at the same place the name of the reigning prince is given as Gotamîputa Śiri Yaññа Sâtakaṇi (Gotamîputra Śrî Yajña Śâtakarṇi).[19] In one of these the year that is given is not legible, but still appears to be the sixteenth of his reign. There is one inscription at Nâsik which is dated in the seventh year of that king.[20] Paṇḍit Bhagvânlâl has brought to light the name of another prince. There is according to him an inscription on the Nânâghâṭ in which is recorded the dedication of a cistern of water in the thirteenth year of Vâsiṭhiputa Chatarapana Sâtakani.

Chatarapana.

Names of princes on the coins found at Kolhâpur.

A large number of coins of copper and lead were discovered a few years ago, buried in what appears to have once been a Buddhist stûpa at Kolhâpur. Another hoard had been found some time previous in about the same locality. The legends on those coins are in characters the forms of which greatly

---

18 No. 19, Jour. B. B. R. A. A. S., Vol. VI. and Vol. XII., p. 409. In the first copy the name is clearly Sakasenasa, but in the second, which is Paṇḍit Bhagvânlâl's rubbing, something like an effaced mark for the vowel *i* appears above the first two consonants. The Paṇḍit, therefore, reads the name as Sirisenasa for Śrîsenasya, but the *k* is distinct even in his copy. *Siki* cannot mean anything, wherefore it appears that the indistinct marks which do not occur in the first copy are due to some flaw in the rock, and do not represent the vowel *i*. Dr. Bhâu Dâji also read the name as Sakasenasa. But the copy of the inscription given in Plate LI. Vol. V. of the Archæological Survey of Western India and marked No. 14 leaves no doubt whatever on the point. The name there is distinctly *Sakasenasa*. Further confirmation if necessary will be found later on. It is therefore clearly a mistake to call the king *Sirisena*.

19 Nos. 4 and 44, Jour. B. B. R. A. S., Vol. VI.

20 No. 4, Jour. B. B. R. A. S., Vol. VII., and Trans. Or. Congr., 1874, p. 339.

resemble those in the cave inscriptions above noticed. Section IV.
They are as follows[21]:

Rañño Vasiṭhîputasa Viḷivâyakurasa.

Rañño Gotamîputasa Viḷivâyakurasa.

Rañño Maḍharîputasa Sevalakurasa.

Here we have the same names as before; but the words Viḷivâyakurasa and Sevalakurasa have not yet been interpreted by any student of Indian antiquities. On a former occasion I put forth a conjecture that they were the names of the viceroys of those kings appointed to govern the country about Kolhâpur.[22] For, coins of two of these princes and of a few others belonging to the same dynasty are found near Dharaṇikoṭ in the Gantur District about the site of Dhanakaṭaka, the old capital. The legends on these do not contain those words, and the coins are of a different type from those found at Kolhâpur. These last, therefore, it appeared to me, were struck on this side of the country, and consequently bore the names of the viceroys under whose authority they were issued. The truth of this conjecture I will demonstrate further on. It will be seen from what is to be stated hereafter that the Vâsiṭhîputa of these coins who had Vilivâyakura for his viceroy can be no other than Vâsishṭhîputra Puḷumâyi. [21] The Gotamîputa must be Gotamîputra Yajña Ŝâtakarṇi of the inscriptions; for the father of Puḷumâyi did not reign on this side of the country, as none of the inscriptions are dated in his

---

21 Jour. B. B. R. A. S., Vol. XIII., p. 305, and Vol. XIV., p. 153-54. There are in my possession coins of lead of the same size as those figured here, and a good many smaller ones in which I find the same legends as those given above. They also were found at Kolhâpur. Some of the smaller ones appear to be of bronze.

22 Jour. B. B. R. A. S., Vol. XIV., p. 154.

Section IV. reign though his exploits are described in the Nâsik Caves. Maḍharîputa must have come after Gotamîputa and not after Vâsiṭhîputa, as is maintained by some scholars ; for his viceroy was a different person from that of the other two. The fact that these two had the same viceroy shows that one of them immediately succeeded the other. Another prince with a different viceroy could not come between them.

Names of princes on the Supârâ coin.

In the stûpa dug out at Supârâ, Paṇḍit Bhagvânlâl found a silver coin in a copper casket. On the obverse of the coin, which bears a well-shaped head of the king, we have the legend Raññno Gotamiputasa Siri Yañña Sâtakanisa, which means " [this coin is] of the king Gotamîputra Śrî Yajña Śâtakarṇi." This therefore is the prince in whose name the coin was issued. There is another legend on the reverse which though some of the letters are not distinct appears to be *Gotamiputa-Kumâru-Yañña - Sâtakani-Chaturapanasa* the sense of which is " [this coin is] of Chaturapana Yañña Sâtakani, prince of Gotamîputa."[23] The coin was thus like the Kolhâpur coins issued in the names

---

[23] The nether portions of the letters *chaturapanasa* only are impressed on the coin so that the reading is somewhat doubtful; but *panasa* is distinct enough. Paṇḍit Bhagvânlâl puts *Chaturapanasa* at the beginning of the legend and reads *Chaturapanasa Gotamiputa Kumâru Yañña Sâtakaṇi* which he translates "Yajña Śâtakarṇi, son of Gotamîputa, and prince of Chaturapana;" and states his belief that Chaturapana was the name of Yajña Śrî's father. But to connect Kumâru, which forms a part of a compound with the genitive, Chaturapanasa, is grammatically not allowable; while the genitive which is always required to show whose coin it is, is wanting. Hence Chaturapanasa is the last word and the whole is a compound, Kumâru is probably a mistake for Kumâra and Yañña Sâtakani is the father's name placed before Chaturapanasa to show that he was his son. (Jour. B. B. R. A. S., Vol. XV., pp. 305-6.)

Section IV.

of two persons ; of whom Yajña Śrî Sâtakarṇi was the reigning sovereign, as his name appears round the bust, and Chaturapana who was his son represented him as viceroy in the province in which the coin was issued, and which from the shape and get-up of the coin appears to have been once ruled over by the Kshatrapas of Ujjayinî or Kâṭhiâwâḍ.

Chaturapana in a Kânheri Inscription.

There is an inscription at Kãnheri which is in a mutilated condition, but which with the help of Mr. West's eye copy and an impression given in one of Dr. Burgess' Reports has been partially restored by Dr. Bühler. Therein is made the dedication of a water cistern by Śateraka who was the confidential counsellor of the Queen of Vâsishṭhîputra Śâtakarṇi, who belonged to the family of the Karddamakas and was the daughter of a Mahâkshatrapa whose name is obliterated. The opening letters of the second line have also been effaced, but what we might expect to find there is the name of her son, after we have had those of her husband, family, and father. From the letters in West's copy which look like *Sakarâja* one might think the son meant was Śakasena ; still the conjecture is somewhat hazardous.[24] The name of this Vâsisṭhî [22] putra is Śâtakarṇi, wherefore he was not Puḷumâyi, but very likely Chatushparṇa (Chatarapana) Śâtakarṇi.

Thus then, from these inscriptions and coins we arrive at the names of the following kings arranged

---

[24] Jour. B. B. R. A. S., Vol. VI. and Archaeol. S. of W.I., Vol. V., Inscription No. 11 ; also p. 78 of the latter. There would be nothing improbable in it if we here read the name of Śakasena. For this name and that of his mother Maḍhari point to a connection with the Śakas whose representatives the Kshatrapas were, and this connection is unfolded in this inscription.

Section IV. in the chronological order indicated by the forms of the characters used and by other circumstances:

Kṛishṇarâja.

Sâtakarṇi.

Kshaharâta Nahapâna and his son-in-law Ushavadâta.

Gotamîputra Sâtakarṇi.

Vâsishṭhîputra Puḷumâyi.

Gotamîputra Srî Yajña Sâtakarṇi.

Vasishṭîputra Chatushparṇa (Chaturapana or Chatarapana) Sâtakarṇi.

Maḍharîputra Sakasena.

Besides these, we have the name of Simuka Sâtavâhana, a king that reigned earlier than the second in the above list. We shall hereafter assign to him his proper place.

[23] SECTION V.

NATIVE AND FOREIGN PRINCES MENTIONED IN THE INSCRIPTIONS.—IDENTIFICATION OF THE FORMER WITH THE ANDHRABHṚITYAS OF THE PURÂNAS.

Section V.

Nahapâna, a Śaka.

THE first thing that will strike one on looking at the list given at the end of the last section, is that the name Kshaharâta Nahapâna is not Indian but foreign. The title Kshatrapa or Mahâkshatrapa also used in the case of that king, is not Indian, though it is the Sanskritised form of a foreign one, very likely the Persian *Satrap*. From the statement in the inscription of Gotamîputra that he destroyed the Śakas, Yavanas, and Pahlavas, it appears that the country was at that time very much exposed to the inroads of these foreigners. Yavanas were the Bactrian Greeks, but Kshaharâta Nahapâna does not look a Greek name. He must, therefore, have been either a Śaka or Pahlava. Again, we are told that Gotamîputra left no remnant of the race of Khagârâta or Khakhârâta which name seems to be the same as Kshaharâta or Khaharâta as it is spelled in the Kârli and Junnar inscriptions. It follows, therefore, that the Śakas or Pahlavas made themselves masters of the country some time between the second king in the above list and Gotamîputra Sâtakarṇi, and that they were driven out by Gotamîputra who, by thus recovering the provinces lost to his dynasty, re-established, as stated in the inscription, the glory of the Sâtavâhana race to which he belonged. All the other kings named above belonged to that dynasty.

Śakas and Pahlavas overthrown by Gotamîputra.

Purâṇic dynasties.

Now, in the Purâṇas we have lists of kings and dynasties that ruled over the country. The earliest dynasty with which we are here concerned is the

Section V. Maurya founded by Chandragupta in B.C. 320, as determined by his relations with Seleucus, one of the generals and successors of Alexander the Great. It ruled over Northern India for 137 years according to the Purâṇas, and the last king Bṛihadratha was murdered by his general Pushyamitra or Pushpamitra, who founded the Śuṅga dynasty. This was in power for 112 years and was succeeded by the Kâṇva family which ruled for forty-five years. The Kâṇvas were overthrown by Sipraka, Sindhuka, or Śisuka, as he is variously named, who founded what the Purâṇas call the dynasty of the Andhrabhṛityas, that is, Andhras who were once servants or dependents. The second king of this dynasty was Kṛishṇa according to all, the third was Śâtakarṇi or Śrîsâtakarṇi according to the Vâyu or Vishṇu, while the Bhâgavata corrupts the name slightly to Śântakarṇa. The Mâtsya interposes three more kings between Kṛishṇa and Śâtakarṇi, while the Vishṇu has another Śâtakarṇi to correspond with that of the Mâtsya. Gotamîputra is the thirteenth prince according to the Vâyu, fifteenth according to the Bhâgavata, seventeenth according to the Vishṇu, and twenty-second according to the Mâtsya. Pulimat, Purimat or Pulomat was his successor [24] according to the Vishṇu, the Bhâgavata, or the Mâtsya. These are so many mislections for the Puḷumâyi of our inscriptions and coins. The Vâyu omits his name altogether. His successor was Śiva Śrî according to the Vishṇu and the Mátsya, while the Bhâgavata calls him Vedaśiras, and the Vâyu does not notice him. Yajña Śrî occurs in all, being placed after Śivaskandha, the successor of Śiva Sri, by all except the Vâyu, which assigns to him the next place after Gotamîputra.

Thus then, the names occurring in the inscriptions and on the coins as well as the order sufficiently

Section V.

The Sâtavâhanas of the inscriptions same as the Andhrabhṛityas of the Purâṇas.

agree with those given in the Purâṇas under the Andrabhṛitya dynasty to justify us in believing that the kings mentioned in both are the same. There is, however, no trace of Chatushparṇa Sâtakarṇi unless we are to identify him with Chaṇḍaśrî Sâtakarṇi. The name Maḍharîputra Ṣakasena also does not occur in the Purâṇas ; and he appears to have belonged to a branch of the dynasty. We shall hereafter assign to him his place in the list. Simuka, whose name occurs in the Nânâghât inscription, and who, as I have already observed, was an earlier occupant of the throne than the reigning prince Sâtakarṇi the third in the Purâṇic list, must be the same as Śiśuka, the founder of the dynasty. For the Devanâgarî *ma* is often so carelessly written as to look like *sa* ; hence the true Simuka was corrupted to Sisuka, Śisuka, or Śiśuka, in the course of time. The Sindhuka of the Vâyu and the Sipraka of the Vishṇu are further corruptions. This identification is rendered probable also by the consideration that he who caused the cave to be constructed, and the statues of himself and the younger princes to be carved, might, to give dignity to his race, be expected to get the founder of the dynasty also represented there, especially as he was removed only one degree from him. In this manner the Andhrabhṛitya dynasty of the Purâṇas is the same as the Sâtavâhana dynasty of the inscriptions.

[25] SECTION VI.

CHRONOLOGY OF THE ANDHRABHṚITYAS OR ŚÂTAVÂHANAS.

Section VI.

The dynasty of Nahapâna not the same as that of the Satraps of Ujjayinî and Kâṭhiâvâḍ.

THE next question we have to consider is as regards the dates of these princes. In my paper on the Nâsik cave inscriptions[1], I have accepted A.D. 319 as the date of Gotamîputra's accession, arrived at by taking B.C. 315 as the year in which Chandragupta founded the dynasty of the Mauryas at Pâṭaliputra, and 664 years to have elapsed between him and Gotamîputra, since the periods assigned in the Purâṇas to that dynasty and the subsequent ones, and the durations of the reigns of the Andhrabhṛitya princes who proceeded Gotamîputra according to the Mâtsya when added, give 664. The "race of Khagârâta," which Gotamîputra is, as observed before, represented in one of the Nâsik inscriptions to have exterminated, I identified with the dynasty of the Kshatrapas whose coins are found in Kâṭhiâvâḍ, as well as a few inscriptions, since Kshaharâta or Khagârâta was also a Kshatrapa and had been placed at the head of the dynasty by previous writers. The latest date on the coins of those princes then known was 250, which referred to the Śaka era, is A.D. 328. This comes so close to Gotamîputra's A.D. 319, that the two seemed to corroborate each other. But there are several objections to this view, some of which occurred to me even then. (1)—The inscriptions and coins of the Kshatrapa dynasty concur in carrying the genealogy backward to Chashṭana and no further, and as yet nothing has turned up to show that any connection existed

---

1 Trans. Or. Congr., 1874.

Section VI.

between him and Nahapâna. (2)—If the Kshatrapa or Satrap dynasty held sway over Mahârâshṭra for about three hundred years as it did over Kâṭhiâvâḍ, we might reasonably expect to find in that country inscriptions or coins of most of the princes, but a few coins of the later ones only have been discovered in a village near Karâḍh[2] and no inscription whatever. (3)—Rudradâman in his Junâgaḍ inscription calls a Ŝâtakarṇi, 'lord of Dakshiṇapatha', which he would not have done if he had been the ruler of even a part of the Dekkan. (4)—And the dates occurring on some Satrap coins recenty discovered are said to be 300 and 304[3] which referred to the Ŝaka era A.D. 378 and 382, that is, the Satraps were in power even long after A.D. 340, which is the date of Gotamî-putra's death according to the Purâṇic accounts. For these reasons it would appear that the "race" of Khagârâta or Nahapâna which Gotamîputra put an end to and which ruled over this country before him, could not have been the dynasty of the Satraps. (5)—Besides, according to my former view, the interval between Nahapâna and Gotamîputra is about 200 years ; but the difference in form between the characters in Ushavadâta's and Gotamîputra's inscriptions is not great enough for that period. Hence the two princes must be brought closer together.

Ptolemy's Siro Polemios the same as Siri Puḷumâyi and his Baleocuros the same as

[26] From the Greek geographer Ptolemy we learn that in his time the country inland from the western coast was divided into two divisions of which the northern was governed by Siro Polemios whose capital was Paiṭhaṇ, and the southern by Baleocuros who lived in Hippocura. Siro Polemios is evidently

---

2 Jour. B. B. R. A. S., Vol. VII., p. 16.

3 Ind. Ant. Vol. VI, p. 57, Note, and Genl. Cunningham's Arch. Report, Vol. XI., p. 127.

Section VI.

Viḷivâya-kura.

the same name as the Siri Puḷumâvi or Puḷumâyi of the inscriptions corresponding to the Pulomat, or Puḷimat of the Purâṇas. But there were two kings who bore that name, one the son of Gotamîputra, mentioned in the inscriptions, and another an earlier prince of the Andhrabhṛitya dynasty. This last does not appear to have been a prince of any note ; wherefore very likely the former is the one spoken of by Ptolemy. But the question is almost settled by the mention of Baleocuros as the Governor of the southern provinces. We have seen that in the legends on the Kolhâpur coins the name Viḷivâyakura is associated with that of Puḷumâyi and of Gotamîputra. Viḷivâyakura is the same as Baleocura, and I have already stated that the reason why his name, in my opinion, occurs along with those of the two princes of the Śâtavâhana dynasty, and on Kolhâpur coins alone, while it does not occur on those found in the lower Godâvarî districts, is that he was the viceroy of those princes ruling over the country about Kolhâpur. This country answers to the southern division mentioned by the Greek geographer as being governed by Baleocuros. The Siro Polemios therefore of Ptolemy is the same as the Puḷumâyi of the inscriptions and coins.

Puḷumâyi began to reign about 130 A. D.

Ptolemy died in A.D. 163, and is said to have written his work after A.D. 151. Puḷumâyi, therefore, must have been on the throne some time before this last date. We will now proceed to reconcile this date with those mentioned in the inscriptions, and to determine more particularly the date of Puḷumâyi's accession. Some of Ushavadâta's benefactions were founded in the years 40, 41 and 42, and the latest date connected with Nahapâna is that in the inscription of his minister Ayama at Junnar, *viz.*, 46. These dates should, I think, be referred to the Śaka era. For, we have seen that before the time of Gotamîputra, the country was subject to the inroads of Śakas and other foreign tribes, and the Scythians who are identified with the Śakas had, according to the Greek geographers, established a kingdom in Sind and even in Râjputânâ. The era known by the name of the Śaka and referred to in all the early copper-plategrants as the era of the Śaka king or kings must have been established by the most powerful of the Śaka invaders,[4] who for the first time Section VI.

[4] Prof. Oldenberg thinks Kanishka to be the founder of the era; but this view is, I think, untenable. (1)—A dynasty of three kings only cannot perpetuate an era. The dynasty of the Guptas composed of seven kings was in power for more than a hundred and fifty years, but their era died a natural death in the course of a few centuries. (2)—The characters in Kanishka's inscriptions, especially the *ya* as conjoined with a preceding consonant, are later than those we find in the first century. One has simply to compare Inscription No. 1 in Plate XIII. of the third volume of General Cunningham's Arch. Reports with No. 4 to see the great difference in the forms of the letters in the times of the earliest Kshatrapas and of Kanishka. The former belongs to the time of the Kshatrapa Śodâsa and the letters are almost like those we find in Ushavadâta's inscriptions at Nâsik; while those in the latter, which is dated in the ninth year of Kanishka, are considerably later; and both the inscriptions exist in Mathurâ. (3)—There is no ground to believe that Kanishka reigned over Gujarât and Mahârâshtra, but the Śaka era began to be used very early, especially in the last country. (4)—The Guptas whose gold coinage is a close imitation of that of the Indo-Scythian dynasty, came to power in A.D. 319: while the last of the three kings Kanishka, Hushka, and Vâsudeva must, if the reign of the first began in A.D. 78, have ceased to reign about A.D. 178, *i.e.*, about 100 years after the foundation of the dynasty. And the latest date of Vâsudeva is 89. If so, an interval of 140 years must have elapsed between the last of the Indo-Scythian kings and the first Gupta; but the close resemblance in the coinage necessitates the supposition

Section VI. [27] obtained a permanent footing in the country, and Nahapâna and Chashṭana[5] or his father must have been his Satraps appointed to rule over Western India, and Mâlvâ. On this supposition the latest date of Nahapâna must correspond to A.D. 124. Gotamîputra or Puḷumâyi therefore must have acquired possession of this country after that year. The earliest date of Puḷumâyi occurring in the inscriptions is the second year of his reign; and since the inscription could not have borne that date if Nahapâna or his successors had been in power, it is clear that Puḷumâyi began to reign after the overthrow of the latter. Now, we also learn from Ptolemy that Tiastenes reigned at Ozene about the time when he wrote, and was therefore a contemporary of Puḷumâyi. Tiastenes has, I think, been reasonably identified with Chashṭana. But accord-

---

that it was much shorter. Albiruni's statement that the initial date of the Gupta era was 241 Śaka, *i.e.*, 319 A.D., has been pronounced unreliable by some antiquarians. As to this point and the era of the Satrap dates, see Appendix A.

5 Professor Oldenberg considers Chashṭana to be a Satrap appointed by Gotamîputra, a supposition which is unwarrantable, since a prince like Gotamîputra whose aim was to expel and destroy foreigners cannot be expected to appoint a foreigner, as Chashṭana's name indicates he was, to be a viceroy, and to use a foreign title; and we have seen that Baleocuros, who was a viceroy of that monarch or of his son, does not use that title. Rudradâman, the grandson of Chashṭana, appointed, as we see from his Junâgaḍ inscription, a Pahlava of the name of Suviśâkha, who was the son of Kûlaipa, to govern Surâshṭra and Ânarta. This circumstance confirms what we gather from other sources, namely, that this was a dynasty of princes of a foreign origin, who had adopted Hindu manners and even names, had in some cases entered into marriage alliance with native royal families, and were domiciled in the country.

ing to the Junâgaḍ inscription noticed above, Chashṭana's grandson Rudradâman was the reigning prince in the year 72, which, taking the era to be the Śaka, is 150 A.D. Chashṭana and Puḷumâyi therefore could not have been contemporaries in 150 A.D. Ptolemy's account must, in consequence, refer to a period much earlier, *i.e.* to about the year 132 A.D., since about eighteen or twenty years at least must be supposed to have elapsed between the date of his information when Chashṭana was on the throne and the year 150 A.D. when his grandson was in possession of it, his son Jayadâman having occupied it for some time in the interval. Again, in the nineteenth year of Puḷumâyi, Gotamîputra was in possession, according to the large inscription at Nâsik, of a good many of those provinces which, according to the Junâgaḍ inscription, were conquered and ruled over by Rudradâman. The date 72 in the inscription seems to refer to the sweeping away by a storm and excessive rain of the dyke on one side of the lake therein mentioned and not to the cutting of the inscription on the rock. So that it is doubtful whether Rudradâman had conquered those [28] provinces before 72 or did so after 72 and before the incision of the inscription. Supposing he conquered them before 72, the nineteenth year of Puḷumâyi must correspond at least to the second or third year before A.D. 150, that is, Puḷumâyi must have begun to reign, at the latest, about the year A.D. 130. And even if we understand him to have conquered them after 72, Puḷumâyi's accession cannot be placed much later, for the interval between Chashṭana who was Puḷumâyi's contemporary and his grandson Rudradâman who was reigning in 150 A.D. will be considerably shortened. Nahapâna or his successor must thus have been overthrown by

Section VI.

Gotamîputra or Puḷumâyi about five or six years at the most after his latest recorded date, *viz.* A.D. 124.

The history of the relations of these princes appears to be this. Nahapâna was a Satrap ruling over Mahârâshṭra. His capital was probably Junnar since the inscriptions at the place show the town to have been in a flourishing condition about that time, and we have a record there of the gift of his minister. He must have died soon after 46 Śaka or A.D. 124.

Relations of Gotamîputra and his successors with Nahapâna, Chashṭana and Rudradâman.

Gotamîputra and Puḷumâyi came from the south-east to regain the provinces lost to their family, overthrew Nahapâna's successor, whoever he was, killed all his heirs, and re-established their power over this side of the country. This appears to be what is meant by Gotamîputra's having been represented in the Nâsik inscription to have "left no remnant of the race of Khagarâta," and to have "regained the prestige of his family." Chashṭana founded or belonged to another dynasty of Satraps which reigned at Ujjayinî. In the Junâgaḍ inscription, men of all castes are represented to have gone to Rudradâman and chosen him their lord for their protection ;[6] and he is spoken of as having re-established the kingdom that had been lost,[7] himself assumed the title of the Great

---

6 The expression is सर्ववर्णैरभिगम्य रक्षणार्थं पतित्वे वृतेन. Ind. Ant., Vol. VII., p. 260, 1, 9.

7 In Paṇḍit Bhagavânlâl's transcript in Vol. VII., Ind. Ant., the reading is भ्रष्टराजप्रतिष्ठापकेन. But in a foot-note Dr. Bühler says that the correct reading may be राज्य for राज. In Dr. Bhâu Dâji's copy of the inscription the ज्य is distinct, p. 118, Vol. VII, Jour. B. B. R. A. S. Bhâu Dâji and Paṇḍit Bhagvânlâl translate this expression by "obtained glory of great exploits by the re-establishment of *deposed kings*," (p. 20, Vol. VII., Jour. B. B. R. A. S.), and "he who has restored to their thrones

Kshatrapa, conquered Akarâvantî, Anûpa, Surâshṭra, Aparânta and other provinces which, as we have seen, were owned by Gotamîputra, and some more; and as having twice subdued Śâtakarṇi, the lord of Dakshinâpatha, but still not destroyed him in consequence of his connection[8] with him not being remote [29] and acquired a good name on that account. The meaning of all this appears to me to be this. Gotamîputra Śâtakarṇi, after having destroyed Nahapâna or his successor, turned his arms against another dynasty of foreigners that was ruling at Ujjayinî. Or the Kshatrapa sovereign of Ujjayinî, Chashṭana, or very probably his son Jayadâman, having observed the growing power of Gotamîputra or Puḷumâyi who had put an end to a kindred family of rulers, and desirous of preventing his further growth, must have attacked him. A fact such as this must be the basis of the popular stories about a king of Ujjayinî having attacked Śâlivâhana at Paiṭhaṇ and been defeated by him. Śâlivâhana is but

Section VI.

---

deposed kings," (p. 260 *a*, Vol. VII., Ind. Ant.). If राज were the reading, this translation would of course be correct, but with राज्य it is far-fetched. There is nothing here to show that the lost *râjya* or kingdom re-established by Rudradâman was any other person's than his own. So that, it looks natural to understand him to have re-established (his own) lost kingdom.

8 The reading is संबंधावदूरया. It is allowable to insert त and take it as संबंधावदूरतया. But the sense of the word, which is "remoteness," will not suit the context; as he could not have "acquired a good name," *i.e.*, been esteemed by people for not destroying the Lord of the Dekkan on account of the remoteness of the connection. Remoteness or distance of the country would compel one to let his enemy alone, and there could be no virtue in it. The व therefore in the word must have crept in through mistake; wherefore the true reading must be संबंधाद्दूरतया.

Section VI. another mode of pronouncing Sâtavâhana ;[9] and Puḷumâyi or Gotamîputra was a Sâtavâhana. The ruler of Ujjayinî was defeated and pursued by the victorious Gotamîputra into his own dominions, when the latter subjugated Avantî, Anûpa, Surâshṭra and Aparânta, and dethroned Jayadâman. For a time he and his successors held sway over the territories owned by Chashṭana, but subsequently Rudradâman collected a band of followers, the same as those that are represented in the inscription as having chosen him their lord, and driving away the Sâtavâhanas, regained his lost kingdom and got himself crowned as Mahâkshatrapa. But as appears from the Supârâ coin of Yajña Srî which bears such striking resemblance to the Kshatrapa coins and is so unlike the Kolhâpur coins of that monarch, large or small, and from the fact that his son Chaturapana was his viceroy or representative, the Sâtavâhanas retained possession of a part at least of the Kshatrapa territories up to the time of Yajña Srî. They even entered into blood relationship with the Kshatrapas, as we learn from the Kânheri inscription, which speaks of the wife of Vâśishṭhîputra Sâtakarṇi being the daughter of a Mahâkshatrapa. But Rudradâman pursued his victories and according to his Junâgaḍ inscription twice conquered Sâtakarṇi the lord of Dakshiṇâpatha, but did not destroy him, and acquired a good name by his forbearance towards one whose connection with him was not remote. Thus the lord of Dakshiṇâpatha that he conquered was Yajña Srî Sâtakarṇi. He could not have been his son Chaturapana ; for the expression "non-remoteness of the connection" suits the former better than the latter, as Chaturapana's wife was the daughter of a

9 Hemachandra's Prâkṛit Grammar.

Mahâkshatrapa, perhaps his own and the connection with him was positively close. The re-acquisition of his lost kingdom by Rudradâman took place after the nineteenth year of Puḷumâyi's reign, that is, after about A.D. 149. It is in this way alone that the scraps of information derived from the Greek writers and gathered from inscriptions, coins, and popular legends, as well as the dates, can be made to harmonize with each other. **Section VI.**

Dates of the Andhrabhṛityas as determined from the Purâṇic accounts.

But the date thus assigned to Gotamîputra is not consistent with that derived from the Mâtsya Purâṇa. Our next endeavour, therefore, should be to ascertain whether none of the Purâṇas agrees sufficiently with the conclusion arrived at, and, if any does, to account for the [30] great discrepancy between it and the Mâtsya and others. That there is very little agreement among them as regards the Andhrabhṛitya dynasty, I have already indicated above. The genesis of our Purâṇic literature seems to be this. Certain versified accounts of certain things, purporting to be narrated by a bard to Ṛishis assembled together at a sacrificial session, were handed down orally from generation to generation ; and these were after some time committed to writing. The later Purâṇas, devoted to the exaltation of a particular deity and to the inculcation of certain doctrines, derived their accounts of these things from the earliest written Purâṇas and not from the oral tradition. Of the works of this class which I am going to compare for our present purpose, the oldest appears to me to be the Vâyu, and next to it the Mâtsya. The Vishṇu is later, and the Bhâgavata, the latest. The text of the old Purâṇas gradually became corrupt, and the authors of the later ones were in some cases misled by their incorrect readings

Section VI. into putting forth statements at variance with the original account. Now the four Purâṇas just mentioned contain general statements about the several dynasties, giving the number of princes belonging to each and its duration in years, and also mention the names of those princes more particularly ; while the Vâyu and the Mâtsya give in addition the number of years for which each reigned. Often there is a discrepancy between the general and the particular statements. The duration assigned by

Duration of the Maurya dynasty.

them all to the Maurya dynasty, founded by Chandragupta whose date as determined by his relations with the successors of Alexander the Great is justly characterised by Professor MaxMüller as the sheet-anchor of Indian chronology, is 137 years. The number of reigning princes given by the Vâyu is nine, and by the rest, ten ; but the names actually enumerated in the Vishṇu only are ten, while the Vâyu and the Bhâgavata give nine, and the Mâtsya, only four. The total of the years assigned to each prince by the Vâyu is 133 years ; so that it is not unlikely that a short reign of four years may have dropped out from the text of that Purâṇa. Thus the general statement about ten princes and 137 years seems to be corroborated, and it appears pretty clear that the text of the Mâtsya has in this case undergone a good deal of corruption. Thus, if with Dr. Kern we take B.C. 322 as the date of the foundation of the Maurya dynasty, its overthrow and the foundation of the next or the Śuṅga family must

Of the Śuṅgas.

have occurred in the year B.C. 185. The Śuṅgas are generally stated in all the Purâṇas to have been ten and to have reigned for 112 years, though the expression used in the Bhâgavata is not "112 years," but "more than a hundred years." In the actual

Section VI.

enumeration, the Mâtsya omits two, and the Bhâgavata, one ; and the total of the years assigned to each prince in the Vâyu exceeds 112. There is evidently some mistake here ; but if we take the general statement to be the correct tradition handed down, the dynasty became extinct in B.C. 73. The dynasty next mentioned is that of the Kâṇvas or Kâṇvâyanas. There were four princes of this line, and they reigned for forty-five years, though the Bhâgavata, through a mistake to be explained hereafter, makes the period to be 345 years. They were [31] followed by the Andhrabhṛityas. But here, there is a statement in the Vâyu and the Mâtsya, the like of which does not occur in the account of the other dynasties. The founder of the Andhrabhṛityas, Sindhuka, according to the first Purâṇa, and Śiśuka, according to the other, is said to have uprooted not only the Kâṇvas, but "whatever was left of the power of the Śuṅgas."[10] And the Kâṇvas are pointedly spoken of as Śuṅgabhṛityas or "servants of the Śuṅgas.[11] It, therefore, appears likely that when the princes of the Śuṅga family became weak, the Kâṇvas usurped the whole power and ruled like the Peshwas in modern times, not uprooting the dynasty of their masters but reducing them to the character of nominal sovereigns ; and this supposition is strengthened by the fact that like the Peshwas

Of the Kâṇvas.

---

10 काण्वायनस्त (मंत) तो भृत्यः सुशर्माणं प्रसह्य तम्। शुङ्गानां चैव यच्छेषं क्षपयित्वा बलं तदा॥ सिन्धुको ह्यन्ध्रजातीयः प्राप्स्यतीमां वसुंधराम्॥
Vâyu.

"A servant of the race of the Andhras having destroyed Suśarman of the Kâṇva family with main force and whatever will have been left of the power of the Śuṅgas, will obtain possession of the earth." The statement in the Mâtsya is similar.

11 चत्वारः शुङ्गभृत्यास्ते नृपाः काण्वायना द्विजाः। Vâyu.

Section VI.

they were Brâhmaṇs and not Kshatriyas. Thus then these dynasties reigned contemporaneously, and hence the 112 years that tradition assigns to the Śuṅgas includes the 45 assigned to the Kâṇvas. The Śuṅgas and the Kâṇvas, therefore, were uprooted, and the family of the Andhrabhṛityas came to power in B.C. 73. In a general way, the number of princes belonging to this line is given as thirty in the Vâyu, the Vishṇu, and the Bhâgavata, and twenty-nine in the Mâtsya ; and the total duration is stated to be 411 years in the first, 456 in the second and the third, and 460 in the fourth. The disagreement here is not great, wherefore the tradition as to thirty princes and about 456 years may be accepted as correct. But the discrepancy between this general statement and the more particular accounts that follow, as well as the disagreement between the several Purâṇas in this last, is very great. This will be apparent from the following table :—

Of the Andhrabhṛityas

[32] Thus, the Vâyu has seventeen princes and 272 years and a half ; and the Mâtsya, thirty and 448 and a half. The Vishṇu gives twenty-four names and the Bhâgavata, twenty-two. This last Purâṇa has in many cases corrupted the names and confounded Hâla with the Arishṭakarman of the Vishṇu, whom it names Anishṭakarman Hâleya. It also omits the fifth prince of the Vishṇu Purâṇa. The details given in the Mâtsya come very close to the general tradition and thus confirm it. Should we then attribute the very great discrepancy between these details and those of the Vâyu to the corruption of the text of the latter? Two or three names might drop away in this manner, but the omission of thirteen names and the reduction of the total duration by 176 years must I think be accounted for in

Vâyu.		Mâtsya.		Vishṇu.	Bhâgavata.
Names.	Duration of reign in years.	Names.	Duration of reign in years.	Names.	Names.
Sindhuka ...	23	Śiśuka	23	Śipraka	Name not given; but mentioned as a Vṛishala or Śûdra.
Kṛishṇa ...	10	Kṛishṇa	18	Kṛishṇa	Kṛishṇa.
		Mallakarṇi	10 or 18	Srî Sâtakarṇi ...	Śântakarṇa.
		Purṇotsaṅga	18	Pûrṇotsaṅga	Paurṇamâsa.
		Skandhastambhi ...	18		
Śâtakarṇî ...	56	Śâtakarṇi	56	Śâtakarṇi.	
		Lambodara	18	Lambodara	Lambodara.

Vâyu.		Mâtsya.		Vishṇu.	Bhâgavata.
Names.	Duration of reign in years.	Names.	Duration of reign in years.	Names.	Names.
Apîlava ...	12	Apîtaka	12	Ivîlaka	Hivîlaka.
		Meghasvâti	18	Meghasvâti	Meghasvâti.
		Svâti	18		
		Skandasvâti	7		
		Mṛigendras vâtikarṇa	3		
		Kuntalasvâti	8		
		Svâtikarṇa	1		
Paṭimâvi. ...	24	Puḷomâvi	36	Paṭumat	Aṭamâna.
Nemikṛishṇa ...	25	Gaurakṛishṇa or Naurikṛishṇa.	25	Arishṭakarman ...	Anishṭakarman Hâleya.
Hâla ...	1	Hâla	5	Hâla	
Saptaka or Mandalaka.	5	Mandulaka	5	Pattalaka	Talaka.
Purîkasheṇa ...	21	Purindrasena ...	5	Pravillasena	Purîshabhîru.
Śâtakarṇi ...	1	Sundara Svâtikarṇa ...	1	Sundara	Sunandana.
Chakora Śâtakarṇi	½	Chakora Svâtikarṇa ...	½	Chakora	Chakora.
Śivasvâti ...	28	Śivasvâti	28	Śivasvâti	Śivasvâti.
Gautamîputra ...	21	Gautamîputra ...	21	Gomatîputra	Gomatîputra.
		Pulomat	28	Pulimat	Purimân (mat).
		Śivaśrî	7	Śivaśrî	Medaśiras.
		Śivaskanda	7	Śivaskandha	Śivaskanda.
Yajñaśrî Śâtakarṇi	29	Yajñaśrî Śâtakarṇi ...	29, 9 or 20	Yajñaśrî	Yajñaśrî.
Vijaya ...	6	Vijaya	6	Vijaya	Vijaya.
Daṇḍaśrî Śâtakarṇi	3	Chaṇḍaśrî Śâtakarṇi ...	10	Chandraśri	Chandravijña.
Pulomavi ...	7	Pulomavit	7	Pulomârchis	Sulomadhi.

some other way. Besides the tradition about 456 years, there is a statement in the Vâyu Purâṇa, in a verse below, to the effect that the "Andhras will have possession of the earth for three hundred years,"[12] which seems to point to another. That such a tradition existed is indicated by the mistake in the Bhâgavata by which the Kâṇvas are assigned three hundred and forty-five years. The original account, which the author of this Purâṇa must have [33] seen, probably assigned forty-five years to the Kâṇvas and three hundred to the next or Andhra-bhṛitya dynasty. But since that dynasty was also assigned another duration, *viz.* 456 years, he connected the "the three hundred" with the preceding, and gave 345 years to the Kâṇvâyana family. Now, the manner in which the two traditions are to be reconciled is by supposing that the longer period is made up by putting together the reigns of all the princes belonging to the several branches of the Andhrabhṛitya dynasty. That the younger princes often reigned at Paiṭhaṇ and the elderly ones at Dhanakaṭaka appears clear when we compare the inscriptions with the statement in Ptolemy. When the throne at the principal seat became vacant, the Paiṭhaṇ princes succeeded. But some probably died before their elders and never became kings of Dhanakaṭaka. From an inscription found at Banavâsî by Dr. Burgess it would appear that another branch of that dynasty ruled over Kânarâ. The period of three hundred years and the seventeen names given in the Vâyu Purâṇa refer probably to the main branch. The Mâtsya seems to me to put together the princes of all the branches, and thus makes them out to be thirty. The total of the years

Section VI.

Two traditions about the duration of the Andhra-bhṛitya dynasty—456 and 300 years.

The lower period refers to the main branch of the family.

12 अन्ध्रा भोक्ष्यन्ति वसुधां शते द्वे च शतं च वै । Vâyu.

Section VI. assigned to the several reigns in the Vâyu is 272½, and if we should suppose one or two reigns lasting for about twenty-eight years to have dropped out by the corruption of the text, it would become 300½. Thus then the Vâyu and the Mâtsya Purâṇas each give a correct account, but of different things. The Vishṇu, which gives twenty-four princes, is not entitled to so much credit as the Vâyu. It is a later work and the author's purpose being sectarian, he probably did not care so much for the accuracy of his details, and hence omitted even the duration of each reign. The Bhâgavata is still more careless, as has already been shown.

Date of the accession and death of Gotamîputra.

If then we take the account in the Vâyu Purâṇa to refer to the main branch of the dynasty and consequently generally correct, the period that intervened between the rise of the Śâtavâhanas or Andhrabhṛityas and the end of the reign of Śivasvâti is 206 years.[13] The dynasty must, as we have seen, have been founded in B.C. 73, wherefore the end of Śivasvâti's reign and the accession of Gotamîputra must be placed in A.D. 133. We have seen that Puḷumâyi, whose capital was Paiṭhaṇ according to Ptolemy, and who from the inscriptions appears to have been king of this part of the country and to have reigned contemporaneously with his father, must have begun to reign at Paiṭhaṇ about 130 A.D. The father and the son drove the foreigners from the Dekkan, and the son was established as the ruler of the regained provinces, Gotamîputra expecting to succeed to the throne at the original seat of the family. Gotamîputra reigned for twenty-one years according to the Purâṇas, wherefore he must have died in 154 A.D. He was alive, as stated before, in

13 By adding up the numbers in the table.

the eighteenth year of Puḷumâyi, *i. e.* in 148, and also in the nineteenth when the cave temple was dedicated, and not alive in the twenty-fourth, *i. e.* in 154, according to the two inscriptions [**34**] mentioned before. Ptolemy's mention of Puḷumâyi I have already referred to about the year 132 ; so that, the date deduced from this source, and those derived from Gotamîputra's and Puḷumâyi's inscriptions at Nâsik and Rudradâman's at Junâgaḍ on the supposition that the era used in this last is the Śaka, as well as those derived from the Purâṇas may thus be shown to be consistent with each other. The dates of all the princes whose names we find in the inscriptions may therefore be thus arranged :

Of the other princes mentioned in the inscriptions.

Simuka began to reign in B.C. 73 and ceased in B.C. 50.
Kṛishṇa began in B.C. 50 and ceased in B.C. 40.
Śâtakarṇi (third in the Vâyu P.) began in B.C. 40 and ceased in A.D. 16.
Nahapâna Kshaharâta.
Gotamîputra began in A.D. 133 and ceased in A.D. 154.

Of Puḷumâyi.

If the twenty-eight years assigned to Puḷumâyi in the Mâtsya Purâṇa are to be reckoned from the year of Gotamîputra's death, he must be considered to have begun to reign at Dhanakaṭaka in A.D. 154, and to have ceased in A.D. 182. He reigned at Paiṭhaṇ from A.D. 130 to A.D. 154, that is, for about twenty-four years, and we have seen that the latest year of his reign recorded in the inscriptions at Nâsik and Kârli is the twenty-fourth. Altogether then his reign lasted for fifty-two years. But if the twenty-eight include the twenty-four for which he ruled at Paiṭhaṇ, he must have died in 158. This supposition looks very probable. He was succeeded by Śivaśrî, whose coin found in the Tailaṅgaṇa districts has been described by Mr. Thomas in the Indian Antiquary, Vol. IX., p. 64. He appears to have been Puḷumâyi's

Puḷumâyi's successors.

Section VI.

brother, since he also is styled on the coin Vâsiṭhîputa, i.e., Vâsishṭhîputra, or the son of Vâsishṭhî. He had a reign of seven years and must have died in A.D. 165. Śivaskanda was the next king, to whom also seven years have been assigned. There is no trace of these two princes on this side of the country ; while the name of the next, Yajña Śrî, occurs frequently as we have seen in inscriptions and coins.

Yajña Śrî.

He appears to have been Puḷumâyi's immediate successor at Paiṭhaṇ. His full name was Gotamîputra Yajña Śrî Sâtakarṇi, and he is, as observed before, the Gotamîputra of the Kolhâpur coins. Some copies of the Mâtsya assign him twenty-nine years, others nine, and twenty, and the Vâyu, twenty-nine ; while the Brahmâṇḍa allows him nineteen. Probably he reigned in Mahârâshṭra for eighteen or nineteen years, since the sixteenth year of his reign is his latest recorded date, and for twenty-nine years at Dhanakaṭaka since, according to our supposition, the Vâyu Purâṇa gives an account of the Dhanakaṭaka branch and his coins are found in Tailaṅgaṇa. And this is confirmed by what we have already said. Puḷumâyi reigned at Dhanakaṭaka for four years and his two successors for fourteen. All this while, *i.e.*, for eighteen years, Yajña Śrî was ruler of Mahârâshṭra. He must thus have ceased to reign in the last country in about A.D. 172 and died in about A.D. 202. The next three reigns lasted, according to the Vâyu, for sixteen years. No trace of any of these has yet been found on this side of the country ; but coins of Chandra Śrî are found near the original seat of government, and two of these are described by Mr. Thomas in the paper mentioned above. Thus the [35] latest Andhrabhṛitya date is A.D. 218.

Maḍharîputa Sakasena.

Maḍharîputa Sakasena of the Kânheri inscription, the same

as the Maḍharîputa of the Kolhâpur coins, has been identified with Śiva Śrî, the successor of Puḷumâyi, by Paṇḍit Bhagvânlâl, and I also at one time concurred with him. But the identification is not, I think, tenable. He was probably led to it by his reading Sirîsena for Sakasena ; but I have shown that the reading is incorrect. Mr. Thomas has described a specimen of eleven coins found at Amrâvatî near Dharaṇikoṭ, the legend on which he reads as *Sakasakasa,* but it is not unlikely *Sakasenasa,* "of Sakasena." Besides, Maḍharîputra Śakasena could not have been the immediate successor of Puḷmâyi for a reason which I have already given. One of the Kolhâpur coins figured by Paṇḍit Bhagvânlâl Indraji bears the names of both Gotamîputa and Maḍharîputa, showing that the piece originally bearing the name of one of them was re-stamped with the name of the other. Mr. Thomas thinks that it was originally Maḍharîputa's coin. I think it was Gotamîputa's ; for, if we see the other figured coins we shall find that they are so stamped as to leave some space between the rim and the legend. This in the present case is utilized and the name of Maḍharîputa stamped close to the rim, which shows that the thing was done later. Maḍharîputra Śakasena, therefore, must have been a successor of Gotamîputra Yajña Śri Śâtakarṇi. But, as we have seen, none of his three Purâṇic successors bore the name, and the name Śakasena is one which has nothing like it on the long list of the Andhrabhṛityas. Still that king must have reigned at Dhanakaṭaka also if my surmise that Mr. Thomas' Sakasaka is the same as Sakasena is correct. In the same manner, as observed before, Chatushparṇa Śâtakarṇi's name does not appear in the Purâṇas. But the Puraṇâs

Section VI.

Chaturapana

Section VI. cannot be expected to give accurate information on these points. In the Mâtsya Purâṇa another Andhra dynasty of "seven princes sprung from the servants of the original Andhrabhṛitya family will," it is said, "come into power after that family becomes extinct."[14] The Vâyu has got a similar verse the reading of which, however, is corrupt ; but it appears that this new dynasty is there meant to be spoken of as having sprung from the Andhrabhṛitya family itself and must have constituted a separate branch cut off from the main line. And we can very well understand from the points already made out how such a branch could have constituted itself after Yajña Śrî's ceasing to reign. Vâsishṭhîputra Śâtakarṇi whom I have identified with Chaturapana married a Kshatrapa lady. The Kshatrapas, as I have before observed, were foreigners, most probably Śakas who had become Hindus. Maḍharîputra was not unlikely the son of that lady. And thus he and his father Chaturapana formed, from the very fact of this marriage, a distinct line of princes. Chaturapana appears to have succeeded Yajña Śrî ; and Maḍharîputra to have reigned after Chaturapana. The durations of these reigns cannot be made out, but the latest date of the former is the thirteenth year of his reign, which probably corresponds [36] to 185 A.D. and of the latter the eighth. The dates of the later Śâtavâhanas are therefore these :

Dates of the later Śâtavâhanas.

In Mahârâshṭra.

Puḷumâyi	A.D. 130—A.D. 154.
Yajña Śrî	A.D. 154—A.D. 172.
Chatushparṇa or Chaturapana ...	A.D. 172—was reigning in A.D. 185.
Maḍharîputra ... ... About	A.D. 190—was reigning in about A.D. 197.

14 अन्ध्राणां संस्थिता (ते?) राज्ये तेषां भृत्यान्वये नृपाः । सप्तैवान्ध्रा भविष्यन्ति.

In Tailaṅgaṇa.

Puḷumâyi	... ...	A.D. 154—A.D. 158.
Śiva Śrî	... ...	A.D. 158—A.D. 165.
Śivaskanda	... ...	A.D. 165—A.D. 172.
Yajña Śrî	... ...	A.D. 172—A.D. 202.
Vijaya	... ...	A.D. 202—A.D. 208.
Chandra Śrî	... ...	A.D. 208—A.D. 211.
Pulomavi	... ...	A.D. 211—A.D. 218.

Thus then, the Andhrabhṛityas or Śâtavâhanas ruled over the Dekkan from B.C. 73 to about A.D. 218, *i.e.*, for about three centuries. For some time, however, they were dispossessed of the country by foreigners who belonged to the Śaka tribe. How long these were in power it is difficult to determine. If the Śaka era was established by the foreign conqueror after his subjugation of the country, and if his Satrap Nahapâna or his successor was overthrown by Gotamîputra or Puḷumâyi, six or seven years after Nahapâna's latest date, *viz.* 46, the foreigners held possession of this country only for about fifty-three years.

[37] SECTION VII.

POLITICAL AND LITERARY TRADITIONS ABOUT THE ŚÂTAVÂHANAS OR ŚÂLIVÂHANAS.

Section VII.

THE period during which the Śâtavâhanas or Andhrabhṛityas ruled over Mahârâshṭra must have been a prosperous one in the history of the country. Hence several traditions with regard to different kings of this dynasty have been preserved. But that Śâlivâhana or Śâtavâhana was a family name has been forgotten, and different princes of the dynasty have been confounded and identified. Thus Hemachandra in his Deśikośa gives Śâlivâhana, Śâlana, Hâla, and Kuntala as the names of one individual; but we see from the list given above that the last two were borne by different princes, and both of them were Śâlivâhanas. In his grammar he gives Śâlivâhana as a Prâkṛit corruption of Śâtavâhana. In modern times the Śaka era is called the Śâlivâhana

Śâlivâhana Śaka.

era or an era founded by Śâlivâhana. When it began to be attributed to him it is difficult to determine precisely. All the copper-plate grants up to the eleventh century speak of the era as Śakanṛipakâla, *i.e.*, the era of the Śaka king, or Śakakâla, *i.e.*, the era of the Śaka, and in an inscription at Bâdâmî it is stated to be the era beginning from "the coronation of the Śaka king." Subsequently, the simple expression "Śâke, in the year of the Śaka," was used, and thereafter Śake or "in the Śaka." The word Śaka thus came to be understood as equivalent to "an era" generally, the original sense being forgotten. And since the era had to be connected with some great king it was associated with the name of Śâlivâhana whom tradition had represented to be

Section VII.

Legend about Sâlivâhana.

such a king ; and thus we now use the expression Sâlivâhana Saka, which etymologically can have no sense and is made up of the names of two royal families. The current legend makes Sâlivâhana the son of a Brâhmaṇ girl who was a sojourner at Paiṭhaṇ and lived with her two brothers in the house of a potter. On one occasion she went to the Godâvarî to bathe, when Sesha, the king of serpents, becoming enamoured of her, transformed himself into a man and embraced her. In due course she gave birth to Sâlivâhana, who was brought up in the house of the potter.[1] Some time after, king Vikramâditya of Ujjayinî, to whom a certain deity had revealed that he was destined to die at the hands of the son of a girl of two years, sent about his Vetâla or king of Ghosts to find out if there was such a child anywhere. The Vetâla saw Sâlivâhana playing with his girlish mother and informed Vikramâditya. Thereupon he invaded Paiṭhaṇ with a large army, but Sâlivâhana infused life into clay figures of horses, elephants, and men, by means of a charm communicated to him by his father, the king of serpents, encountered [38] Vikramâditya, and defeated him. This descent of a king of Ujjayin on Paiṭhaṇ I have already alluded to and endeavoured to explain. The Sâlivâhana referred to in this tradition appears to be Puḷumâyi who in conjunction with his father freed the country from the Sakas and fought with Chashṭana or Jayadâman and Ṛudradâman whose capital appears to have been Ujjayinî. It was in consequence of some faint reminiscence of Puḷumâyi Sâlivâhana's relations with the

1 The story about the girl and her serpent-lover is in the Kathâsaritsâgara mentioned with reference to Guṇâḍhya who was the son of the girl. Sâtavâhana's origin is given differently.

Section VII.

Śakas and their Satrap kings that his name was attached to the era first used by his adversaries.

Sâtavâhana's name in connection with the Bṛihatkathâ.

There are also several literary traditions connected with the name of Sâtavâhana or Sâlivâhana. A work of the name of Bṛihatkathâ written in that form of the Prâkṛit which is called the Paiśâchî or the language of goblins is mentioned by Daṇḍin in his work the Kâvyâdarśa.[2] Somadeva, the author of the Kathâsaritsâgara, and Kshemendra, the author of another Bṛihatkathâ, profess to have derived their stories from this Paiśâchî Bṛihatkathâ. The stories comprised in this are said to have been communicated to Guṇâḍhya, who for some time had been minister to Sâtavâhana, by a ghost of the name of Kâṇabhûti. They were written in blood and arranged in seven books. Guṇâḍhya offered them to king Sâtavâhana, but he refused to receive such a ghastly work written in blood and in the language of goblins, whereupon Guṇâḍhya burnt six of them. Some time after, king Sâtavâhana having been informed of the charming nature of those stories went to Guṇâḍhya and asked for them. But the last or seventh book alone remained, and this the king obtained from his pupils with his permission.[3]

Composition of the Kâtantra Grammar.

It is narrated in the Kathâsaritsâgara that while Sâtavâhana was, on one occasion, bathing with his wives in a tank in a pleasure-garden, he threw water at one of them. As she was tired, she told the king not to besprinkle her with water, using the words *modakaiḥ paritâḍaya mâm*. The king not understanding that the first word was composed of two, *mâ* "do not" and *udakaih* "with waters," but taking it to be one word meaning "pieces of sweetmeat," caused sweetmeat to be brought and began to throw

2 भूतभाषामयीं प्राहुरद्भुतार्थां बृहत्कथाम्.

3 Kathâsaritsâgara, II. 8.

pieces at the queen. Thereupon she laughed and told the king that he did not know the phonetic rules of Sanskrit, and that while she meant to tell him not to besprinkle her with water, he had understood her to say that she wanted him to throw pieces of sweetmeat at her. There was no occasion for sweetmeat at the place, and this ought to have led the king to the true sense ; but he was not. Thereupon the king was ashamed of his own ignorance while his queen was so learned, and became disconsolate. Guṇâḍhya and Śarvavarman, who were his ministers, were informed of the cause ; and the former promised to teach him grammar in six years, though it was a study of twelve. Śarvavarman, however, offered to teach the subject in six months, and his offer was accepted ; but as it was not possible to do so, Śarvavarman propitiated the god Kârtikeya or Skanda by his [39] self-mortifications, and the god communicated to him the first Sûtra of a new grammar *Siddho Varṇasamâmnâyaḥ*. Thereupon Śarvavarman repeated the other Sûtras, when Kârtikeya said that if he had not been so hasty and allowed him to repeat the whole, the new grammar would have become superior to Pâṇini's ; but since it could not be so now, it would be a small treatise—*Kâtantra,* and would also be called *Kâlâpaka* after the tail of his peacock. This new grammar Śarvavarman taught to the king.[4] The same story is told by Târânâtha in his "History of Buddhism,"[5] but he makes the name of the king to be Udayana, and of Śarvavarman, Saptavarman ; while the competitor of Śarvavarman is represented by him to be Vararuchi instead of Guṇâdhya. But Udayana is represented as a king reigning in Southern India and Sâtavâhana in the form of

4 Kathâsaritsâgara, VI. 108 & ff.

5 Schiefner's Translation, p. 73 & ff.

Section VII. Śântivâhana is also mentioned in connection with the story as a southern king in whose dominions Vararuchi lived. As Udayana frequently figures in Buddhistic stories, the southern prince Śâtavâhana is confounded with him, and this seems to be indicated by the fact that this Udayana is represented to have ruled over a country in the south, though the usual Udayana is a northern prince. It will thus appear that the Kâtantra grammar was composed by Śarvavarman at the request of a prince of the Śatavâhana family. And this same thing appears to be alluded to even by Hwan Thsang when he says in connection with the shortening of the originally large work on grammar by Pâṇini and others, "lately a Brâhmaṇ of South India, at the request of a king of South India, reduced them further to 2,500 ślokas. This work is widely spread, and used throughout all the frontier provinces, but the well-read scholars of India do not follow it as their guide in practice."[6]

Hâla's Saptaśatî.

There is a work written in the old Mahârâshṭrî dialect called Saptaśatî, which is of the nature of an anthology consisting of Gâthâs or stanzas in the Âryâ metre, mostly on love matters. The author of this is in the third verse mentioned as Hâla, and ordinarily he is spoken of as Śâlivâhana. Bâṇa speaks of it in a verse in the introduction to his Harshacharita as "an imperishable and refined repository of good sayings composed by Śâlivâhana." Verses from it are quoted in Dhanika's commentary on the Daśarûpaka, in the Sarasvati Kaṇṭhâbharaṇa, and in the Kâvyaprakâśa. There is, it will be observed, in the list of the Andhrabhṛitya princes, one of the name of Hâla, who probably was either the author of the work or to whom it was dedicated by a court-poet.

---

6 Life of Hwan Thsang, Beal's Trans., p. 122.

Section VII.

From these traditions we may, I think, safely conclude that literature flourished under the rule of the Andhrabhṛityas, and that the Prâkṛits or spoken languages, especially the Mahârâshṭrî, were probably for the first time used for literary purposes. In Vâtsyâyana's Kâmasûtra or Institutes of Love, Kuntala Śâtakarṇi Śâtavâhana is spoken of as having killed Malayavatî, who is called [40] Mahâdevî, and consequently must have been his chief queen, by means of a pair of scissors in connection with certain amorous sports.[7] The name Kuntala occurs in the list given in the Mâtsya Purâṇa.

Kuntala Śâtakarṇi.

7 कर्तर्या कुन्तलः शातकर्णिः शातवाहनो महादेवीं मलयवतीं [जघान] Prof. Aufrecht's quotation in the Oxf. Cat., p. 217 b., does not contain the name मलयवतीं, and he supplies गणिकां from the preceding clause; but a Gaṇikâ or courtezan cannot be called Mahâdevî.

[41] SECTION VIII.

Religious, social, and economic condition of Mahârâshtṛa under the Andhrabhṛityas or Śâtavâhanas.

Section VIII.

Founders of Benefactions

During this period the religion of Buddha was in a flourishing condition. Princes and chiefs calling themselves Mahâbhojas and Mahâraṭṭhis, merchants (Naigamas), goldsmiths (Suvarṇakâras), carpenters (Vardhakas), corn-dealers (Dhânyakaśreṇis) druggists (Gândhikas), and ordinary householders (Gṛihasthas) caused at their expense temples and monasteries to be excavated out of the solid rock for the use of the followers of that religion. It has been mentioned that in the first part of this period the country was exposed to the inroads of foreign tribes, such as Yavanas or Bactrian Greeks, Śakas, and Pahlavas. These afterwards settled in the country and adopted the Buddhist religion. For, among the donors and benefactors whose names are recorded in the cave inscriptions, there are a good many Śakas and Yavanas. But some and especially the Śakas seem to have adopted Brâhmaṇism. The Buddhist temples were provided with *chaityas* or tombs in imitation of those in which some relic of Buddha was buried, and these were objects of worship. The monasteries contained cells intended as residences for Bhikshus or mendicant priests. These travelled over the

Wandering Buddhist mendicants.

country during the year and spent the four rainy months at one of these monastic establishments. In the month of Śrâvaṇa the monks held the ceremony of robing, at which the old clothes were thrown away and new ones worn. To provide these for them, charitable persons deposited, as we have seen, sums of money with certain guilds with directions that out of the interest new robes should be purchased and given to the priests. Villages were assigned by kings and their officers for the support of these religious establishments. The mendicant priests often travelled by sea ; and hence at the head of several of the creeks in the Konkan we have cave monasteries intended as Dharmaśâlâs or rest-houses for them. We have such caves at Chipḷuṇ, Mahâḍ, and Kuḍeṁ situated respectively on the Dâbhoḷ, the Bâṇkoṭ, and the Râjpurî creeks. For those who landed at the head of the Bombay harbour or at Ghoḍbandar, there were the Kânheri caves. Section VIII.

Brâhmaṇism equally with Buddhism in a flourishing condition.

Brâhmaṇism also flourished side by side with Buddhism. In the inscription at Nâsik in which Ushavadâta dedicates the cave monastery excavated at his expense for the use of the itinerant "priests of the four quarters," he speaks, as we have seen, of his many charities to Brâhmaṇs. The same notions as regards these matters prevailed then as now. Ushavadâta fed a hundred thousand Brâhmaṇs as the Mahârâj Sindia did about thirty years ago. It was considered highly meritorious to get Brâhmaṇs married at one's expense then as now. Gotamîputra also, in the same inscription which records a benefaction in favour of the Buddhists, is spoken of as the only protector of Brâhmaṇs, and as having like Ushavadâta [42] put them in the way of increasing their race. Kings and princes thus appear to have patronized the followers of both the religions, and in none of the inscriptions is there an indication of an open hostility between them.

Trade and Commerce.

Trade and commerce must also have been in a flourishing condition during this early period. Ships from the western countries came, according to the author of the Periplus, to Barugaza or Bharu-

Section VIII.

Identification of towns and cities.

kachchha, the modern Bharoch ; and the merchandize brought by them was thence carried to the inland countries. Onyx stone in large quantities from Paiṭhaṇ, and ordinary cottons, muslins, mallow-coloured cottons, and other articles of local production from Tagara, were carried in waggons to Barugaza and thence exported to the west. Paiṭhaṇ is placed by the author of the Periplus at the distance of twenty days' journey to the south of Barugaza, and is spoken of as the greatest city in Dakhinabades or Dakshiṇâpatha, and Tagara, ten days' east of Paiṭhaṇ.[1] This town has not yet been identified. Its name does not occur in any of the cave inscriptions, but it is mentioned in a copper-plate grant of the first half of the seventh century ; and princes of a dynasty known by the name of Śilâhâra call themselves "sovereigns of Tagara, the best of towns," in all their grants. Some have identified it with Devagiri and others with Junnar, but in both cases its bearing from Paiṭhaṇ as given by the Greek geographers has not been taken into account. I have elsewhere discussed the question, and have proposed Dhârur in the Nizâm's territory as the site of the ancient city. The other sea-port towns mentioned in the Periplus are Souppara, the modern Supâreṁ or Supârâ near Bassein and the Śorparaka of the inscriptions and the Purâṇas, where interesting Buddhistic relics were dug out by Mr. Campbell and Paṇḍit Bhagvânlâl ; Kalliena, the modern Kalyâṇ, which must have been a place of great commercial importance since a good many of the donors whose names are inscribed in the caves at Kânheri and some mentioned in the caves at

1 Ind. Ant., Vol. VIII., pp. 143, 144.

Junnar were merchants residing in Kalyâṇ ;[2] Semulla identified with Chembur by some and with Chaul by others ; Mandagora, very likely the same as the modern Mâṇḍâḍ, originally Mandagaḍa, situated on the Râjapurî creek near Kuḍeṁ where we have the caves ; Palaipatmai, which probably was the same as Pâl which is near Mahâd ; Melizeigara, the second part of the name of which can at once be recognized as Jayagaḍ and which must be identified with that place whatever the first part Meli may mean ; Buzantion, and others. Buzantion is probably the Vaijayantî[3] of the inscriptions, but with what modern town it is to be identified it is difficult to say. Vaijayantî is mentioned in the Kadamba copper-plates translated by Mr. Telang,[4] and was most probably some place in North Kânara. [43] In a grant of the Vijayanagar dynasty, Mâdhava, the great counsellor of king Harihara, is represented to have been appointed viceroy of Jayantîpura.[5] He then conquered Goa and seems to have made that his capital.[5] Jayantîpura is said to be another name for Banavâsî. In the Sabhâparvan of the Mahâbhârata, Banavâsî is spoken of as if it were the name of a country, and immediately after it, Jayantî is mentioned as a town.[6] If then Jayantî and Vaijayantî were two forms of the same name, Vaijayantî was probably the modern Banavâsî, or perhaps in consideration of the facts that the name of

Section VIII.

2 See the inscriptions in Jour. B. B. R. A. S., Vol. VI., and in Arch. Surv., W. India, No. 10.

3 Kârli No. 1, Arch. Surv. West. Ind., No. 10.

4 Jour. B. B. R. A. S., Vol. XII. pp. 318 and 321.

5 Jour. B. B. R. A. S., Vol. IV., p. 115.

6 Chap. XXXI, vv. 69 and 70, Bom. Ed. The Vanavâsinaḥ at the end of v. 69 refers to the town or country of Banavâsî and ought properly to appear as Vanavâsikân. In the Purâṇas, too, Vanavâsikâḥ is given as the name of a people.

Section VIII.

Vaijayantî occurs in an inscription at Kârli and also that the Greek geographers in mentioning the places of note on the coast could not have run at once from Jayagaḍ to the southern limit of North Kânarâ, Vaijayantî may be identified with Vijayadurg. But these objections are not of very great weight.

Inland towns.

It is not possible to ascertain the names of all the towns in the inland country that were in a flourishing condition during the time we have been speaking of. Besides Paiṭhaṇ and Tagara there was Nâsik, which is mentioned in an inscription in one of the caves at the place and also at Beḍsâ. The district about the town was called Govardhana. Junnar was another flourishing town, as is attested by the number of cave-temples at the place. But what its name was we do not know. The name Junnar, Junanara, Jûrṇanagara, or Jîrṇanagara, which means the old town, must have been given to it after it had lost its importance. I have already expressed my belief that it was the capital of Nahapâna. Puḷumâyi, who overthrew the dynasty of Nahapâna, is in one of the Nâsik inscriptions styled "lord of Navanara," meant probably for Navanagara or the new town. That he reigned at Paiṭhaṇ we know from Ptolemy, and also from the many traditions about Śâlivâhana which locate the person or persons bearing that name at that city. The Navanara, then, of the inscription was probably another name given to the town when Puḷumâyi re-established his dynasty, and, in contrast with it, Nahapâna's capital was called the "Old Town." Or perhaps Puḷumâyi windened the old town of Paiṭhaṇ and called the new extension Navanara. What town existed near the group of caves at Kârli and the adjoining places, we do not know. But the place spoken of in connection with the monastic establishment is in an inscription named Valuraka,[7] and the district in which it was situated is called Mâmalâhâra,[8] or the district of Mâmala, the modern Mâvaḷ. Further south there was the town of Karahâṭaka, the modern Karhâḍ, which is mentioned in an inscription at Kuḍeṁ[9] and also in the Mahâbhârata.[10] Kolhâpur also must have been a flourishing town in those days, since a Buddhistic stûpa containing the coins [44] we have already noticed and other remains of antiquity have been found there. The old name of the place is unknown. Either Karhâḍ or Kolhâpur must be the Hippocura of Ptolemy in which he locates Baleocuros whom we have identified with the Viḷivâyakura of the Kolhâpur coins. Section VIII.

Persons engaged in trade and commerce probably acquired large fortunes. The great *chaitya* cave at Kârli was caused to be constructed by a Śeth (Śreshṭhin) of Vaijayantî, and in other places also, especially at Kânheri, their gifts were costly. There were in those days guilds of trades such as those of weavers, druggists, corn-dealers, oil-manufacturers, &c. Their organization seems to have been complete and effective, since, as already mentioned, they received permanent deposits of money and paid interest on them from generation to generation. Self-government by means of such guilds and village communities has always formed an important factor of the political administration of the country. A *nigamasabhâ* or town-corporation is also mentioned in one of Ushavadâta's Nâsik inscriptions, which shows that something like municipal institutions existed in those early days. It is also worthy of Trade-guilds.

7 No. 14, Kârli. Arch. Surv. West. Ind., No. 10.

8 *Ibid.* No. 19.

9 No. 20, Kuḍâ Caves. Arch. Surv. West. Ind., No. 10.

10 In the place above referred to.

Section VIII.

remark that the yearly interest on the 2000 *kârshâpaṇas* deposited by Ushavadâta was 100 *kârshâpaṇas*, and in another case that on 1000 and 75 showing that the rate of interest was not so high as it has been in recent times, but varied from five to seven and a half per cent. per annum. If the rate of interest depends on the degree of security and bears an inverse ratio to the efficiency of government, it appears that the country was well governed notwithstanding political revolutions. To this result the efficient local organization spoken of above, which no changes of dynasties ever affected, must no doubt have contributed in a large measure.

Rate of Interest.

Communication between different parts of the country.

Communication between the several provinces does not appear to have been very difficult. Benefactions of persons residing in Vaijayantî or Banavâsî, and Ṡorparaka or Supârâ, are recorded in the cave at Kârli ; of a Nâsik merchant at Beḍsâ ; of some inhabitants of Bharukachchha and Kalyâṇ at Junnar ; of natives of Northern India and Dâttâmitrî, which I have elsewhere shown was situated in Lower Sindh, at Nâsik ; and of an iron-monger of Karahâkaḍa or Karhâḍ at Kuḍeṁ. On the other hand, gifts of natives of Nâsik and Karhâḍ are recorded on the stûpa at Bharhut which lies midway between Jabalpur and Allahâbâd.[11] Unless there were frequent communications between these places, it is not possible that the natives of one should make religious endowments at another.

11 Cunningham's Stupa of Bharhut, pp. 131, 135, 136, 138, 139.

[45] SECTION IX.

PROBABLE HISTORY OF THE PERIOD BETWEEN THE EXTINCTION OF THE ANDHRABHṚITYAS AND THE RISE OF THE CHÂLUKYAS.

For about three centuries after the extinction of the Andhrabhṛityas, we have no specific information about the dynasties that ruled over the country. The Mâtsya and the Vâyu, as observed before, place seven princes of a branch of the Andhrabhṛityas after them, and I have given reasons to believe that the Maḍharîputra of the inscription and the coins referred to before was one of them. This branch seems to have been in possession of the whole extent of the country that was ruled over by their predecessors. If the fact, noticed before, of some coins of the later Kshatrapa kings being found in a village near Karhâḍ is to be regarded as evidence of their sway over this country and not to be attributed merely to commercial intercourse, the Kshatrapa dynasty also must be considered to have obtained possession of a portion at least of the Dekkan after the Śâtavâhanas. The earliest of these princes is Vijaya Sâha[1] (or Sena) whose date is 144[2] which, if the era is that of the Śaka kings, corresponds to A.D. 222, while the latest date we have assigned to the Śâtavâhanas is about A.D. 218. The last of the princes whose coins are found near Karhâḍ is Viśva Sâha (Sena), one of whose coins has the date 214 and another 224, corresponding to A.D. 292 and A.D. 302.[3] About this time princes of Section IX.

1 Jour. B. B. R. A. S., Vol. VII., p. 17.

2 *Ibid.* p. 28 (No. 10).

3 *Ibid.* No. 15.

Section IX.

Âbhîras.

the race of Âbhîras or cowherds must have come into power. Ten of them are mentioned in the Purâṇas. In the Nâsik caves there is an inscription dated in the ninth year of Vîrasena Âbhîra, the son of Damarî and of Śivadatta Âbhîra.[4] The characters in the inscription, though they do not differ much from those in the inscriptions of the later Andhra-bhṛitya kings, must be regarded as more modern. The language is Sanskrit, which I regard as an indication of a later era. When the popular dialect became different from the Pâli, or the Pâli became less sacred, the people fell back upon the original Sanskrit for such purposes as those of recording religious gifts ; and thus in all the later grants we find the Sanskrit used, while, from the times of Aśoka to the extinction of the Andhrabhṛityas, the language used was mostly the Pâli, or, to speak more accurately, one or more of the Prâkṛits of the period. The Âbhîras were in power for sixty-seven years according to the Vâyu Purâṇa. Many other dynasties are mentioned in the Purâṇas as having ruled over the country. But the information given there is much more confused than in the case of the previous families. It appears that the dynasties that ruled over different parts of India at the same time are put together and confused with those that succeeded each other, so that it is not possible without extraneous assistance to determine their chronological relations.

Râshṭrakûṭas.

[46] We have seen from the cave inscriptions that from remote times tribes of Kshatriyas calling themselves Bhojas and Raṭṭhis or Râshṭrikas were predominant in the country. In the northern part of the Dekkan or Mahârâshṭra these called them-

4 Jour. B. B. R. A. S., Vol. VII., No. 15, and Trans. Inter. Con. 1874, p. 341.

selves "the Great Raṭṭhis or Mahâraṭṭhis, the ancient Marâṭhâs," but in other places the name in use must have been Raṭṭhis or Raṭṭhas, since we know of more modern chiefs in the Southern Marâṭhâ Country who called themselves by that name. Some of the Raṭṭha tribes must have formed themselves into a family or group (kûṭa) and called themselves Raṭṭhakûḍa, and later on Râṭhoḍa, the Sanskrit original of which is Râshṭrakûta. Or the Râshṭrakûta family was so called because it was the main branch of the race of the Raṭṭhas that had spread over the whole country. These native chiefs that ruled over the country must have been held in subjection by the Andhrabhṛityas during the continuance of their power, and also by the later Kshatrapas. But after the dynasties became extinct they must have resumed their independence. The Âbhîras held sway for some time and over a part of the country only ; for the tradition of Gauḷi or cowherd rulers which very probably refers to them is confined to the Nâsik and Khândeś districts. The Râshṭrakûṭas probably rose to power about the same time as the Âbhîras. Hence in the inscriptions on the Miraj plates and the Yevur tablet first brought to light by Mr. Wathen and Sir Walter Elliot,[5] respectively, it is stated that Jaysiṁha, the founder of the Châlukya dynasty in the Dekkan, established himself in the country after having vanquished Indra, the son of Kṛishṇa of the Râshṭrakûṭa family. The Châlukya dynasty was, as will hereafter be seen, founded in the beginning of the sixth century of the Christian era. From about the end of the third to the beginning of the

---

[5] Jour. R. A. S., Vols. II., III., IV.; Ind. Ant., Vol. VIII., p. 12.

Section IX. sixth century, therefore, the Dekkan was ruled over by princes of the Râshṭrakûṭa family.

Traikûṭakas. An inscription on copper-plates found in the *chaitya* of one of the caves at Kânheri is dated in the 245th year of a dynasty, which, if the word has been correctly lithographed, is called Strakûṭaka.[6] But the published copy of the inscription was made in the time of Dr. Bird and the plates themselves are not now available for re-examination. This Strakûṭaka, may be a mislection for Râshṭrakûṭa. But it is not unlikely Traikûṭaka, as the late Paṇḍit Bhagvânlâl contended. He has published a copper-plate charter issued from the camp of the victorious army of Traikûṭakas by a prince of the name of Darhasena[7] in the year 207. Traikûṭaka was thus probably the name of a race and the prince belonged to it. And the Kânheri inscription would show that this dynasty had an era of its own. From the form of the characters in the inscription, it appears that it was engraved in the latter part of the fifth century of the Christian era ; so that the Traikûṭaka dynasty was founded about the middle of [47] the third century, *i.e.*, after the extinction of the Śâtavâhanas. But further information about the dynasty is not available ; and we do not know over what extent of country it ruled. But since the epoch of the era appears to be the same as that of the era used by the kings of Chedi, possibly the race of the Haihayas or Kalachuris which ruled over that province rose to power about 249 A.D. and held sway over a part of the Dekkan including the western coast up to the country of Lâṭ. They were

---

6 Jour. B. B. R. A. S., Vol., V., p. 16, of the copies of the Kânheri inscription.

7 Jour. B. B. R. A. S., Vol. XVI., p. 346.

afterwards driven away by some other race and had to confine themselves to Chedi. The resemblance between the names Tripura the capital of the dynasty and Trikûṭa is perhaps not fortuitous. Section IX.

[48] SECTION X.

The Early Châlukyas.

Section X.

Legendary origin.

We will next proceed to an account of the princes who belonged to the dynasty called Chalikya, Chalukya, or Châlukya.[1] A large number of inscriptions on copper-plates and stone tablets have amply elucidated the history of this dynasty. The legendary origin of this family is thus given by

---

1 Dr. Fleet draws a distinction between Chalukya and Châlukya and asserts that "this last form belongs only to the restored dynasty commencing with Taila II" and that "it does not occur in any of the genuine early inscriptions." But it does belong to the earlier dynasty also, and is found in genuine early inscriptions. The best way to determine the point whether the first syllable was च or चा is to refer to verses containing the name, the metre of which will show the quantity unmistakeably. The inscriptions of the earlier dynasty are in prose; we must therefore refer to the versified grants of the Râshṭrakûṭas which speak of the dynasty supplanted by them. In the Râdhanpur grant of Govinda III. (Ind. ant., Vol. VI., p. 65), we have यश्चालुक्यकुलादनून &c., in verse 3. In the Navasârî grant edited by me (Jour. B. B. R. A. S., Vol. XVIII., p. 257), we have चालुक्यवंशजलधेः स्वयमेव लक्ष्मीः &c. In three of the five grants of the eastern branch of the early dynasty edited by Dr. Hultzsch we have चालुक्यानां कुलम् (South Indian Inscriptions, Vol. I., pp. 44, 47 & 57). The form चलुक्य is also frequently used. The distinction between च and चा and the difference in sense in consequence of the lengthening of the vowel which Dr. Fleet points out have place in the pure Sanskrit of Pâṇini and of the Brâhmaṇas; but there is no room for them in names that came into use in the Prâkṛit period long after Sanskrit became a dead language. Chalukya was some vernacular name which was Sanskritized into the various forms we actually find.

Section X.

Bilhaṇa, the author of the Vikramâṅkadevacharita, or life of Vikramâditya a prince of the later or restored Châlukya line. On one occasion when Brahmadeva was engaged in his morning devotions, Indra came up to him and complained of the sinfulness of the world in which no man performed the sacrificial rites or gave oblations to the gods. Brahmadeva looked at his *chuluka* or the hand hollowed for the reception of water in the course of his devotional exercise, and from it sprang a mighty warrior who became the progenitor of the Châlukya race. Some time after, two great heroes of the name of Hârîta and Mânavya were born in the family and they raised it to very great distinction. The original seat of the dynasty was Ayodhyâ, and in the course of time a branch of it established itself in the south.

As stated in the opening lines of all the copper-plate grants of this family, the Châlukyas belonged to the Gotra or race of Mânavya and were the descendants of Hârîti. They were under the guardianship of the Seven Mothers and were led to prosperity by the god Kârtikeya. They obtained from Nârâyaṇa a standard with a boar represented on it, and fighting under that standard they subjugated all kings. The Yevur tablet and the Miraj plates, referred to above, agree with Bilhaṇa in representing Ayodhyâ as the original seat of the family. But since these were almost contemporaneous with the poet, all the three represent only the tradition that was current in the eleventh century. The first prince who raised the family to [49] distinction in the south was Jayasiṁha. He fought several battles with the reigning princes, and, among them, those belonging to the Râshṭrakûṭa family, if the Yevur tablet is to be trusted, and acquired the

Jayasiṁha, the first prince.

Section X.

Raṇarâga. sovereignty of the country. After him reigned Raṇarâga, who was a prince of great valour and had a stately and gigantic person. He was succeeded

Pulakeśi I. by his son Pulakeśi, who performed a great Aśvamedha or horse-sacrifice and attended equally to the concerns of this world and the next. He made Vâtâpipura, which has been identified with Bâdâmî in the Kalâdgi district, his capital. He appears to have been the first great prince of the family; for, in all the subsequent grants the genealogy begins with him. His full title was Satyâśraya Śrî Pulakeśi Vallabha Mahârâja. Of these words, *Vallabha* appears to be the title of all princes of this dynasty. In some cases, *Vallabha* had *Pṛithvî* prefixed to it, so that the expression meant "the Lover or Husband of the Earth." *Satyâśraya* or "the Support of Truth" was inherited by some of the later princes. Pulakeśi's son

Kîrtivarman. Kîrtivarman succeeded to the throne after him. He subjugated a family of princes of the name of Nalas; but over what province it ruled we do not know. He also subdued the Mauryas, who, from a statement in an inscription at Aihole[2] upon which this account is principally based, seem to have been chiefs of northern Konkan, and reduced also the Kadambas of Banavâsî in North Kânarâ.

Kîrtivarman had three sons at least, who were

Maṅgalîśa. all young when he died. His brother Maṅgalîśa therefore came to the throne after him. Maṅgalîśa vanquished the Kalachuris, a family of princes ruling over the country of Chedi, the capital of which was Tripura or Tevur near Jabalpur. Buddha son of Śaṁkaragaṇa, whom he is represented in one grant[3] to have conquered and put to flight must

---

2 Ind. Ant., Vol. VIII., p. 241

3 Ind. Ant., Vol. VII., p. 161. See also Vol. XIX., p. 17.

have been a Kalachuri prince, as the name Śaṁkaragaṇa frequently occurs in the genealogy of the dynasty. Maṅgalîśa is said to have carried his arms to both the eastern and the western seas. On the coast of the latter he conquered what is called Revatîdvîpa, or the Island of Revatî. A copper-plate grant by a governor of this island was found near Goa,[4] from which it would appear that Revatî was very probably the old name of Reḍî[5] situated a few miles to the south of Vengurleṁ. In an inscription in a cave-temple at Bâdâmî, it is stated that the temple[6] was caused to be excavated by Maṅgalîśa. He there placed an idol of Vishṇu, and on the occasion of its consecration granted a village, out of the revenues of which a ceremony called Nârâyaṇabali was to be performed and sixteen Brâhmaṇs to be fed every day, and the residue to be devoted to the maintenance of recluses. This inscription is dated in the twelfth year of some reign when 500 years of the Śaka era had elapsed. The reign in the [50] twelfth year of which the cave-temple was consecrated is taken to be the reign of Maṅgalîśa. On this supposition Maṅgalîśa began to reign in 489 Śaka ; but I have elsewhere[7] brought forward what I consider to be very strong arguments to show that Maṅgalîśa could not have come to the throne so early as that, and the only criticism[8] that I have seen on my observations seems to me to be very unsatisfactory and serves only to confirm my statement. The reign referred to, therefore, is that

---

4 Jour. B. B. R. A. S., Vol. X., pp. 365-6.

5 Revatî should, according to the usual rules, be corrupted to Revaḍî or Re-a-ḍi and then to Reḍî.

6 Ind. Ant., Vol. III., p. 305.

7 Jour. B. B. R. A. S., Vol. XIV., pp. 23-25.

8 Ind. Ant., Vol. X., 57-58.

Section IX. of Kîrtivarman, and if its twelfth year fell in 500 Śaka, Kîrtivarman must have come to the throne in 489 Śaka corresponding to A.D. 567. In that inscription Maṅgalîśa assigns all the good fruits of his charities to his brother in the presence of the gods Âditya and Agni and of the assembled crowd of men, and claims to himself only the fruit arising from serving his brother faithfully. In the copper-plate grant of the governor of Revatî, referred to above, Śaka 532 is mentioned as the twentieth year of the reign of a prince who, from the titles given there and from the fact that Maṅgalîśa had about that period conquered the island, must have belonged to the Châlukya family. He could not have been Kîrtivarman, for the island was not conquered in his time, neither could he be the successor of Maṅgalîśa who, as I shall presently state, got possession of the throne in 533 Śaka. He must therefore have been Maṅgalîśa himself, and if Śaka 532 was the twentieth year of his reign, he must have begun to reign in 513 Śaka.[9] Kîrtivarman

---

[9] See also the arguments used by me in the paper referred to above. In a recently published article Dr. Fleet places the accession of Maṅgalîśa in 521 Śaka current, being led to it by the occurrence in an inscription of that prince of the words राज्य पञ्चमश्री वर्षे प्रवर्त्तमाने सिद्धार्थे. I have carefully examined the facsimile of the inscription given in the article; and am satisfied that this is by no means the correct reading. राज्य and प्रवर्त्तमाने are the only words that are certain and perhaps the word श्री also. But पञ्चम is highly doubtful; the letter which Dr. Fleet reads म is exactly like that which he reads ञ्च; and there is some vacant space after ञ्च and म in which something like another letter appears. Similarly the सि of सिद्धार्थे is hardly visible as an independent letter, and the next two letters are also doubtful. Besides in no other inscription of the early Châlukyas does the cyclic year appear. (See Ind. Ant., Vol. XIX., p. 9 and ff.)

thus reigned from 489 Śaka or A.D. 567 to 513 Śaka or A.D. 591, that is, for twenty-four years. **Section X.**

Death of Maṅgalîśa.

In the latter years of his reign Maṅgalîśa seems to have been engaged in intrigues to keep his brother's son Pulakeśi off from the succession and to place his own son on the throne. But Pulakeśi, who had grown to be a prince of remarkable abilities, baffled all his intrigues, and by the use of energy and counsel he neutralized all the advantage that Maṅgalîśa had by the actual possession of power, and in the attempt to secure the throne for his son, Maṅgalîśa lost his own life and his kingdom.

Pulakeśi II.

Pulakeśi, the son of Kîrtivarman, succeeded. His full title was Satyâśraya Śrî Pṛithvî-Vallabha Mahârâja. From a copper-plate[10] **[51]** grant executed in the third year of his reign and in 535 Śaka, he appears to have come to the throne in 533 Śaka or A.D. 611. After Maṅgalîśa's death, the enemies whom his valour had kept in subjection rose on all sides. A prince of the name of Appâyika and another named Govinda who very probably belonged to the Râshṭrakûṭa race, since that name occurs frequently in the genealogy of that family, attacked the new Châlukya king. The former, who had horses from the northern seas in his army, fled away in fear when opposed by the powerful forces of Pulakeśi, and the latter surrendered to him and becoming his ally was received into favour and rewarded.[11] He then turned his arms against the Kadambas, attacked Banavâsî, their capital, and reduced it. The prince of the Gaṅga family which

---

10 Ind. Ant., Vol. VI., p. 73.

11 Ind. Ant., Vol. VIII., p. 242, line 8 of the inscription. From the words *cha, ekena* and *apareṇa* it is clear that two persons are here meant. But Dr. Fleet in his translation makes both of them one, which is a mistake; and the translation, I must say, is unintelligible.

Section X. ruled over the Chera[12] country situated about the modern province of Maisur, and the head of the Alupa[13] race which probably held the province of Malabâr, became his allies. He then sent his forces against the Mauryas of the Konkan, who were vanquished without any difficulty. With a fleet of hundreds of ships he attacked Purî,[14] which was the mistress of the western sea, and reduced it. The kings of Lâṭa, Mâlava, and Gûrjara were conquered and became his dependents. About this time, there was a powerful monarch in Northern India whose name was Harshavardhana. He was king of Kanoj, but in the course of time made himself the paramount sovereign of the north. He then endeavoured to extend his power to the south of the Narmadâ, but was opposed by Pulakeśi, who killed many of his elephants and defeated his army. Thenceforward, Pulakeśi received or assumed the title of Parameśvara or lord paramount. This achievement was by the later kings of the dynasty considered the most important, and that alone is mentioned in their copper-plate grants in the description of Pulakeśi II. Pulakeśi appears to have kept a strong force on the banks of the Narmadâ to guard the frontiers. Thus, by his policy as well as valour, he became the supreme lord of the three countries called Mahârâshṭrakas containing ninety-nine thousand villages. The kings of Kosala and

---

12 Ind. Ant., Vol. I., p. 363, and Vol. VII., p. 168.

13 The name of the royal family seems to be preserved in the name of the modern town of Alupai on the Malabâr Coâst.

14 The town is called the Lakshimî of the Western Ocean. It was probably the capital of the Maurya king of the Konkan and afterwards of the Śilâhâras.

Section X.

Kaliṅga[15] trembled at his approach and surrendered to him. After some time he marched with a large army against the king of Kâñchîpura or Conjeveram and laid siege to the town. He then crossed the Kâverî and invaded the country of the Cholas, the Pâṇḍyas, and the Keralas. But these appear to have become his allies. After having in this manner established his supremacy throughout the south, he entered his capital and reigned in peace. The date of the inscription from which the greater [52] portion of this narrative is taken is 556 Śaka, corresponding to A.D. 634, so that Pulakeśi's career of conquest had closed before A.D. 634.

Hwan Thsang's account.

It was in the reign of this king that Hwan Thsang, the Chinese Buddhist pilgrim, visited India. In the course of his travels through the country he visited Mahârâshṭra, which he calls *Mo-ho-la-cha*. He saw Pulakeśi, whom he thus describes: "He is of the race of *Tsa-ta-li* (Kshatriyas) ; his name is *Pu-lo-ki-she ;* his ideas are large and profound and he extends widely his sympathy and benefactions. His subjects serve him with perfect self-devotion."[16] About Pulakeśi's having withstood the power of Harshavardhana which we have before mentioned on the authority of inscriptions, Hwan Thsang speaks in these words: "At present the great king Śîlâditya (Harshavardhana) carries his victorious arms from the east to the west ; he subdues distant peoples and makes the neighbouring nations fear him ; but the people of this kingdom alone have not submitted. Although he be often at the head of all the troops of the five Indies, though he has summoned the bravest generals of all the kingdoms,

---

15 For the position of these countries, see Sec. III. para. 2.

16 Ind. Ant., Vol. VII., p. 290.

Section X.

and though he has marched himself to punish them, he has not yet been able to vanquish their opposition. From this we may judge of their warlike habits and manners."[17] The Chinese traveller visited Mahârâshṭra about the year A.D. 639, that is, five years after the inscription referred to above was incised. The kingdom, according to him, was six thousand *li* (1200 miles) in circuit and the capital was thirty *li*, and towards the west was situated near a large river. The soil, climate, and the character and general condition of the people of Mahârâshṭra are thus described by him: "The soil is rich and fertile and produces abundance of grain. The climate is warm. The manners are simple and honest. The natives are tall and haughty and supercilious in character. Whoever does them a service may count on their gratitude, but he that offends them will not escape their revenge. If any one insult them they will risk their lives to wipe out that affront. If one apply to them in difficulty they will forget to care for themselves in order to flee to his assistance. When they have an injury to avenge they never fail to give warning to their enemy; after which each puts on his cuirass and grasps his spear in his hand. In battle they pursue the fugitives but do not slay those who give themselves up. When a general has lost a battle, instead of punishing him corporally, they make him wear women's clothes, and by that force him to sacrifice his own life. The state maintains a body of dauntless champions to the number of several hundreds. Each time they prepare for combat they drink wine to intoxicate them, and then one of these men, spear in hand, will defy ten thousand enemies. If they kill a man met upon the road the law does not punish them. When-

[17] Ind. Ant., Vol. VII., p. 291

ever the army commences a campaign these braves march in the van to the sound of the drum. Besides, they intoxicate many hundreds of naturally fierce elephants. At the time of their coming to [53] blows they drink also strong liquor. They run in a body trampling everything under their feet. No enemy can stand before them. The king, proud of possessing these men and elephants, despises and slights the neighbouring kingdoms." Section X.

Pulakeśi II. appears undoubtedly to have been the greatest prince of this dynasty ; and his fame reached even foreign countries. He is represented in an Arabic work to have sent an embassy to Chosroes II., king of Persia, who reigned from A.D. 591 to A.D. 628, in the thirty-sixth year of that prince's reign, and must have received one from him, either before or after.[18] During his reign the power of the Châlukyas was established over a very large extent of country. His younger brother Vishṇuvardhana, otherwise called Vishamasiddhi, seems to have for some time been appointed to rule over the Sâtârâ and Paṇḍharpur districts, since a copper-plate inscription of his found at Sâtârâ records the grant of a village situated on the southern bank of the Bhîmâ.[19] Vishṇuvardhana afterwards obtained the province of Veṅgi between the lower Kṛishṇâ and the Godâvarî, where he founded another flourishing branch of the Châlukya dynasty. Pulakeśi's second brother Jayasiṁha must have been his brother's viceroy in the district about Nâsik. For, in a copper-plate grant found in the Igatpurî tâluka of the district, Nâgavardhana, the son of Jayasiṁha, assigns the village of Balegrâma, which has been identified with the modern Belgâm

Vishṇuvardhana.

Jayasiṁha.

18 Arch. Sur. W. India. No. 9. pp. 90-92.

19 Jour. B. B. R. A. S., Vol. II., p. 11.

Section X.

Tarhâḷâ about twelve miles to the north-east of Igatpurî, for the worship of the god Kâpâlikeśvara.[20] The district in which the village was situated is in the grant called Goparâshṭra. Similarly, Pulakeśi's eldest son Chandrâditya ruled over the province which contained the Sâvantvâḍî district. In a copper-plate grant, Vijayabhaṭṭârikâ, the queen of Chandrâditya, who is styled Pṛithvîvallabha and Mahârâja or great king, assigns to certain Brâhmaṇs a field along with the adjoining *Khajjana* (modern Khâjaṇa) or marshy land in the village of Kocharem situated on the coast about seven miles to the north of Vengurlem. In another grant found at Nerur, she assigns a field in the fifth year of *svarâjya* or "one's own reign." Now the reign referred to by this expression must be her husband's, so spoken of to distinguish it from that of his brother Vikramâditya, the second son of Pulakeśi, who succeeded his father at the chief seat of government. Chandrâditya was a king, as the titles above given show, and it is proper that his crowned queen should speak of his reign as *svarâjya* or her reign. It is not necessary that charities such as those recorded in these grants should, like political offices or rights, be conferred by the reigning prince alone. The religious merit arising from them is sought [54] by women as much as by men ; and hence a woman like Vijayabhaṭṭârikâ might, during the lifetime of her husband, give a field. The fact of her doing so does not necessitate the supposition that she was a ruler or a regent when she made these grants, as has been thought. She was simply the crowned

Chandrâditya.

---

20 Jour. B. B. R. A. S., Vol. II., p. 4, first translated by Bâla Śâstrî and then by me (Jour. B. B. R. A. S., Vol. XIV.), and last of all by Dr. Fleet (Ind. Ant., Vol. IX., p. 123).

Section X.

queen of a reigning monarch at that time. Another son of Pulakeśi named Âdityavarman seems to have ruled over the district near the confluence of the Kṛishṇâ and the Tuṅgabhadrâ,[21] as a copper-plate grant of his issued in the first year of his reign was found in the Karnul District. An undated grant of Pulakeśi found at Chiplun in Southern Konkan has recently been published. In it he sanctions the grant of the village of Âmravâṭaka made by his maternal uncle Śrîvallabha Senânandarâja "the ornament" of the Sendraka race.[22] This appears to be a family of minor chiefs with whom the Châlukyas were connected. A similar grant was made by the next king at the request of the Sendraka chief Devaśakti.[23] Inscriptions of Sendrakas are found in Gujarât also, where probably they went when the power of the Châlukyas was established in that province. The name Sendraka is probably preserved in the modern Marâṭhâ name Sinde.

Âditya-varman.

Sendraka race.

Pulakeśi was succeeded by his second son Vikramâditya. In the grants he is called Pulakeśi's *priyatanaya* or favourite son ; so that it appears that Pulakeśi had arranged that Vikramâditya should succeed him at the principal seat of government, and had assigned an outlying province to his eldest son Chandrâditya. At the beginning of this reign as of the previous ones there was a disturbance ; but it did not come from the princes or chiefs more to the north who seem to have now been permanently humbled, but from the far south. The Pallava king of Kâñchî or Conjeveram and the rulers of the

Vikram-âditya I.

21 Ind. Ant., Vol. X., p. 244, and Jour. B. B. R. A. S., Vol. XVI., p. 223.

22 Epigraphia Indica, Vol. III., p. 51.

23 Jour. B. B. R. A. S., Vol. XVI., p. 228. See also below.

Section X.

Cholas, the Pâṇḍyas, and the Keralas threw off the yoke which Pulakeśi had but loosely placed over them, and rebelled. Vikramâditya, who was a man of abilities and daring adventure, broke the power of the Cholas, Pâṇḍyas, and Keralas. He defeated the Pallava king, captured his capital Kâñchî, and compelled him, who had never before humbled himself before anybody, to do him homage. On the back of his horse Chitrakaṇṭha and sword in hand he is said to have repelled all the enemies that attacked him. In this manner he acquired again the whole of the dominions ruled over by his father, and became the paramount sovereign of the country "between the three seas."[24]

A branch of the Châlukya dynasty established in southern Gujarât.

During the reign of Vikramâditya I. a branch of the Châlukya dynasty was founded in southern Gujarât or the country called Lâṭa in ancient times. Vikramâditya seems to have assigned that province to a younger brother named Jayasiṁhavarman Dharâśraya, [55] who thus was another son of Pulakeśi II.[25] Śryâśraya Śîlâditya son of Jayasiṁha made a grant of land while residing at Navasârî in the year 421,[26] and another in 443 while encamped at Kusumeśvara with his victorious army.[27] In both of these Śryâśraya is called Yuvarâja or prince-regent and not a king. Another son of Jayasiṁha named Vinayâditya Yuddhamalla Jayâśraya Maṅgalarâja issued a similar charter in the Śaka year 653.[28] Pulakeśi, who represents himself as the

---

24 Ind. Ant., Vol. VI., pp. 86, 89, 92; Jour. B. B. R. A. S., Vol. III., p. 203; and Ind. Ant., Vol. IX., pp. 127, 130-131.

25 Jour. B. B. R. A. S., Vol. XVI., p. 2.

26 *Ibid.* pp. 2 & 3.

27 Transactions VII. Or. Congr., p. 226.

28 Jour. B. B. R. A. S., p. 5.

younger brother of Jayâśraya Mañgalarasarâja and as meditating on his feet, granted a village in the year 490.[29] Both are styled kings. From all this it appears that Jayasiṁhavarman though made sovereign of southern Gujarât did not rule over the province himself but made his son Śryâśraya his regent. He held that position for more than twenty-two years; and does not appear to have become king in his own right, as he is not mentioned in Pulakeśi's grant. Pulakeśi, however, seems from his date to be his younger brother. Śryâśraya died before his father; Jayâśraya succeeded the latter as king and he was succeeded by Pulakeśi. The dates 421, 443, and 490, the era of which is not given, would if referred to the Gupta era be equivalent to 739, 761, and 808 of the Christian era respectively; while Jayâśraya's 653 Śaka is 731 A.D. But Vinayâditya the sovereign of the main branch who is mentioned in the grant of 443 died about 697 A.D.;[30] and Jayasiṁha whose Yuvarâja was Śryâśraya will have to be supposed to have lived to 761 A.D. *i.e.*, 81 years after the death of his brother Vikramâditya; while the interval between Pulakeśi and his immediate predecessor Jayâśraya will become 77 years, as Śaka 653 of the latter corresponds to 731 A.D. The Gupta era will, therefore, not do; and we must with the late Paṇḍit Bhagvânlâl refer the dates to the Traikûtaka era of the use of which we have at least two instances. Thus Śryâśraya's dates will be 670 and 692 A.D., of Jayâśraya 731 A.D. and of Pulakeśi 739 A.D., and there will be no incongruity. But the original dates themselves 421 and 490 show the distance of time between Śryâśraya and Pulakeśi to be 69 years; and if we take the later

Section X.

29 Transactions VII. Or. Congr., p. 230.

30 See below.

Section X. date of the former it will be reduced to 47 years. Even this is too much and the only way to account for it is by supposing that the two youngest sons of Jayasiṁha Dharâśraya were born of a young wife married when he was advanced in years. In Pulakeśi's grant it is stated that he vanquished an army of Tâjikas which had destroyed the Saindhava,[31] Kachchhella,[32] Saurâshṭra, Châvoṭaka,[33] Maurya,[34] Gurjara[35] and other kings, and on its way to Dakshiṇâpatha to conquer the southern kings had come to Navasârî to reduce that country first. Thereupon Valla [56] bhanarendra, who must have been Vijayâditya or Vikramâditya II. the reigning sovereign of the main branch, conferred upon him the titles of "Pillar of Dakshiṇâpatha" (Dakshiṇâpathasâdhâra), "Ornament of the family of Chaluka" (Chalukakulâlaṁkâra), "Beloved of the earth" (Pṛithivîvallabha), the "Repeller of the unrepellable" (Anivartakanivartayitri) and "Support of men in the world" (Avanijanâśraya). As "Tâjika" is a name applied to Arabs, from which the name "Tajika" of a branch of astrology borrowed in the first instance from the Arabs is derived, the allusion in this grant is to an Arab invasion. And we have a mention of such invasions between the years 711 A.D. and 750 A.D. by Mahammad Kasim and his successors.[36] Navasârî was the capital of the Châlukyas of Lâṭa or southern Gujarât.

---

31 King of Sindh.

32 Very likely king of Kachchha.

33 King of Anahilpattan of the Châpotkaṭa race.

34 King of the Maurya race; probably ruled over some part of the Konkan and the coast of southern Gujarât.

35 King of the Gurjara race; ruled over the Broach District.

36 Elphinstone's Hist. of India.

A copper-plate grant of the Gujarât Châlukyas found at Kherâ and translated by Prof. Dowson contains the names of three princes, *viz.*, Jayasiṁharâja, Buddhavarmarâja, and Vijayarâja.[37] Scholars and antiquarians have understood the first of these to be the same as Jayasiṁha the founder of the Châlukya dynasty of the Dekkan. But I think the prince meant is Jayasiṁhavarman, the brother of Vikramâditya I. and founder of the Gujarât branch of the dynasty; for nothing has hitherto been discovered connecting the early Châlukya princes with Gujarât. The grant, however, appears to me to be a forgery.[38] The Buddhavarman mentioned in it, if he existed at all, must have been another son of Jayasiṁhavarman, besides the two spoken of above, and he and his son Vijayarâja must have ruled over another part of Gujarât. If the grant is to be regarded as genuine, the date 394 will have to be referred to the Gupta era.

Section X.

A spurious Châlukya grant.

Vinayâditya.

After Vikramâditya I, his son Vinayâditya came to the throne. One of his grants is dated Śaka 611, which was the tenth year of his reign,[39] another in 613 Śaka and in the eleventh year, and a third in 616 Śaka and the fourteenth year.[40] There is also an inscription of his on a stone tablet, the date occurr-

---

37 Jour. R. A. S., Vol. I., p. 268.

38 My reasons are these:—(1) Its style is unlike that of the Châlukya grants. (2) It does not contain the usual invocation to the Boar incarnation. (3) It simply gives the three regulation names, *i.e.*, so many as are prescribed, in the legal treatises. (4) There is a uniform mode of naming the three princes, by adding the suffix *râja*, a mode not to be met with in the genuine Châlukya grants. (5) None of the three princes has a title or *Biruda* as all Châlukya princes from Pulakeśi I. downwards had.

39 Ind. Ant., Vol. VI., p. 86.

40 *Ibid.*, pp. 89, 92.

Section X. ing in which is 608 Śaka and the seventh year of his reign.[41] From these it appears that Vinayâditya came to the throne in 602 Śaka corresponding to A.D. 680, in which year his father Vikramâditya must have ceased to reign. His latest is A.D. 694, but his reign terminated in A.D. 696 as is seen from his son's grants referred to below. During his father's lifetime, Vinayâditya assisted him in his wars with the southern kings and won his love by destroying the forces of the Pallava king and of the other three, *i.e.*, Chola, Pâṇḍya, and Kerala, and tranquilizing the country. Between the eleventh and fourteenth years of his reign (A.D. 692—A.D. 695) he succeeded in making the Pallavas, [57] Kaḷambhras, Keralas, Haihayas, Vilas, Mâlavas, Cholas, Pâṇḍyas, and others as steadfast allies of the Châlukya crown as the Gaṅga family of Chera and the Alupas whose loyalty was for the first time secured by Pulakeśi II.[42] The kings of Kâvera, or Kerala as it is read in some of the grants, of the Pârasîkas, who were probably the Syrians settled on the coast of Malabâr, and of Siṁhala were made tributaries. He also seems, like his grandfather, to have fought with and defeated some paramount sovereign of Northern India whose name is not given, and to have acquired all the insignia of paramountcy, such as a certain standard called *Pâlidhvaja*, the drum called Ḍhakkâ, and others. These events must have taken place after 616 Śaka, since they are not mentioned in his grant of that year, but in those of his successors.[43] A

41 Ind. Ant., Vol. VII., p. 112.

42 This fact is not mentioned in the grant of the eleventh year of his reign (Ind. Ant., Vol. VI., p. 89), while it does occur in that of the fourteenth year (p. 92) and in those of his successors.

43 Ind. Ant., Vol. IX., pp. 127 and 131.

Section X.

chief of the name of Mahârâja Pogilli of the Sendraka family was a feudatory of his in the south about Maisur.[44]

Vijayâditya.

Vinayâditya was succeeded by his son Vijayâditya. He appears to have assisted his grandfather in his campaigns against the southern kings and his father in the expedition into the north. At one time he was captured by his enemies, though they had been defeated and were retreating. Notwithstanding he was in their custody he succeeded in averting anarchy and disturbance in his own country, and when he got off, established his power everywhere and bore all the insignia of supreme sovereignty. There is an inscription at Bâdâmî in which it is stated that during his reign, idols of Brahmâ, Vishṇu, and Maheśvara were put up at Vâtâpipura in Śaka 621 and the third year of his reign. One of his grants was issued in Śaka 622 on the full-moon day of Âshaḍha and in the fourth year of his reign, another in Śaka 627 and in the tenth year, and a third in Śaka 651 on the full-moon day of Phâlguna and in the thirty-fourth year of his reign.[45] On a comparison of all these dates it follows that his reign began in 618 Śaka after the full-moon day of Âshâḍha corresponding to A.D. 696. The first two of these grants, and another which bears no date, were found at Nerur in the Sâvantvâḍî state.[46] Vijayâditya had a long reign of thirty-six years.

Vikramâditya II.

After Vijayâditya, his son Vikramâditya II. ascended the throne. A grant of his, engraved on a stone tablet, is dated in 656 Śaka and in the second

[44] Ind. Ant., Vol. XIX., p. 143.

[45] Ind. Ant., Vol. VII., p. 112.

[46] Ind. Ant., Vol. IX., pp. 127 and 131; and Jour. B. B. R. A. S., Vol. III., p. 203, *et seq.*

Section X.

year of his reign,[47] wherefore he must have come to the throne in 655 Śaka or A.D. 733. Soon after his coronation he had to turn his arms against his hereditary enemy the Pallava king. The name of the prince who reigned at the Pallava capital at this time was Nandipotavarman. Vikramâditya marched against him in haste and encountered him in the Tudâka country. Nandipotavarman was defeated and had to fly away from the battle-field. [58] The Châlukya king got a good deal of spoil in the shape of large quantities of rubies, elephants, and instruments of martial music. He then entered the city of Kâñchî, but did not destroy it. In that city he gave a good deal of money to Brâhmaṇs and to the poor and helpless, and restored to the temples of Râjasiṁheśvara and other gods the gold which, it appears, had been taken away by some previous king. He then fought with the Cholas, the Pâṇḍyas, the Keralas, and the Kaḷabhras, and reduced them.[48] Vikramâditya married two sisters belonging to the family of the Haihayas. The elder of these was called Lokamahâdevî and she built a temple of Śiva under the name of Lokeśvara, at Paṭṭaḍakal in the Kalâdgi district. The younger's name was Trailokyamahâdevî, and she built another in the vicinity dedicated to the same god under the name of Trailokyeśvara. The latter was the mother of Kîrtivarman the next king.[49] Vikramâditya reigned for fourteen years.

Kîrtivarman II.

His son Kîrtivarman II. began to reign in 669 Śaka or A.D. 747, since a grant of his, made in the

[47] Ind. Ant., Vol. VII., p. 107.

[48] Ind. Ant., Vol. VIII., p. 26.

[49] Ind. Ant., Vol. X., p. 165. Epigraphia Indica, Vol. III., p. 5.

Section X.

eleventh year of his reign, bears the date 679 Śaka.[50] He assisted his father in his wars with the Pallavas. On one occasion he marched against the Pallava king with his father's permission. The ruler of Kâñchî, too weak to face him in the battle-field, took refuge in a fortress. His power was broken by the Châlukya king, who returned to his country with a large spoil. During the reign of this prince the Châlukyas were deprived of their power in Mahârâshṭra, and the sovereignty of the country passed from their hands into those of the Râshṭrakûṭa princes. The main branch of the dynasty became extinct ; but it had several minor offshoots, and one of these in the person of Tailapa succeeded in the course of time in regaining supreme power. From this time forward, therefore, we do not meet with any copper-plate grants issued by the Châlukyas ; but Râshṭrakûṭa plates belonging to this intervening period are met with from Râdhanpur in Northern Gujarât to Sâmangaḍ near Kolhâpur and Nâgpur in the Central Provinces. The grant of Kîrtivarman II., from which the above account of that prince is taken, does not allude to the fact of his disgrace, but he must have lost possession of the greater portion of his kingdom before Śaka 679, the date of the grant. The name of the Râshṭrakûṭa monarch who first humbled the Châlukyas was Dantidurga, and the work begun by him was completed by his successor Kṛishṇa. In a copper-plate grant of the former found at Sâmangaḍ he is spoken of as having become paramount sovereign after having vanquished Vallabha.[51] The date occurring in the grant is 675 Śaka. Before that time, therefore, the Châlukyas must have lost

Overthrow of the Châlukyas.

---

50 Ind. Ant., Vol. VIII., p. 27.

51 Jour. B. B. R. A. S., Vol. II., p. 375.

Section X.

their hold over Mahârâshṭra. In the Yevur tablet and the Miraj plates the Châlukyas are spoken of as having lost sovereign power in the reign of Kîrtivarman II. We will therefore here close our account of the early Châlukyas.

Jainism under the Châlukyas.

[59] During the period occupied by the reigns of these early Châlukya princes, the Jaina religion comes into prominence. Ravikîrti, the Jaina who composed the Aihole inscription and represents himself as a poet, was patronized by Pulakeśi II. Vijayâditya gave a village for the maintenance of a Jaina temple to Udayadevapaṇḍita or Niravadyapaṇḍita, the house pupil of Śrîpûjyapâda, who belonged to the Devagaṇa sect of the Mûlasaṁgha, *i.e.* of the Digambara Jainas. Niravadyapaṇḍita is spoken of as a spiritual adviser of Vijayâditya's[52] father, *i.e.* Vinayâditya. Vikramâditya II. repaired a Jaina temple and gave a grant in connection with it to a learned Jaina of the name of Vijayapaṇḍita, who is represented to have silenced his opponents in argument and is styled the only disputant.[53] But Jainism in those days, as at present, probably flourished in the Southern Marâṭhâ Country only. If the Pûjyapâda who was the preceptor of Niravadyapaṇḍita was the famous grammarian of that name, he must have flourished some time before 618 Śaka, the date of Vinayâditya's death, *i.e.* about 600 Śaka or 678 A.D. All that is known about Pûjyapâda and his relations to other Digambara writers is not inconsistent with this date. But another date two hundred years earlier has also been assigned to Pûjyapâda.

Buddhism.

No inscription has yet come to light showing any close relations between the Buddhists and the

---

[52] Ind. Ant., Vol. VII., p. 112.

[53] Ind. Ant., Vol. VII., p. 197.

Section X.

Châlukya princes. But that the religion did prevail, and that there were many Buddhist temples and monasteries, is shown by the account given by Hwan Thsang. Still there is little question that it was in a condition of decline. With the decline of Buddhism came the revival of Brâhmaṇism and especially of the sacrificial religion. The prevalence of the religion of Buddha had brought sacrifices into discredit ; but we now see them rising into importance. Pulakeśi I. is mentioned in all the inscriptions in which his name occurs as having performed a great many sacrifices and even the Aśvamedha. I have elsewhere[54] remarked that the names of most of the famous Brâhmaṇical writers on sacrificial rites have the title of *Svâmin* attached to them ; and that it was in use at a certain period, and was given only to those conversant with the sacrificial lore. The period of the early Châlukyas appears to be that period. Amongst the Brâhmaṇ grantees of these princes we have Nandisvâmin, Lohasvâmin, and Bhallasvâmin ;[55] Dâsasvâmin the son of Jannasvâmin and grandson of Revâsvâmi-Dîkshita ;[56] Devasvâmin, Karkasvâmin, Yajñasvâmin, Nâgammasvâmin, another Devasvâmin, Gargasvâmin, Rudrasvâmin,[57] Prabhâkarasvâmin, Keśavasvâmin,[58] &c. There are others whose names have not this title attached to them. Among these names there are three borne by the great commentators on sacrificial sûtras and rites, viz. Karkasvâmin, Devasvâmin, and Keśavasvâmin. [60] Though it would be hazardous to assume that these writers were

Revival of Brâhmaṇism

54 Report on MSS. for 1884, pp. 31, 32.

55 Ind. Ant., Vol. VI., p. 77.

56 Ind. Ant., Vol. IX., 128.

57 Ind. Ant., Vol. IX., p. 131.

58 B. B. R. A. S., Vol. XVI., pp. 237, 239.

Section X. exactly the persons who are mentioned in the grants with those names, still it admits of no reasonable doubt that they are to be referred to the period when the Châlukyas reigned in Mahârâshṭra ; and probably flourished in the Dekkan or the Telugu and Kanarese countries. For the revival of Brahmaṇism was carried on vigorously in the Southern India. The ritual of the sacrifices must during the previous centuries have become confused, and it was the great object of these writers to settle it by the interpretation of the works of the old Ṛishis.

Purâṇic gods.

And the Purâṇic side of Brahmaṇism also received a great development during this period. Temples in honour of the Purâṇic triad, Brahmâ, Vishṇu, and Maheśvara with a variety of names were constructed in many places. The worship of Śiva in his terrific form seems also to have prevailed, as the Nâsik grant of Nâgavardhana assigning a certain village to the worship of Kâpâlikeśvara, or the god wearing a garland of skulls, would show.

Cave architecture.

Cave architecture came to be used for the purposes of the Purâṇic religion about the time of the early princes of the dynasty, as we see from the cave-temple at Bâdâmî dedicated to the worship of Vishṇu by Maṅgalîśa. The Châlukyas, like their predecessors in previous times, were tolerant towards all religions.

[61] *Genealogy of the early Châlukyas.*

1. JAYASIMHA.

2. RANARÂGA.

3. PULAKEŚI I.—Satyâśraya Śrî Pulakeśi Vallabha.

4. KÎRTIVARMAN I., Śaka 489—513 or A. D. 567—591.

5. MANGALÎŚA, Śaka 513—532 or A. D. 591—610.

Sons of Kîrtivarman I.:

6. PULAKEŚI II.—Satyâśraya Śrî Pṛithvî-vallabha, began to reign in Śaka 532 or A. D. 610, was on the throne in Śaka 556 or A. D. 634, and seen by Hwan Thsang in A. D. 639.

Vishṇuvardhana, founded the eastern Châlukya dynasty.

Jayasiṁha. — Nâgavardhana.

Sons of Pulakeśi II.:

Chandrâditya.

7. VIKRAMÂDITYA I., ceased to reign in Śaka 602 or A. D. 680.

Âdityavarman.

Jayasiṁhavarman.

---

8. VINAYÂDITYA, Śaka 602—619 or A. D. 680—697.

9. VIJAYÂDITYA, Śaka 618—655 or A.D. 696—733.

10. VIKRAMÂDITYA II., Śaka 655—669 or A. D. 733—747.

11. KÎRTIVARMAN II., Śaka 669 or A. D. 747, deprived of supreme sovereignty by Dantidurga before Śaka 675 or A. D. 753.

[62] SECTION XI.

THE RÂSHṬRAKÛṬAS.

Section XI.

THE Râshṭrakûṭas are represented to have belonged to the race of Yadû.[1] According to the Wardhâ plates they were members of the Sâtyaki branch of the race ; and were the direct descendants of a prince of the name of Raṭṭa. He had a son of the name of Râshṭrakûṭa after whom the family was so called. These are clearly imaginary persons ; and as remarked before, the Râshṭrakûṭa family was in all likelihood the main branch of the race of Kshatriyas named Raṭṭhas who gave their name to the country of Mahârâshṭra, and were found in it even in the times of Aśoka the Maurya. The Râshṭrakûṭas were the real native rulers of the country and were sometimes eclipsed by enterprising princes of foreign origin, such as the Śâtavâhanas and the Châlukyas who established themselves in the Dekkan and exercised supreme sovereignty, but were never extirpated. The earliest prince of the dynasty mentioned in the grants hitherto discovered is Govinda I. But in an inscription in the rock-cut temple of the Daśâvatâras at Elurâ the names of two earlier ones, Dantivarman and Indrarâja, occur.[2] The latter was Govinda's father and the former his grandfather. Govinda I. was probably the prince of that name who in Ravikîrti's inscription at Aihole is spoken of as having attacked the Châlukya king Pulakeśi II. and to have afterwards become his ally.

Govinda I.

1 Khârepâṭan plate, Jour. B. B. R. A. S., Vol. I., p. 217; Sângalî plates, B. B. R. A., Vol. IV., p. 111.; Navasârî plates and Wardhâ plates, Jour. B. B. R. A. S., Vol. XVIII. p. 239 *et seq.*

2 Arch. Surv. West. Ind., No. 10, pp. 92—96.

Section XI.

Govinda was succeeded by his son Karka, during whose reign the Brâhmaṇs performed many sacrifices and who seems to have patronized the old Vedic religion. After him his son Indrarâja came to the throne. Indrarâja married a girl who belonged to the Châlukya family, though on her mother's side she was connected with the lunar race, probably that of the Râshṭrakûṭas themselves. From this union sprang Dantidurga, who became king after his father. With a handful of soldiers Dantidurga defeated the army of Karṇâṭaka, which hitherto had achieved very great glory by vanquishing the forces of the kings of Kâñchî, the Keralas, Cholas, and Pâṇḍyas, and of Śrîharsha, the lord paramount of Northern India, and Vajraṭa ;[3] and thus conquered Vallabha or the last Châlukya king Kîrtivarman II. with ease. He thus acquired paramount sovereignty in the south.[4] He also subdued the kings of Kâñchî, Kaliṅga, Kosala, Śrî-Śaila,[5] Mâlava, Lâṭ, and [63] Ṭaṅka. At Ujjayinî he gave large quantities of gold and jewels in charity.[6] A grant of Dantidurga found at Sâmangaḍ in the Kolhâpur district bears the date 675 of the Śaka era, corresponding to A.D. 753.[7]

Karka I.

Indra II.

Dantidurga.

Dantidurga died childless according to a grant found at Karḍâ,[8] and his paternal uncle Kṛishṇarâja succeeded to the throne. Another grant found at

Kṛishṇarâja

3 The army of Karṇâṭaka was thus the army of the Châlukyas.

4 Sâmangaḍ grant, p. 375, Jour. B. B. R. A. S., Vol. II.

5 This must have been the country about Śrî-Śaila which contains the celebrated shrine of Mallikârjuna and which is situated on the lower Kṛishṇa in the Karnul district, Madras Presidency.

6 Arch. Surv. West. Ind., No. 10. *loc. cit.*

7 Referred to above.

8 Jour. R. A. S., Vol. III.

Section XI.

Baroda[9] omits the name of Dantidurga, since the object of the writer was simply to give the pedigree of the reigning monarch, with reference to whom Dantidurga was but a collateral, and not to give the names of all the previous kings. In that grant Kṛishṇarâja is spoken of as having "rooted out" a prince belonging to the same family with himself who had taken to evil ways and to have himself assumed the task of governing for the "benefit of his race." The prince dethroned or destroyed by Kṛishṇarâja could not have been Dantidurga, as has been supposed by some writers, since he was a powerful monarch who for the first time acquired supreme sovereignty for his family. In a grant found at Kâvî, and another found in the Navasârî district, Kṛishṇa is represented to have succeeded to the throne after Dantidurga's death.[10] The prince whom he set aside, therefore, must either have been a son of Dantidurga or some other person with a better claim to the throne than himself. The statement of the Karḍâ plate that Dantidurga died childless may be discredited as being made two hundred years after the occurrence.

Kṛishṇarâja, otherwise called Śubhatuṅga and also Akâlavarsha, carried on the work of Dantidurga and reduced the Châlukyas to complete subjection. In two of the grants[11] he is spoken of "as having with the aid of gods in the form of his counsellors or followers churned the ocean of the Châlukya race which had been resorted to by mountains in the

9 Published in Jour. Beng. A. S., Vol. VIII., pp. 292—303.

10 See stanza 11 (p. 146, Ind. Ant., Vol. V.,) of the first half of which only तस्मिन्दिवं [गते] remains; and lines 15 and 16, Jour. B. B. R. A. S., Vol. XVIII., p. 257, ii. 14, 15.

11 Vaṇi-Dinḍorî, Jour. R. A. S., Vol. V., and Râdhanpur, Ind. Ant., Vol. VI., p. 65.

Section XI.

shape of kings afraid of their wings or power being destroyed[12]—an ocean that was inaccessible to others, —and drawn out from it the Lakshmî"[13] of paramount sovereignty. He is said to have defeated Râhappa who was proud of his own power and prowess, and afterwards assumed the ensigns of supreme sovereignty. Who[14] this person was we have not the means of determining. In the Wardhâ plates he is represented to have constructed many temples of Śiva, [64] which resembled the Kailâsa mountain.[15] In the Baroda grant it is stated that Kṛishṇarâja "caused to be constructed a temple of a wonderful form on the mountain at Elâpura. When the gods moving in their aerial cars saw it they were struck with wonder and constantly thought much over the matter saying to themselves, 'This temple of Śiva is self-existent; for such beauty is not to be found in a work of art.' Even the architect who constructed it was struck with wonder, saying when his heart misgave him as regards making another similar attempt, 'Wonderful! I do not know how it was that I could construct it.' King Kṛishṇa with his own hands again decorated Śambhu (Śiva) placed in that temple, by means of gold, rubies,

Temple of Śiva at Elurâ excavated at the orders of Kṛishṇarâja

---

12 The legend is that in early times mountains had wings, and as they did considerable mischief by their use, Indra set about cutting them. The mountains thereupon took refuge in the sea. The story originated from the double sense which the word *parvata* bears in the Vedas. It denotes "a mountain" and "a cloud" also. Indra was the god who prevented the clouds from flying from place to place, and compelled them to discharge their freight on the earth for the benefit of his human worshippers.

13 Vishṇu churned the ocean with the aid of the gods and drew out Lakshmî from it, whom he married.

14 Ind. Ant., Vol. XII., p. 182, l. 13.

15 *Loc. cit.*

Section XI. and other precious jewels, though he had already been decorated by the wonderful artificial ornaments of the stream of the Gaṅgâ, the moon, and the deadly poison." The ending *pura* in the names of towns, when it undergoes a change at all, is invariably changed to *ur*, as in Sihur for Siṁhapura, Indur for Indrapura, Śirur for Śrîpura, &c. The Elâpura of the inscription, therefore, is Elur ; and the temple described in the grant in such terms must be one of those excavated on the hills at the place, perhaps the temple of Kailâsa itself.[16] Thus it appears that it was Kṛishṇarâja that caused the Kailâsa to be constructed, and the date assigned to

---

16 Dr. Bühler in his paper in Vol. VI., Ind. Ant., simply states that the "grant (Baroda) connects him (Kṛishṇarâja) with the hill at Elâpur, where he seems to have built a fort and a splendid temple of Śiva." He has not identified Elâpura and did not perceive the important significance of this and the next two stanzas. He, however, suspected that one of the verses was badly deciphered. That this and the following verses are somewhat badly deciphered there is no doubt; but the translation in the Bengal Asiatic Society's Journal is far worse and Dr. Bühler was misled by it. Dr. Fleet has published a revised translation (Ind. Ant., Vol. XII., p. 162), but as regards this passage it certainly is no improvement on the first. He also once spoke of "a hill fort" (Ind. Ant., Vol. XI., p. 124), and now thinks Elâpura is in the passage meant to be represented as Kṛishṇarâja's "encampments." He identifies Elâpura with Yellâpur in the North Kânarâ districts. But the manner in which the temple is described according to my translation and also the obvious derivation of Elur from Elâpura, and Elurâ from Elâpuraka, leave little doubt that a rock-cut temple at Elurâ is meant to be spoken of; and actually the existence of a Râshṭrakûṭa inscription in one of the temples confirms my conclusion. That my translation is correct and appropriate, I have shown in an article published in the Indian Antiquary, Vol. XII., p. 228, where the reader will find the point fully discussed.

it by Drs. Fergusson and Burgess simply on architectural grounds is verified. Kṛishṇarâja must have reigned in the last quarter of the seventh century of the Śaka era, *i.e.*, between 753 and 775 A.D. **Section XI.**

Kṛishṇarâja was succeeded by his son Govinda II.[17] Nothing particular is recorded of him in the grants, except, of course, the general praise which is accorded to every prince, however weak and inglorious. It however appears from the Vaṇi-Diṇḍorî and Râdhanpur grants that he was superseded by his younger brother [65] Dhruva, and the grants endeavour to palliate his crime in having thus usurped the throne. The Wardhâ grant states that he gave himself up to sensual pleasures, and left the cares of the kingdom to his younger brother Nirupama ; and thus allowed the sovereignty to drop away from his hands. But subsequently he seems from the Paiṭhan[18] grant to have endeavoured to regain his power with the assistance of the neighbouring princes, when Dhruva vanquished him in a battle and formally assumed the insignia of supreme sovereignty. At the end of a Purâṇa entitled Harivaṁśa of the Digambara Jainas, it is stated that the work was composed by Jinasena in the Śaka year 705 while Vallabha the son of Kṛishṇa was ruling over the south. Govinda II. is in the Kâvî and Paiṭhan grants called Vallabha, while one of the names of Dhruva, the second son of Kṛishṇa I., was Kalivallabha. Govinda II., therefore, must be the

Govinda II.

17 The name of this prince is omitted in the Vaṇi-Diṇḍori and Râdhanpur grants, for the same reason apparently as that for which Dantidurga's is omitted in the Baroda grant; but he is alluded to when they state that Dhruva or Nirupama set aside his elder brother.

18 Epigraphia Indica, Vol. IV., p. 107.

Section XI.

prince alluded to, and he appears thus to have been on the throne in the Śaka year 705, or A.D. 783.[19]

Dhruva was an able and warlike prince. His other names were Nirupama or the "Matchless," Kalivallabha, and Dhârâvarsha. He humbled the Pallava king of Kâñchî and obtained from him a tribute of elephants. He detained in custody the prince of the Gaṅgâ family, which ruled over the Chera country. He also carried his arms into the north against the king of the Vatsas, whose capital must have been Kauśâmbî the modern Kosam near Allahabad, and who had grown haughty by his conquest of a king of the Gauḍa country. He drove the Vatsa prince into the impassable desert of Mârvâḍ and carried away the two state umbrellas which he had won from the Gauḍa king.[20] The Jaina Harivaṁśa represents a Vatsa prince as ruling over the west in Śaka 705. He must have been the same as that vanquished by Nirupama. According to the Navasârî grant Nirupama took away the umbrella of the king of Kosala also; and in the Wardhâ plates he is represented as having three white umbrellas. A stone inscription at Paṭṭadakal was incised in the reign of Nirupama. There he is styled Dhârâvarsha and Kalivallabha.[21] The last name occurs also in the Wardhâ grant and the first in that found at Paiṭhan. This prince does not

---

19 शाकेष्वब्दशतेषु सप्तसु दिशं पञ्चोत्तरेषूत्तरां
पातीन्द्रायुधनाम्नि कृष्णनृपजे श्रीवल्लभे दक्षिणाम् ।
पूर्वां श्रीमदवन्तिभूभृति नृपे वत्सादि (धि) राजेऽपरां
सौर्यां (रा) णामधिमण्डले (लं) जययुते वीरे वराहेऽवति ॥

Râjendralal's Skr. MSS., Vol. VI., p. 80, and MSS. in the Deccan College collections.

20 Vaṇi-Dinḍorî and Râdhanpur plates.

21 Ind. Ant., Vol. XI., p. 125.

Section XI.

appear to have reigned long, as his brother was on the throne in Śaka 705 and his son in Śaka 716, the year in which the Paiṭhan charter was issued.

Govinda III. or Jagat-tunga I.

Dhruva Nirupama was succeeded by his son Govinda III. The Râdhanpur and Vaṇi-Diṇḍorî grants were issued by him in the Śaka year 730 corresponding to A.D. 808[22] while he was at [66] Mayûrakhaṇḍî. This place has been identified with a hill-fort in the Nâsik territory of the name of Morkhaṇḍ. Whether Mayûrakhaṇḍî was the capital of the dynasty in the time of this king cannot be satisfactorily determined. Govinda III. was certainly one of the greatest of the Râshṭrakûṭa princes, and the statement in his grant that during his time the Râshṭrakûṭas became invincible, as the Yâdavas of Purâṇic history did when under the guidance of Kṛishṇa, appears credible. Seeing he had grown up to be a brave prince his father proposed to abdicate the throne in his favour ; but he declined, expressing himself perfectly satisfied with his position as Yuvarâja or prince-regent.[23] When after his father's death he ascended the throne, twelve kings united their forces and rose against him,

---

22 The Saṁvatsara or cyclic year given in the first is *Sarvajit*, the current Śaka year corresponding to which was 730, while in the second it is *Vyaya* corresponding to 729 current. As regards the exact signification to be attached to these dates, see Appendix B.

23 The Kâvî grant, however, states that the father did raise him to the supreme sovereignty which his enemies were endeavouring to deprive his family of, *i.e.*, when he found the enemies of his family too powerful for him, he raised his son to the throne and assigned to him the task of suppressing them. Ind. Ant., Vol. V., p. 147, v. 27. The reading, however, is somewhat corrupt. The enemies spoken of here must be those twelve whom he is represented to have vanquished in the other grants.

Section XI. desirous of striking an effectual blow at the power of the Râshṭrakûṭas. But alone and unassisted, he by his personal valour suddenly inflicted a crushing defeat on them and broke the confederacy. He released the Gaṅga prince of Chera, who had been kept in custody by his father ; but no sooner did he go back to his native country than he put himself into an attitude of hostility. But Govinda III. immediately vanquished him, and threw him into captivity again. Subsequently he marched against the Gûrjara king, who fled away at his approach. Thence he proceeded to Mâlvâ, the king of which country knowing himself to be unable to resist his power surrendered to him. After receiving his obeisance he directed his march to the Vindhyas. When Mârâśarva, the ruler of the adjoining country, who had been watching his movements, heard from his spies that Govinda's army had encamped on the slopes of that mountain, he went up to him, and throwing himself at his feet presented to him his most highly valued heirlooms which no other prince had ever got before. On this occasion Govinda spent the rainy season at a place called Śrîbhavana, which has not been identified. When the rains were over, he marched with his army to the Tuṅgabhadrâ, where he stayed for a short time, and brought the Pallava king of Kâñchî under a more complete subjection than before. Thence he sent a message to the king of Veṅgi, or the country between the lower Kṛishṇâ and the Godâvarî, who probably belonged to the eastern Châlukya dynasty, and he came and attended on him as if he were his servant.[24] This grand victorious march to the north and the south must have taken place before Śaka 726 or A.D.

24 Vaṇi-Diṇḍorî and Râdhanpur plates.

804. For in a copper-plate grant bearing that date found in the Kânarese country, it is stated that when the king (Govinda III.) "having conquered Dantiga who ruled over Kâñchî, had come to levy tribute, and when his encampments were on the banks of the Tuṅgabhadrâ," he allotted some lands to one Śivadhârî at a holy place named Râmeśvara.[25] His expeditions against the neighbouring princes must have been undertaken after [67] Śaka 716 *past*, or 794 A.D., since the Paiṭhan charter which was issued in that year makes no mention of them. Section XI.

Govinda III. thus acquired a large extent of territory and established his supremacy over a number of kings. He appears to have become the paramount sovereign of the whole country from Mâlvâ in the north to Kâñchîpura in the south, and to have under his immediate sway the country between the Narmadâ and the Tuṅgabhadrâ. The Vaṇi-Diṇḍorî plates convey a village situated in the Nâsik district, while those found in the Kânarese country assign some land near the Tuṅgabhadrâ. The province of Lâṭa, situated between the Mahî and the lower Tâpî, was assigned by him to his brother Indra,[26] who became the founder of another branch of the dynasty. Govinda III., as stated in the Baroda grant, made and unmade kings. His secondary names as found in his own grants were Prabhûtavarsha or "Raining profusely," Pṛithvî-vallabha or "the Lover of the Earth," and Śrî-Vallabha. Others will be noticed below. The Baroda grant was issued by Karka, the son of

---

25 Ind. Ant., Vol. XI., pp. 126-7.

26 Kâvi plate, Ind. Ant., Vol. V., p. 147, v. 29; Baroda grant, Jour. Beng. A. S., Vol. VIII., p. 296, v. 21, in which तदा ought to be तद्दत्त as in the Kâvi.

Section XI. Govinda's brother Indra, the king of Lâta. in Śaka 734 or A.D. 812, and the Kâvî grant by Govinda the younger brother of Karka, in Śaka 749 or A.D. 827. We need not notice these princes further, since they belong more to the history of Gujarât than of the Dekkan.

Śarva or Amoghavarsha I.

In several of the grants belonging to this dynasty, the son and successor of Nirupama is stated to be Jagattuṅga. Now, since Govinda III. was one of the greatest princes of this dynasty, it is impossible that he should have been passed over by the writers of these grants. Jagattuṅga, the son of Nirupama, must, therefore, be Govinda himself and no other. After his death his son Amoghavarsha, whose proper name appears to have been Śarva,[27] came to the throne. He seems to have marched against the Châlukyas of Veṅgi and put several of the princes to death.[28] In the Navasârî grant Amoghavarsha is spoken of simply as Vallabha and is styled *Râjarâja* or king of kings and also Vîra-Nârâyaṇa. This last title is justified by the poetic writer of the grant by saying that as the God Nârâyaṇa brought out the earth which was immersed in the ocean, so did Vallabha bring the goddess of sovereignty out of the ocean in the shape of the Châlukyas in which it had sunk. He is also represented to have "burnt" Châlukyas. These also must be allusions to Amoghavarsha's wars with the Châlukyas of Veṅgi ; and he probably conquered some territory belonging to them. In the Karḍâ grant the city of Mânyakheṭa is spoken of as being in a very flourishing condition in his time. There is little question that it was his capital ; but whether

---

27 Ind. Ant., Vol. XII., p. 183, 1. 25.

28 Sâṅgali plates. But the reading is somewhat corrupt.

Section XI.

it was he who founded it and made it the capital of the dynasty cannot be clearly made out from that grant, as the reading given by Mr. Wathen is corrupt. But the Wardhâ plates are clear on the point. In them the successor of Jagattuṅga is called Nṛipatuṅga ; and he is represented to have founded the city of Mânyakheṭa, which "put the [68] city of the gods" to shame. Mânyakheṭa has been properly identified with Mâlkhed in the Nizam's territory. In the Kânheri caves there are three inscriptions, in which the reigning paramount sovereign is represented to be Amoghavarsha. In one of them Pullaśakti of the Śîlâhâra family, and in the other two his son, Kapardin, are mentioned as his dependents ruling over Konkan, which province had been assigned to them by Amoghavarsha. The dates occurring in the last two are Śaka 775 and 799.[29] An inscription at Sirur in the Dhârvâḍ district published by Dr. Fleet is dated Śaka 788, *vyaya*, which is represented as the fifty-second year of the reign of Amoghavarsha;[30] so that the year 799 Śaka of the Kânheri inscription must have been the sixty-third of his reign. The cyclic year *vyaya* corresponds to the Śaka year 788 *past* and 789 *current*. This prince appears thus to have begun to reign in Śaka 737 *past*. In a historical appendix at the end of a Jaina work entitled Uttarapurâṇa, or the latter

---

29 Jour. B. B. R. A. S., Vol. VI., West's copies Nos. 15 and 42; Vol. XIII., p. 11; and Prof. Kielhorn's paper, Ind. Ant., Vol. XIII., p. 133. The cyclic year given with 775 is *Prajâpati*, the current Śaka year corresponding to which, however, was 774. Prof. Kielhorn has recently calculated the true Śaka from the day of the week and fortnight and found it to be 773 expired, *i.e.*, 774 current.

30 Ind. Ant., Vol. XII., p. 216.

Section XI. half of the Mahâpurâṇa, by Guṇabhadra, Amoghavarsha is represented to have been a devoted worshipper of a holy Jaina saint named Jinasena, who was the preceptor of Guṇabhadra, and wrote the Âdipurâṇa or the first part of the same work.[31] Jinasena himself at the end of his poem the Pârśvâbhyudaya gives expression to a wish that Amoghavarsha may reign for a long time. An important work on the philosophy of the Digambara Jainas entitled Jayadhavalâ is represented at the end to have been composed when 759 years of the Śaka king had elapsed, in the reign of Amoghavarsha. In the introductory portion of a Jaina mathematical work entitled Sârasaṁgraha by Virâchârya, Amoghavarsha is highly praised for his power and his virtues, and is spoken of as a follower of the Jaina doctrine (Syâdvâda).[32] He is mentioned there also by his other name Nṛipatuṅga. The authorship of a small tract consisting of questions and answers on moral subjects, entitled Praśnottara-ratnamâlikâ, which has

---

31 Several copies of this Purâṇa have been purchased by me for Government. The stanza in which Amoghavarsha is alluded to is this :—

यस्य प्रांशुनखांशुजालविसरद्धारान्तराविर्भव-
त्पादाम्भोजरजःपिशङ्गमुकुटप्रत्यग्ररत्नद्युतिः ।
संस्मर्ता स्वममोघवर्षनृपतिः पूतोऽहमद्येत्यलं
स श्रीमाञ्जिनसेनपूज्यभगवत्पादो जगन्मङ्गलम् ॥

"The king Amoghavarsha remembered himself to have been purified that day when the lustre of the gems was heightened in consequence of his diadem becoming reddish by the dust-pollen of [Jinasena's] foot-lotuses appearing in the stream [of waterlike lustre] flowing from the collection of the brilliant rays of his nails;—enough—that prosperous Jinasena with the worshipful and revered feet is the blessing of the world."

32 This and the two preceding references I owe to the kindness of Mr. K. B. Pathak.

Section XI.

been claimed for Śaṁkarâchârya and one Śaṁkaraguru by the Brâhmaṇs, and for Vimala by the Śvetâmbaras, is attributed [69] to king Amoghavarsha by the Digambara Jainas. At the end of the Digambara copies occurs a stanza, in which it is stated that Amoghavarsha composed the Ratnamâlikâ after he had abdicated the throne in consequence of the growth of the ascetic spirit[33] in him. There is another Amoghavarsha in the dynasty who is represented as being of a thoughtful and religious temper. But he reigned for a short time and does not appear to have had any connection with the Jainas. There is a translation of the work in the Thibetan language, and there, too, the tract is attributed to Amoghavarsha, who is represented as a great king. The Thibetan translation of the name has been retranslated, however, into Amoghodaya by Schiefner; but if he had known the Digambara tradition, he would have put it as Amoghavarsha.[34] From all this it appears that of all the Râshṭrakûṭa princes, Amoghavarsha was the greatest patron of the Digambara Jainas; and the statement that he adopted the Jaina faith seems to be true.

Kṛishṇa II. or Akâlavarsha.

Amoghavarsha's son and successor was Akâlavarsha. He married the daughter of Kokkala, king of Chedi, who belonged to the Haihaya race, and by her had a son named Jagattuṅga. Akâlavarsha's proper name was Kṛishṇa as is evident from the Navasârî grant and also from the Wardhâ and the Karḍâ plates. He is the Kṛishṇarâja during whose

---

33 See my Report on the search for Sanskrit MSS. for 1883-84; Notes, &c., p. ii. The stanza is

विवेकात्त्यक्तराज्येन राज्ञेयं रत्नमालिका ।
रचितामोघवर्षेण सुधियां सदलंकृतिः ॥

34 Weber's Indische Streifen, Vol. I., p. 210.

Section XI. reign a tributary chief of the name of Ṛithvîrâma made a grant of land to a Jaina temple which he had caused to be constructed in the Śaka year 797 at Saundatti.[35] Another Jaina temple was built by a Vaiśya or Bania named Chikârya during his reign in Śaka 824 at Muḷgunda in the Dhârvâḍ district, and in the inscription which records this fact he is styled Kṛishṇa Vallabha.[36] Kṛishṇa or Akâlavarsha appears to have been a powerful prince. He is represented as having frightened the Gûrjara, humbled the pride of the Lâta, taught humility to the Gauḍas, deprived the people on the sea-coast of their repose, and exacted obedience from the Andhra, Kaliṅga, Gâṅga, and Magadha.[37]

In the reign of this prince the Jaina Purâṇa noticed above was consecrated in Śaka 820, the cyclic year being Piṅgala,[38] by Lokasena [70] the

---

35 Jour. B. B. R. A. S., Vol. X., p. 200. The cyclic year mentioned is Manmatha, which corresponds to Śaka 797 *past*.

36 *Ib.*, p. 192. The cyclic year is Dundubhi, which fell in 825 current.

37 Wardhâ and Navasâri plates. Jour. B. B. R. A. S., Vol. XVIII., pp. 239-269.

38 अकालवर्षभूपाले पालयत्यखिलामिलाम्।
तस्मिन्विध्वस्तनिःशेषद्विषि वीध्रयशोजुषि॥
धर्म *v. l.*

* * * * *

शकनृपकालाभ्यन्तरविंशत्यधिकाष्टशतमिताब्दान्ते।
मङ्गलमहार्थकारिणि पिङ्गलनामनि समस्तजनसुखदे

* * * * *

निष्ठितं भव्यवर्यैः
प्राप्तेज्यं शास्त्रसारं जगति विजयते पुण्यमेतत्पुराणम्॥

"Victorious in the world is this holy Purâṇa, the essence of the Sâstras which was finished and worshipped by the best among respectable [men]* * * in the year Pingala that brings about great prosperity and confers happiness on pupil of Guṇabhadra, who was the author of the second part. In the historical appendix, "the lofty elephants of Akâlavarsha" are represented "to have drunk the waters of the Ganges rendered fragrant by being mixed with the humour flowing from their temples, and, as if not having their thirst quenched, to have resorted to the Kaumâra forest (in the extreme south), which was full of sandal trees set in gentle motion by the breezes blowing over the sea waves, and into the shade of which the rays of the sun did not penetrate."[39] The date 833 Śaka has also been assigned to Akâlavarsha.[40] It will have been seen that an inscription at Saundatti represents Kṛishṇarâja to have been the reigning prince in Śaka 797, while one in the Kânheri caves speaks of his father Amoghavarsha as being on the throne two years later, *i.e.*, in 799. This discrepancy must be due to the fact mentioned in the Ratnamâlikâ that the latter had abdicated the throne in his old age. The real reigning prince therefore in Śaka 797 and 799 must have been Akâlavarsha his son ; but the writer of the Kânheri inscription must in the latter year have put in Amoghavarsha's name, as he was not dead, and his having abdicated had probably no significance in his eyes.

Section XI.

Akâlavarsha's son was Jagattuṅga. But he did **Jagattuṅga.**

all mankind, at the end of the year measured by 820 of the era of the Śaka king * * * , while that king Akâlavarsha, all of whose enemies were destroyed and whose fame was pure (*or* who acquired religious merit and fame) was protecting the whole earth."

The cyclic year Piṅgala corresponded to 820 Śaka *current*.

39 यस्योत्तुङ्गमतंगजा निजमदस्रोतस्विनीसंगमा-
द्गाङ्गं वारि कलङ्कितं कटु मुहुः पीत्वाप्यगच्छत्तृषः ।
कौमारं घनचन्दनं वनमपांपत्युस्तरंगानिलै-
र्मन्दान्दोलितमस्तभास्करकरच्छायं समाशिश्रियन् ॥

40 Ind. Ant., Vol. XI., p. 109.

Section XI. not ascend the throne as appears from the fact that his name is not mentioned in the list of kings given in the Khârepâtaṇ grant, after Akâlavarsha, but that of Indra, who is spoken of as Akâlavarsha's grandson, while Jagattuṅga is mentioned in another connection below. And in the Navasârî grant Indra is represented as "meditating on the feet" of Akâlavarsha, and not of Jagattuṅga though he was his father, which shows that he was the immediate successor of Akâlavarsha. But the Wardhâ grant is explicit. It tells us that Jagattuṅga had a beautiful person, and that he died without having [71] ascended the throne. Jagattuṅga married Lakshmî, the daughter of his maternal uncle, the son of Kokkala, who is called Raṇavigraha in the Sâṅgalî and Navasârî grants, and Śaṁkaragaṇa in the Karḍâ plates. But it will be presently shown that the Karḍâ plates contain many mistakes and are the source of a good deal of confusion in the history of this dynasty.

Indra III. From this union sprang Indra, who succeeded his grandfather. His title was Nityavarsha according to the Navasârî grant ; and his son Govinda IV. is in the Sâṅgalî grant spoken of as "meditating on the feet" of Nityavarsha, which also shows that that was Indra's title. Nityavarsha is the donor in the Navasârî grant. He is represented as residing at his capital Mânyakheṭa, but to have on the occasion gone to Kurundaka, identified with the modern Kaḍoda on the banks of the Tâpî, for his Paṭṭabandhotsava. This must have been the festival in honour of his coronation. At Kurundaka he granted that and many other villages, and restored four hundred more which had once been given in charity but had been resumed by former kings. He also gave away twenty lacs of Drammas in charity after having weighed himself against gold. The village conveyed by the Navasârî grant is Tenna situated in the Lâṭ country. It has been identified with Tenâ in the Navasârî division of the Baroda State. The grant was issued in Śaka 836 ; so that Indra appears to have come to the throne in that year. Another set of copper-plates found in the Navasârî district records the grant of the village of Gumra identified with the modern Bagumra by the same prince. The grant was issued at the same time as the other, and the contents *mutatis mutandis* are exactly the same.[41] From these grants of villages in the Navasârî district which must have formed a part of the old country of Lâṭa, and from the statement in the Wardhâ plates that Kṛishṇa or Akâlavarsha humbled the pride of the Lâṭa prince, it appears that the main branch of the Râshṭrakûṭas reigning at Mânyakheṭa must have in Akâlavarsha's time supplanted or reduced to a humble position the dynasty of their kinsmen in Gujarât, which had been founded in the time of Jagattuṅga or Govinda III. Indra was the reigning monarch in Śaka 838, the cyclic year being *Dhâtu,* as appears from an inscription published by Dr. Fleet.[42]

As regards the next king there is some confusion in the Karḍâ plates. The Sâṅgalî grant, however, is clear. Indra married a lady from the Haihaya family of Chedi again. Her name was Vijâṁbâ ;[43] and she was the daughter of Aṅgaṇadeva, the son of Arjuna, who was the eldest son of Kokkala, men-

41 Jour. B. B. R. A. S., Vol. XVIII., p. 261 *et seq.*

42 Ind. Ant., Vol. XII., p. 224.

43 Dr. Fleet in his revised transcript and translation of the Sângalî grant calls her Dvijâmbâ, but in the facsimile given by him the name is distinctly Vijâmbâ in both the places where it occurs. The Sanskrit of Vijâmbâ is Vidyâmbâ. Ind. Ant., Vol. XII., p. 250.

Section XI.

tioned above. By her Indra had a son named Govinda, who is the last king noticed in the Sâṅgalî grant, since it was issued by him. But according to the Khârepâṭaṇ grant, Govinda was the younger brother of a prince named [72] Amoghavarsha.[44]

Amoghavarsha II

The immediate successor of Indra, therefore, was Amoghavarsha, and after him his younger brother Govinda came to the throne. And this is confirmed by the Karḍâ plates also. Amoghavarsha and Govinda are there meant to be mentioned as the two sons of Ambâ, who is the same as the Vijâmbâ of the Sâṅgalî plate. But in the text of the grant Govinda and Ambâ form one compound, so that the translators of the grant call the lady Govindâmbâ, which certainly is an unique or an absurd name. Thus they drop king Govinda altogether.[45] But the

---

44 Dr. Fleet in his genealogical table at p. 109, Vol. XI., Ind. Ant., speaks of Govinda's brother as unnamed. But he is named Amoghavarsha in the Khârepâṭan grant, and also in that of Karḍâ, if properly understood.

45 The 14th stanza, the latter part of which I have construed as in the text, is

चैद्यां मातुलशंकरगणात्मजायामभूज्जगत्तुङ्गात् ।
श्रीमानमोघवर्षो गोविन्दां बाभिधानायां ॥

Now the first line of this is, as it stands, out of place and must contain some mistakes. For, (1) it contains, in substance, a repetition of what we have in the first line of stanza 12, and (2) if it is read here as it is, we shall have to make Ambâ a wife of Jagattuṅga along with Lakshmî, who has been represented as his wife in stanza 12, and understand her to be Lakshmî's sister, the father of both being Śaṁkaragaṇa. But Ambâ or Vijâmbâ is in the Sâṅgalî grant clearly spoken of as the daughter of Aṅgaṇadeva, the son of Arjuna, who was the brother of Raṇavigraha, the father of Lakshmî; that is, Ambâ was the daughter of Lakshmî's first cousin. She is also distinctly represented as the wife of Indra and the mother of Govinda IV. Again, if we take the lines as they are, the result will be that the Karḍâ grant makes no mention of Indra's wife Vijâmbâ and

Section XI.

Wardhâ grant is explicit on the point. From it we learn that Amoghavarsha was the elder brother of Govinda, but that he died immediately after his father, as if "out of love for him," and then Govinda came to the throne. The Sâṅgali grant of Govinda IV., as he must be called, does not mention Amoghavarsha by name; but states that "though Govinda had the power, he did not act with any reprehensible cruelty towards his elder brother, and did not render himself infamous by incest, or assume the nature of a devil by casting aside considerations of purity and impurity, but became Sâhasâṅka by his matchless enterprise and liberality." What this

Govinda IV.

of his sons Amoghavarsha and Govinda IV., the latter of whom reigned, as we shall see, for at least fifteen years. Such an omission is not likely. Then, again, the Sâṅgalî grant makes no allusion whatever to Jagattuṅga's marriage with a lady of the name of Govindâmbâ. And the second line श्रीमानमोघवर्षो गोविन्दाम्बाभिधानायाम्। looks as if the intention of the writer of it was set forth the names of the two sons of Indra, Amoghavarsha and Govinda, and of their mother Ambâ or Vijâmbâ. And it seems to me that the following stanza, in which the liberality of a monarch has been praised refers to Govinda IV., who, as noticed in the text below, was called Suvarṇavarsha by people, because he "rained down gold." The name of that prince, therefore, must occur in the verse immediately previous. The first line must, it is clear to me, have crept in through mistake. If it were not read here, the second would be applicable to the king mentioned immediately before, *i.e.*, Indra, and the whole would be consistent with the information derived from the Sâṅgalî grant. The emendation I make in the second line is to read न्दों for न्दां and then Ambâ would be released from her incongruous association with Govinda, and the whole would be consistent and intelligible. There must be other mistakes also in the Karḍâ grant. Very probably a verse or two are omitted here, as also after the next stanza, where Kṛishṇarâja is abruptly introduced and spoken of parenthetically.

Section XI. statement exactly means it is difficult to say. But probably Govinda was believed to have encompassed his brother's death, and the other accusations referred to were whispered against him; and this is [73] intended as a defence. The Khârepâṭaṇ and Wardhâ grants agree in representing Govinda as a prince addicted to sensual pleasures. The former says that he was "the abode of the dramatic sentiment of love and was always surrounded by crowds of beautiful women," and the latter that he was "the source of the sportive pleasures of Love, his mind was enchained by the eyes of women, he displeased all men by his vicious courses, and his health being undermined, he met with an untimely death." The words used have double senses from which it would appear that the affairs of the state also fell into confusion and hastened his destruction. But the Sâṅgalî grant which was issued by him has of course nothing but praise for him. Govinda's other names were Prabhûtavarsha and Suvarṇavarsha (raining gold) and probably Sâhâsaṅka also. The grant was issued in Śaka 855, or A.D. 933, in the Vijaya[46] year of the cycle, while he was at his capital Mânyakheṭa. Govinda IV. was on the throne in Śaka 841, as appears from an inscription published by Dr. Fleet, in which under the name of Prabhûtavarsha he is represented as the reigning sovereign.[47] The inscription, however, is dated 840 Śaka; but from the cyclic year Pramâthin, which is also given,

46 The current Śaka year was 856.

47 Ind. Ant., Vol. XII., p. 222. Dr. Fleet, however, identifies this Prabhûtavarsha with Jagattuṅga the son of Akâlavarsha or Kṛishṇa II., and father of Nityavarsha. But as we have seen Nityavarsha was on the throne in Śaka 836 and 838, wherefore his father could not have been the reigning prince in Śaka 840 or 841. Besides, as I have shown, Jagattuṅga did not ascend the throne at all.

Section XI.

it must be understood that the year meant is 841 Śaka. It will appear from this that Indra or Nityavarsha, who succeeded his grandfather in Śaka 836, had a very short reign, and his eldest son, Amoghavarsha, could have been on the throne only for a few months. Govinda IV. like Amoghavarsha I. was at war with the Châlukyas of Veṅgi.[48] Another inscription represents Govinda IV. as the reigning monarch in Śaka 851.[49]

Baddiga or Amoghavarsha III.

From the Khârepâṭaṇ plates it appears that Govinda IV. was succeeded by his (paternal uncle) Baddiga, the second son of Jagattuṅga. He is represented to have been a virtuous prince, serene like a sage. He was succeeded by his son Kṛishṇarâja, and after his death his younger brother Khoṭika became king. The Karḍâ grant is somewhat confusing here, but when properly understood it is perfectly consistent with that of Khârepâṭaṇ. It states: "When the elder brother Kṛishṇarâjadeva went to heaven, Khoṭṭigadeva, who was begotten by the king Amoghavarsha on Kaṇdakadevî, the daughter of Yuvarâja, became king."[50] Here the expression "elder brother" must be taken as related to Khoṭṭigadeva and not to the preceding king,[51] whoever he may have been. Khoṭika therefore was, even [74] according to the Karḍâ grant, the younger brother

Kṛishṇa III. and Khotika

48 Ind. Ant., Vol. XII., p. 249, and my note on Professor Peterson's Report on MSS. for 1883-84, p. 48.

49 Ind. Ant., Vol. XII., p. 249.

50 ऐन्द्रपदजिगीषयेव स्वर्गमधिरूढे च ज्येष्ठे भ्रातरि श्रीमत्कृष्णराजदेवे
युवराजदेवदुहितरि कन्दकदेव्याममोघवर्षनृपा-
ज्जातः खोट्टिगदेवो नृपतिरभूद्भुवनविख्यातः ॥ १६ ॥

51 For, the clause containing that expression is dependent on the principal sentence, which is in the next or 16th stanza and the subject of which is Khoṭṭigadeva. See the passage in the last note.

Section XI. of Kṛishṇarâja. But he is represented to have been the son of Amoghavarsha, while Kṛishṇarâja is spoken of in the Khârepâṭaṇ plates as the son of Baddiga. In an inscription at Saloṭgi, Kṛishṇarâja, the son of Amoghavarsha, is represented to have been reigning at Mânyakheṭa in 867 Śaka,[52] that is, twelve years after the Sâṇgalî grant of Govinda IV. was issued. He must have been the same prince as that mentioned in the grants we have been examining. For the Kṛishṇa of these was the second king after Govinda IV. His father Baddiga, who was Govinda's uncle, must have been an old man when he succeeded, and consequently must have reigned for a very short time. Hence his son Kṛishṇa came to be king within twelve years after Govinda's grant ; and there is no other Kṛishṇa mentioned in the grants who is likely to have been on the throne in 867 Śaka. If, then, the Kṛishṇa of the grants is the same as the Kṛishṇa of the Saloṭgi inscription, here we have evidence that his father's name was Amoghavarsha ; so that the Baddiga of the Khârepâṭaṇ plates was the same as the Amoghavarsha of the Karḍâ plates. Kṛishṇarâja and Khoṭika were thus brothers, and it would appear from the wording of the statement in the Karḍâ plates that they were the sons of the same father but of different mothers.[53]

---

52 Ind. Ant., Vol. I., p. 205, *et seq.* The cyclic year given is Plavaṅga, which followed next after Śaka 869 and the current year corresponding to which was 870. According to another system, which however was rarely used in Southern India, it was Plavaṅga in a part of the year 867 Śaka *expired.*

53 Dr. Fleet, following Mr. Wathen's translation, makes Kṛishṇa, whom he calls Kṛishṇa III., the elder brother of Amoghavarsha and thus a son of Jagattuṅga. But in the Khârepâṭaṇ grant he is distinctly represented as the son of Baddiga who was the son of Jagattuṅga, and in the

And these points have been placed beyond the possibility of doubt by the Wardhâ grant. After Govinda's death, we are told, the feudatory chiefs entreated Amoghavarsha the son of Jagattuṅga, who Section XI.

Wardhâ plates as the son of Amoghavarsha, the son of Amoghavarsha, the son of Jagattuṅga, and was thus a grandson of Jagattuṅga. He is also represented as Khoṭika's elder brother. I have shown in the text that the expression "elder brother," occurring in the Karḍâ grant, should by the rules of construction be taken as referring to Khoṭṭiga and in this way that grant becomes perfectly consistent with that of Khârepâṭaṇ. The Amoghavarsha who was the son of Jagattuṅga is that spoken of in the sixteenth stanza of the Karḍâ grant, and was different from the one mentioned in the fourteenth, who was the son of Indra and nephew of that Amoghavarsha, as I have shown above. Dr. Fleet brings in another Kṛishṇa and makes him the younger brother of Khoṭika, and identifies him with Nirupama (see the text below) and with the Kṛishṇa whose dates range from Śaka 867 to 878. What his authority is I do not know. But the Khârepâṭaṇ grant mentions one Kṛishṇa only, the elder brother of Khoṭika and son of Baddiga. The Karḍâ also mentions one only, and as to his relation with the other princes, I have shown that that grant agrees with the Khârepâṭaṇ plates. The Kṛishṇa whose dates range from 867 to 878 is to be identified with the elder brother of Khoṭika and is not to be considered a different prince unalluded to in the grants. Nirupama, the younger brother of Khoṭika, is not and cannot have been this Kṛishṇa, because his elder brother and the elder brother of Khoṭiga was called Kṛishṇa, and he too could not have been called by the same name. Nirupama does not appear to have been a reigning prince, for in the Karḍâ plates he is only parenthetically introduced as the father of Kakka, who was a reigning prince; and in the Khârepâṭaṇ grant he is not mentioned at all by name, but Kakkala is said to be the son of the brother of Khoṭika. Kṛishṇa, on the other hand, was on the throne from 867 to 878 Śaka according to the stone inscriptions. Again if Khoṭika was the elder brother of this Nirupama-Kṛishṇa it is impossible that he should be reigning in 893 Śaka, while Kṛishṇa should be

Section XI. was [75] "first among the wise" and the "best of serene sages", to assume the reins of power. He was assisted in the government by his son Kṛishṇa, who though but a crown-prince wielded very great power. The enemies who transgressed his commands were punished; he put to death Dantiga and Bappuka who had grown insolent. He thoroughly subdued the Gâṅga prince; and planted what appears to be a colony of the Âryas in his dominions. Hearing of the ease with which he captured the strongholds in the south, the Gûrjara prince, who was preparing to take the fortresses of Kâlanjara and Chitrakûṭa in the

---

on the throne from 867 to 878 Śaka, that is, before his elder brother. Kṛishṇ, therefore, was the elder of the two as stated in the Khârepâṭaṇ grant, and Khoṭika the younger. Dr. Fleet, however, being under the belief that this last was the elder brother, gives the following explanation of the discrepancy in the dates:—"Koṭṭiga or Khoṭṭiga left no issue, and this explains why the date of his inscription now published is considerably later than the dates obtained for Kṛishṇa IV.; viz., there being no probability of Koṭṭiga leaving any issue, first his younger brother Kṛishṇa IV. was joined with him in the government and then the latter's son Kakka III."—(Ind. Ant., Vol. XII., p. 255). This supposition is not supported by any circumstance; on the contrary it is utterly discountenanced by the inscriptions of Kṛishṇa which represent him to be the "Supreme king of great kings," (Ind. Ant., Vol. XII., p. 258) and to have been reigning at the time at Mânyakheṭa and governing the kingdom (Ind. Ant., Vol. I., p. 210). Otherwise, they would have spoken of him as *Yuvarâja*. Thus there were not two Kṛishṇas but only one. He was the son of Baddiga or Amoghavarsha, not his brother. His earliest date is that of the Warḍhâ grant, *i.e.*, 862 Śaka and the latest 881 that of the Yaśastilaka. He was the same monarch as that spoken of in the Saloṭgi and other stone inscriptions bearing the dates 867, 873, and 878 Śaka. Khoṭiga was his younger brother, and Nirupama the youngest.

north, had to give up the enterprize. All feudatory chiefs between the eastern and the western oceans and between the Himâlaya and Siṁhala (Ceylon) paid obeisance to him. After he had thus rendered the power of his family firm, his father died, and he ascended the throne. The Wardhâ plates announce the grant of a village to the north-west of Nâgpur near the modern Mohagaon made by Kṛishṇarâja, who is also called Akâlavarsha, in the name of his brother Jagattuṅga to a Brâhmaṇ of the Kâṇva school of the White Yajurveda on the 5th of the dark half of Vaiśâkha in Śaka 862, corresponding to 940 A.D., the cyclic year being Śârvari. This prince is called Śri-Vallabha also in the grant.

Section XI.

Kṛishṇarâja was the reigning monarch in Śaka 873 and 878.[54] At the end of a Jaina work called Yaśastilaka by Somadeva it is stated that it was finished on the 13th of Chaitra when 881 years of the era of the Śaka king had elapsed, the cyçlic year being Siddhârthin, during the reign of a feudatory of Kṛishṇarâjadeva. Kṛishṇarâjadeva is spoken of as reigning gloriously, having subdued the Pâṇḍyas, Siṁhala, the Cholas, the Cheras and others.[55] Khoṭika, his brother, was on the throne in Śaka 893 *Prajâpati*.[56]

Kakkala or Karka II.

Khoṭika was succeeded, according to the Khârepâṭaṇ grant, by Kakkala, the son of his brother. The name of this brother was Nirupama according to the Karḍâ grant. Kakkala is said to have been a brave soldier ; but he was conquered in battle by Tailapa, who belonged to the Châlukya race, and thus the sovereignty of the Dekkan passed

---

54 Ind. Ant., Vol. XII., p. 257, and Vol. XI., p. 109.

55 Prof. Peterson's Report, *loc. cit.*

56 Ind. Ant., Vol. XII., p. 225.

Section XI.

Overthrow of the Râshṭrakûṭas.

from the hands of the Râshṭrakûṭas once more [76] into those of the Châlukyas. The Karḍâ grant, which was made in the reign of Kakkala, is dated Śaka 894 or A.D. 972. And another inscription represents him as being on the throne in 896 *current*,[57] the cyclic year being *Śrîmukha*. But in this year or Śaka 895 *past* Tailapa attained sovereign powers.[58] The Râshṭrakûṭas were thus supreme masters of this country from about A.D. 748 to A.D. 973, that is, for nearly two hundred and twenty-five years.

Religion under the Râshṭrakûṭas.

That the princes of this race were very powerful there can be little doubt. The rock-cut temples at Elurâ still attest their power and magnificence. Under them the worship of the Purâṇic gods rose into much greater importance than before. The days when kings and princes got temples and monasteries cut out of the solid rock for the use of the followers of Gotama Buddha had gone by, never to return. Instead of them we have during this period temples excavated or constructed on a more magnificent scale and dedicated to the worship of Śiva and Vishṇu. Several of the grants of these Râshṭrakûṭa princes praise their bounty and mention their having constructed temples. Still, as the Kânheri inscriptions of the reign of Amoghavarsha I. show, Buddhism had its votaries and benefactors, though the religion had evidently sunk into unimportance. Jainism, on the other hand, retained the prominence it had acquired during the Châlukya period, or even made greater progress. Amoghavarsha was, as we have seen, a great patron of it, and was perhaps a convert to it ; and some of the minor chiefs and the lower castes,

---

57 Ind. Ant., Vol. XII., p. 270.

58 The cyclic year mentioned along with the first of these two dates in Aṅgiras the current Śaka year corresponding to which was 895.

Section XI.

especially the traders, were its devoted adherents. The form of Jainism that prevailed in the country was mostly that professed by the Digambara sect. A good many of the extant Digambara works were, as we have seen, composed during this period.

It is remarkable that, unlike the grants of the early Châlukya princes, those of the Râshṭrakûṭas contain accounts in verse of the ancestors of the grantor, and most of the verses are of the nature of those we find in the ordinary artificial poems in Sanskrit literature, possessing the same merits and faults. The Râshṭrakûṭas, therefore, must have been patrons of learning, and probably had poets in their service. One of the three Kṛishṇas belonging to the dynasty is the hero of an artificial poem by Halâyudha entitled the *Kavirahasya*, the purpose of which is to explain the distinction as regards sense and conjugational peculiarities between roots having the same external form. He is spoken of as the paramount sovereign of Dakshiṇâpatha.[59] Prof. Westergaard, however, thought [77] him to be the Kṛishṇarâya of the Vijayanagar dynasty who reigned in the first quarter of the sixteenth century. But in the *Kavirahasya* he is spoken of in one place as "having sprung from the Râshṭrakûṭa race,"[60] and is in another called "the ornament of the lunar

Kṛishṇa of the Râshṭrakûṭa race, the hero of the *Kavirahasya*.

---

59 अस्त्यगस्त्यमुनिज्योत्स्नापवित्रे दक्षिणापथे ।
कृष्णराज इति ख्यातो राजा साम्राज्यदीक्षितः ॥

"In Dakshiṇâpatha, which is rendered holy by the light of the sage Agastya, there was a king of the name of Kṛishṇarâja who was crowned as a paramount sovereign."

60 तोलयत्यतुलं शक्त्या यो भारं भुवनेश्वरः ।
कस्तं तुलयति स्थाम्ना राष्ट्रकूटकुलोद्भवम् ॥

"Who will equal in strength that lord of the world sprung from the Râshṭrakûṭa race, who by his power bears an incomparable burden."

Section XI.

Balharâs identified with the Râshṭrakûṭas.

race,"[61] which description is of course not applicable to the Vijayanagar prince.

Arabic travellers of the tenth century mention a powerful dynasty of the name of Balharâs who ruled at a place called Mânkir. The name of the city would show that the Râshṭrakûṭas, whose capital was Mânyakheṭa or Mânkhed, were meant. But Balharâ, the name of the dynasty, has not been identified with any that might be considered to be applicable to the Râshṭrakûṭas. But to me the identification does not appear difficult. The Râshṭrakûṭas appear clearly to have assumed the title of *Vallabha* which was used by their predecessors the Châlukyas. We have seen that Govinda II. is called Vallabha in two grants, Amoghavarsha I. in a third, and Kṛishṇa III. in a fourth. In an inscription on a stone tablet at Lakshmeśvar, Govinda III. is called *Śri-Vallabha,*[62] while in the Râdhanpur plates he is spoken of as *Vallabha-narendra.* In the Sâṅgalî and Karḍâ grants also the reigning king is styled Vallabha-narendra, while in other inscriptions we find the title *Pṛithivîvallabha* alone used. Now Vallabha-narendra means "the king Vallabha," and is the same as *Vallabharâja*, the words *râja (n) and narendra* both denoting "a king". Vallabha-râja should by the rules of Prâkṛit or vernacular pronunciation, become *Vallaha-rây, Ballaha-rây,* or *Balha-rây.* This last is the same as the Balharâ of the Arabs.

---

61 सोमं सुनोति यज्ञेषु सोमवंशविभूषण:

"That ornament of the lunar race extracts the juice of Soma in sacrifices."

62 Ind. Ant., Vol. XI., p. 156.

[78] The genealogy of the Râshṭrakûṭas is shown in the following table:— **Section XI.**

- 1. Dantivarman.
  - 2. Indra I.
    - 3. Govinda I.
      - 4. Karka I.
        - 5. Indra II.
          - 6. DANTIDURGA. (675 Ś.)
        - 7. KṚISHṆA I. Akâlavarsha, or Śubhatunga.
          - 8. GOVINDA II. (705 Ś.)
          - 9. DHRUVA, Nirupama, or Dhârâvarsha.
            - 10. GOVINDA III. Jagattuṅga I. or Prabhûtavarsha, (716, 726 & 730 Ś.)
              - 11. ŚARVA NṚIPATUNGA or Amoghavarsha I, (759, 773, 788 & 799 Ś.)
                - 12. KṚISHṆA II. or Akâlavarsha (797, 820, 824 & 833 Ś.)
                  - *Jagattuṅga.*
                    - 13. INDRA III. or Nityavarsha. (836 & 838 Ś.)
                      - 14. AMOGHAVARSHA II.
                      - 15. GOVINDA IV. (841, 851 & 855 Ś.)
                    - 16. BADDIGA or Amoghavarsha III.
                      - 17. KṚISHṆA III. or Akâlavarsha. (862, 867, 873, 878 & 881 Ś.)
                      - 18. KHOṬIKA. (893 Ś.)
                      - *Nirupama.*
                        - 19. KAKKALA, Karka II, or Amoghavarsha IV. (894 & 895 Ś.)
            - Indra.
              - Karka (724 Ś.)
              - Govinda. (749 Ś.)
              - (Karka and Govinda:) Gujarât Branch.

(*a*) The names of those who were supreme sovereign in the Dekkan are printed in capitals.
(*b*) The names of those who were kings before the attainment of supreme power are printed in small letters.
(*c*) The order of succession is represented by the numbers.
(*d*) The names of those who did not ascend the throne at all, have hee print ed in Italics.

[79] SECTION XII.

The Later Châlukyas.

Section XII.

We left the history of the kings of the Châlukya race at Kîrtivarman II. Between him and Tailapa, who wrested the supreme sovereignty of the Dekkan from Kakkala, the last of the Râshṭrakûṭa kings, the Miraj copperplate grant and the Yevur tablet place six kings. Kîrtivarman ascended the throne in Śaka 669 and was reigning in 679, before which time he had been reduced to the condition of a minor chief; and Tailapa regained sovereign power in 895 Śaka.[1] We have thus seven princes only between 669 and 895, *i.e.*, for 226 years. This gives an average reign of 32 years to each, which is far too much. This was the darkest period in the history of the Châlukya dynasty, and probably no correct account of the succession was kept. Where the dynasty reigned and what the extent of its power was, cannot be satisfactorily determined in the absence of the usual contemporary evidence, viz., inscriptions. There must have been several branches of the Châlukya family, and it is even a question whether Tailapa sprang from the main branch. I am inclined to believe that he belonged to quite a collateral and unimportant branch, and that the main branch became extinct. For, the princes of the earlier dynasty always traced their descent to Hârîti and spoke of themselves as belonging to the Mânavya race; while these later Châlukyas traced their pedigree to Satyâśraya only, and those two names do not occur in their inscriptions except in the Miraj grant and its copies, where an effort is made to begin at the beginning. But evidently the writer of that grant had not sufficient materials at his command, since, as above stated, he

The later Châlukya dynasty, not a continuation of the earlier.

[1] Jour. R. A. S., Vol. IV., p. 4.

places six princes only between Kîrtivarman II. and Tailapa. There is little question that there was no continuity of tradition. The titles Jagadekamalla, Tribhuvanamalla, &c., which the later Châlukyas assumed mark them off distinctively from princes of the earlier dynasty, who had none like them. In a copper-plate grant dated Śaka 735 found in Maisur a Châlukya prince of the name of Vimalâditya, the son of Yaśovarman and grandson of Balavarman, is mentioned. To ward off the evil influence of Saturn from Vimalâditya, a village was granted to a Jaina sage on behalf of a Jaina temple by Govinda III., the Râshṭrakûṭa king, at the request of Châkirâja of the Gaṅga family, the maternal uncle of Vimalâditya.[2] These three Châlukya names do not occur in the usual genealogy of the family. This therefore appears to have been an independent branch. Another independent offshoot ruled over a province called Jola, a portion of which at least is included in the modern district of Dhârvâḍ. In the Kanarese Bhârata [80] written in 863 Śaka by a Jaina poet of the name of Pampa, Arikesarin belonging to this branch, is mentioned by the poet as his patron. The genealogy there given is as follows:—

Yuddhamalla
|
Arikesarin
|
Narasiṁha
|
Dugdhamalla
|
Baddiga
|
Yuddhamalla
|
Narasiṁha
|
Arikesarin

2 Ind. Ant., Vol. XII., p. 11.

Section XII.

Châlukya prince mentioned in a Vedântic work.

At the end of a work entitled Saṁkshepaśârîraka, the author Sarvajñâtman, the pupil of Sureśvara, who himself was a pupil of the great Śaṁkarâchârya, states that he composed it while "the prosperous king of the Kshatriya race, the Âditya (sun) of the race of Manu whose orders were never disobeyed, was ruling over the earth."[3] This description would apply with propriety to such a king as Âdityavarman, Vikramâditya I., Vinayâditya, Vijayâditya, or Vikramâditya II. of the early Châlukya dynasty, since they were very powerful princes and were "Âdityas of the race of Manu." For the Mânavya race to which they belonged may be understood as "the race of Manu." But Śaṁkarâchârya is said to have lived between Śaka 710 and 742, wherefore his grand-pupil must have flourished about the year 800 of that era, while Vikramâditya II., the latest of the four, ceased to reign in 669 Śaka. Supposing then that the date assigned to Śaṁkarâchârya is correct, the king meant by Sarvajñâtman must be one of those placed by the Miraj grant between Kîrtivarman II. and Tailapa. He may be Vikramâditya, the third prince after Kîrtivarman II.,[4] but if the description is considered hardly applicable to a minor chief, Śaṁkarâchârya's date must be pushed backwards so as to place the pupil of his pupil in the reign of one of the five princes of the early Châlukya dynasty mentioned above.

---

3 श्रीदेवेश्वरपादपङ्कजरजःसंपर्कपूताशयः
सर्वज्ञात्मगिराङ्कितो मुनिवरः संक्षेपशारीरकम् ।
चक्रे सज्जनबुद्धिवर्धनमिदं राजन्यवंश्ये नृपे
श्रीमत्यक्षतशासने मनुकुलादित्ये भुवं शासति ॥

The Devaśara spoken of in the first line is Sureśvara, the pupil of Śaṁkarâchârya.

4 See the genealogy at the end of this Section.

Section XII.

Tailapa's expeditions.

Tailapa seems to have carried his arms into the country of the Cholas[5] and humbled the king of Chedi.[6] He despatched an expedition into Gujarât, under a general of the name of Bârapa, against Mûlarâja, the founder of the Châlukya dynasty of Anahilapattana, [81] who for some time was hard pressed ; but according to the Gujarât chroniclers the general was eventually defeated with slaughter.[7] Someśvara, the author of the Kîrtikaumudî, speaks of Bârapa as the general of the lord of Lâṭa, from which it would appear that Tailapa was in possession of that country.[8] Tailapa invaded Mâlvâ also, which at this time was governed by Muñja, the uncle of the celebrated Bhoja. Muñja, instead of strictly confining himself to the defensive, took the offensive, and, against the counsels of his aged minister Rudrâditya, crossed the Godâvarî with a large army. He was encountered by Tailapa, who inflicted a crushing defeat on him and took him prisoner. At first Muñja was treated with consideration by his captor ; but an attempt to effect his escape having been detected, he was subjected to indignities, made to beg from door to door, and finally beheaded.[9] This event is alluded to in one of Tailapa's inscriptions.[10] Tailapa reigned for twenty-four years.[11] One of his feudatory chiefs granted a piece of land to a Jaina temple that he had constructed at

---

5 Ind. Ant., Vol. V., p. 17.

6 Ind. Ant., Vol. VIII., p. 15.

7 Râsa Mâlâ, Chap. IV., p. 38, new Ed.

8 Kîrtikaumudî, II. 3.

9 Merutuṅga's Bhojaprabandha and Bhojacharitra by Râjavallabha.

10 Jour. R. A. S., Vol. IV., p. 12, and Ind. Ant., Vol. XXI., p. 168.

11 Jour. R. S. Vol. IV., p. 4.

Section XII. Saundatti[12] in the Belgaum district, in the year 902 Śaka or A.D. 980.

Satyâśraya. Tailapa married Jâkabbâ, the daughter of the last Râshṭrakûṭa king, and had by her two sons, whose names were Satyâśraya and Daśavarman.[13] The former succeeded him in 919 Śaka or A.D. 997. Nothing particular is mentioned of him in any of the inscriptions. The Khârepâṭaṇ grant, which we have so often referred to, was issued in his reign in Śaka 930 by a dependent chief of the Śilâhâra family which ruled over southern Konkan.[14]

Vikramâditya I. Satyâśraya died without issue and was succeeded by Vikramâditya I.[15] the son of his younger brother Daśavarman by his wife Bhagavatî. The earliest of his inscriptions is dated Śaka 930, which is also the latest date of his predecessor. He therefore succeeded to the throne in that year, *i.e.*, in 1008 A.D., and appears to have reigned for only a short time.[16] He

Jayasiṁha. was succeeded by his brother Jayasiṁha or Jagadekamalla, who in an inscription dated 941 Śaka, *i.e.*, 1019 A.D., is represented to have put to flight or broken the confederacy of Mâlava and is styled "the moon of the lotus which was King Bhoja," that is, one who humbled him.[17] He is also spoken of as having beaten the Cholas and the Cheras. The Miraj grant was executed by him five years later, *i.e.*, in Śaka 946, when "after having subdued the

---

12 Jour. B. B. R. A. S., Vol. X., p. 210.

13 Miraj plates; Jour. R. A. S., Vol. III., p. 262, st. 30-35; Ind. Ant., Vol. VIII., pp. 15-17.

14 Jour. B. B. R. A. S., Vol. I., p. 209.

15 I call him Vikramâditya I. and not Vikramâditya V., as others do, because I would keep the two dynasties distinct for the reasons given in the text above. I shall call Vikramâditya Tribhuvanamalla, Vikramâditya II, and so on.

16 Jour. R. A. S., Vol. IV., p. 4.

17 Ind. Ant., Vol. V., p. 17.

powerful Chola, the lord of the Dramila country, and taken away everything belonging to the ruler of the seven Konkans, he had encamped with his victorious army at [82] Kolhâpur in the course of a march to the northern countries to vanquish them."[18] The latest date of this prince is Śaka 962.[19]

Section XII.

Someśvara or Âhavamalla.

Jayasiṁha ceased to reign in 962 Śaka, or 1040 A.D., and was succeeded by his son Someśvara I., who assumed the titles of Âhavamalla and Trailokyamalla. As usual with the Châlukya princes the first enemy he had to turn his arms against was the king of the Cholas.[20] He is then represented by Bilhaṇa to have marched against Dhârâ, the capital of Bhoja, and captured it. Bhoja was compelled to abandon the city. These hostilities with the king of Mâlvâ seem to have been inherited by this king and his predecessor from Tailapa, who had caused Muñja to be put to death. Bhoja was but a boy when this event took place. It is narrated in the Bhojacharitra that after he had come of age and begun to administer the affairs of his kingdom, on one occasion a dramatic play representing the fate of Muñja was acted before him, and thereupon he resolved to avenge his uncle's death. He invaded the Dekkan with a large army, captured Tailapa, subjected him to the same indignities to which Muñja had been subjected by

---

18 *Loc. cit.* Dramila is another form of Draviḍa. There is some mistake here in the original. The letters are यं-चंद्रमिलाधिपतिं. Dr. Fleet takes यं as one word and चंद्रमिलाधिपतिं as another, but यं cannot be construed and Chandramila is unknown. The first word must be यंचं, a mistake for some such word as अंचं, "down," "below," and the second *Dramilâdhipatim*.

19 Ind. Ant., Vol. XIX., p. 164.

20 Bilhaṇa's Vikramâṅka Charitra, I., 90; Jour. R. A S Vol. IV., p. 13.

Section XII.

him, and finally executed him.[21] Bhoja, who ruled over Mâlvâ for about fifty-three years, was but a minor when Muñja died. Muñja was on the throne in 994 A.D.,[22] while Tailapa died or ceased to reign in 997 A.D. He must therefore have been slain by the latter between 994 and 997 A.D., and Tailapa did not survive Muñja for a sufficiently long time to allow of Bhoja's attaining majority and fighting with him. Hence Bhoja could not have wreaked vengeance on Tailapa. But the wars of Jayasiṁha and Someśvara I. with him show that the tradition recorded in the Bhojacharitra must have been correct to this extent, that to avenge his uncle's death the king of Mâlvâ formed a confederacy with some neighbouring princes and attacked the dominions of the Châlukyas. Perhaps he captured Vikramâditya I., of whom we know so little, and put him to death. It was probably on that account that Jayasiṁha took arms against him and broke the confederacy, as represented in the inscription dated 941 Śaka.

Attack against Ḍâhala and the southern countries.

After some time Someśvara attacked Chedi or Ḍâhala, the capital of which was Tevur or Tripura, and deposed or slew Karṇa.[23] King Bhoja must have died before this event ; for, just about the time of his death, Karṇa had formed a confederacy with Bhîmadeva I. of Gujarât with a view to attack Mâlvâ from two sides, and sacked Dhârâ after his death.[24] Bilhaṇa next represents the Châlukya prince to have marched against the countries on the sea-coast, [83] probably the western. These he conquered, and

21 Bhojácharitra, I., 50-56.

22 My Report on the search for MSS. during 1882-83, p. 45.

23 Bilhana's Vikr., I., 102-103.

24 Merutuṅga's Bhojaprabandha; Râsa Mâlâ, VI., p. 69, new Ed.

having erected a triumphal column there, proceeded by the sea-shore to the extremity of the peninsula. In his progress through that part of the country the king of the Draviḍas or Cholas attacked him, but was defeated. Someśvara thereupon proceeded to his capital Kâñchî, which he captured, and the Chola king had to flee away to save his life.[25] Âhavamalla's operations against Bhoja and the Cholas are alluded to in an inscription, and he is also represented to have fought with the king of Kânyakubja or Kanoj and compelled him to betake himself to the caverns of mountains for safety.[26] **Section XII.**

Âhavamalla or Someśvara founded the city of Kalyâṇa and made it his capital. Bilhaṇa mentions the fact,[27] and the name of the city does not occur in any inscription of a date earlier than 975 Śaka, when Someśvara was reigning.[28] In the course of time three sons were born to Âhavamalla, the eldest of whom was named Someśvara, the second Vikramâditya, and the third Jayasiṁha.[29] The ablest of these was Vikramâditya, and Âhavamalla intended to raise him to the dignity of *Yuvarâja* or prince-regent in supersession of his elder brother; but

Sons of Âhavamalla.

---

25 Vikr. Ch., I., 107-116.

26 Ind. Ant., Vol. VIII., p. 19.

27 Bilhaṇa's Vikr. Ch., II., I. The natural construction appears to be to take परार्ध्यं "most excellent" as an *attributive* adjective, not *predicative*, and take चकार as the predicate. The sense then will be: "He made (founded) the most excellent city named Kalyâna."

28 See Dr. Fleet's remarks on the point, Ind. Ant., Vol. VIII., p. 105. The word *Kalyâṇa* occurring in the Saloṭgi inscription (Ind. Ant., Vol. I., p. 210), is also, like that in Kîrtivarman's grant, to be taken in the sense of "good," "benefit," "beneficial," and not as the name of a town as Mr. Páṇḍit and Dr. Bühler have done.

29 Bilhaṇa's Vikr. Ch., II., 57-58 and 85; III., 1, 25.

Section XII.

Vikramâditya's military operations.

Bilhaṇa tells us he declined the honour.[30] Someśvara therefore was installed as prince-regent, but the real work was done by Vikramâditya, who was invariably employed by his father to fight his battles. The first thing he did was to march as usual against the Cholas, whose king was defeated and deprived of his kingdom. The king of Mâlvâ, who had been driven from his country by somebody whose name is not given, sought Vikramâditya's assistance. That prince put down his enemies and placed him on the throne.[31] Vikramâditya is said to have invaded the Gauḍa country or Bengal and Kâmarûpa or Assam.[32] In the more detailed description of his career of conquest, Bilhaṇa tells us, he first marched against the Keralas, whom he conquered.[33] The king of Siṁhala submitted to him at his approach ;[34] then he took the city of Gaṅgakuṇḍa and proceeded to the country of the Cholas, the prince of which fled and took refuge in the caverns of mountains. Vikramâditya then entered Kâñchî and plundered it ; and thence directed his march to Veṅgi, and to Chakrakoṭa.[35]

Âhavamalla's death.

While Vikramâditya was so employed, Âhavamalla was seized with a strong fever. When he ovserved his end approaching, he caused himself to be taken to the banks of the Tuṅgabhadrâ. He [84] bathed in the waters of the river and gave away a great deal of gold in charity. Then entering the river again, he proceeded until the water reached his neck, and, in the din caused by the waves and a number of musical instruments, drowned himself.[36]

---

30 *Ib.*, III., 26-32, 35-41, and 48-51.

31 *Ib.*, III., 55-67.

32 *Ib.*, III., 74.

33 *Ib.*, IV., 2, 18.

34 *Ib.*, IV., 20.

35 *Ib.*, IV., 21-30. For the situation of Veṅgi, see *supra*, p. 53.

36 Bilhaṇa's Vikr. Ch., IV., 46-68. This mode of death is known by the name of *Jalasamâdhi*.

This event must have taken place in Śaka 991, corresponding to 1069 A.D.[37] Âhavamalla, according to Bilhaṇa, performed a great many sacrifices and was very liberal to men of learning.[38] On account of his virtues, poets made him the hero of the tales, poems, and dramas composed by them.[39]

Section XII.

Someśvara proclaimed king.

Someśvara, the eldest son of Âhavamalla, having been prince-regent, ascended the throne as a matter of course, and assumed the title of Bhuvanaikamalla. Vikramâditya received intelligence of his father's death while returning from Veṅgi. He hastened to the capital and was received with affection by his brother. Vikramâditya made over to him all the spoils he had won in the course of his conquests, and for some time there was a good understanding between the brothers. But Someśvara was a weak and tyrannical prince. He oppressed his subjects and lost their affection. He would not be guided by the counsels of wiser and better men ; and the kingdom of Kuntala lost a good deal of its importance and influence. Vikramâditya, unable to control his brother and suspecting his intentions towards himself, left the capital with his younger brother Jayasiṁha and a large army.[40] Someśvara II. sent his forces after him, but they were defeated by Vikramâditya with great slaughter.[41] The prince then proceeded to the banks of the Tuṅgabhadrâ, and, after some time, directed his march towards the country of the Cholas. On the way he stopped at Banavâsî, where he enjoyed himself for some time, and then started for the country of Malaya. Jaya-

Quarrels between the brothers.

37 Jour. R. A. S., Vol. IV., p. 4.

38 Bilhaṇa's Vikr. Ch., I., 97-99; IV., 52.

39 *Ib.*, I., 88.

40 *Ib.*, IV., 88-119; V., I.

41 *Ib.*, V., 5-8.

Section XII.

Submission of Jayakeśi of Goa to Vikramâditya.

keśi is represented to have submitted to Vikramâditya and "given him more wealth than he desired, and thus to have rendered lasting the smile on the face of the Konkan ladies."[42] Jayakeśi appears thus to have been king of the Konkan, and was the same as the first king of that name, who in the copper-plate grants of the Goa Kadambas, published by Dr. Fleet, is spoken of as having entered into an alliance with the Châlukya and Chola kings and made Gopakapattana or Goa his capital. Vikramâditya or Tribhuvanamalla in after-life gave his daughter Mallalamahâdevî in marriage to his grandson, who also was called Jayakeśi ; and this circumstance is mentioned in all the three grants, since the connection with the paramount sovereign of the Dekkan raised the dignity of the family.[43] The king of the Alupas[44] also rendered his obeisance to the Châlukya prince, who showed him marks of favour. He then subjugated the Keralas or people of Malabâr, and turned towards the country of the Draviḍas or Cholas. Being informed of this, the Chola prince sent a herald with proposals of peace, offering [85] his daughter in marriage to Vikramâditya. These were accepted by the latter, and at the solicitations of the Chola he fell back on the Tuṅgabhadrâ, where the prince arrived with his daughter and concluded an alliance.[45]

Alliance with the Chola prince.

Revolution in the Chola kingdom.

Some time after, the king of the Cholas died and there was a revolution in the kingdom. When the Châlukya prince heard of this he immediately proceeded to Kâñchî, and placing the son of his father-in-law on the throne, remained there for a month to

---

[42] *Ib.*, V., 10, 18-25.

[43] Jour. B. B. R. A. S., Vol. IX., pp. 242, 268, 279.

[44] See *supra*, p. 88, note 13.

[45] Bilhaṇa's Vikr. Ch., V. 26-29, 46, 56, 60, 73, 79-89.

suppress his enemies and render his position secure. A short time after his return to the Tuṅgabhadrâ, however, Râjiga, the king of Veṅgi, observing that the nobility of the Chola prince were disaffected, seized the opportunity, and, having deposed him, usurped the sovereignty of the country. To embarrass Vikramâditya and prevent his descent on Kâñchî, Râjiga incited his brother Someśvara II. to attack him from behind. Vikramâditya, however, marched on, and, by the time he came in sight of the Draviḍa forces, Someśvara overtook him in his rear. He had a very large army, which was well equipped.[46] Bilhaṇa, who is, of course, anxious to show his patron to be guiltless in this fratricidal war, represents him to be deeply afflicted when he saw that his brother had made common cause with his enemy, and to have endeavoured to dissuade him from the course on which he had embarked. Someśvara made a show of yielding to his brother's expostulations, seeking however in the meanwhile for a favourable opportunity to strike a decisive blow.[47] But Vikramâditya finally resolved to give a fight to the armies of both. Then a bloody battle ensued, Vikramâditya proved victorious, the new king of the Draviḍas fled, and Someśvara was taken prisoner. The Châlukya prince then returned to the Tuṅgabhadrâ, and after some hesitation dethroned Someśvara and had himself crowned king. To his younger brother Jayasiṁha he assigned the province of Banavâsî.[48] These events took place in the cyclic year *Nala*, Śaka 998, or A.D. 1076.[49]

Section XII.

Alliance between Râjiga and Someśvara II. against Vikramâditya.

Battle of Vikramâditya with his brother and Râjiga.

Coronation of Vikramâditya.

---

46 *Ib.*, VI., 7-54.

47 *Ib.*, VI., 56-61.

48 *Ib.*, VI., 90-93, 98-99.

49 Jour. R. A. S., Vol. IV., p. 4; Ind. Ant., Vol. VIII., p. 189. The current Śaka year was 999. Dr. Fleet thinks

Section XII.

Reign of Vikramâditya II.

Vikramâditya II. then entered Kalyâṇa and had a long and upon the whole a peaceful reign of fifty years.[50] He assumed the title of Tribhuvanamalla, and is known by the names of Kalivikrama and Parmâḍirâya also. He abolished the Śaka era and established his own ; but it fell into disuse not long after his death. Some time after his accession, he went to Karahâṭaka or Karhâḍ and married the daughter of the Śilâhâra king who reigned at the place. Her [86] name was Chandralekhâ and she was a woman of rare beauty. Bilhaṇa represents her to have held a *svayaṁvara* where a great many kings assembled, out of whom she chose the Châlukya prince and placed the nuptial wreath round his neck. Whether the *svayaṁvara* was real, or imagined by the poet to give himself an opportunity for the display of his poetic and descriptive powers, it is not possible to decide. Chandralekhâ is spoken of in the inscriptions as Chandraladevî, and many other wives of Tribhuvanamalla are mentioned besides her. The revenues of certain villages were assigned to them for their private expenses.[61]

---

that the festival of his *Paṭṭabandha* or coronation, grants on account of which are recorded as made on the 5th day of the bright half of Phâlguna in the Nala year, in an inscription at Vaḍageri, was the annual festival. But this is a mere assumption. One would expect in such a case the word *vârshikotsava*. The *utsava* or festival spoken of must be that which followed the ceremony. The date in this inscription refers to the grant, and does not, in my opinion, show at all the day on which the coronation ceremony took place. All we can gather from this inscription and that at Araleśvara is that the *Nala* Saṁvatsara was the first year of his reign.

[50] Jour. R. A. S., Vol. IV., p. 14.

[61] Jour. R. A. S., Vol. IV., p. 15, and Bilhaṇa's Vikr. Ch., VIII.—XI.

Section XII.

Rebellion of Jayasiṁha, Vikrama's brother.

Some years after, Vikrama's brother Jayasiṁha, who had been appointed his viceroy at Banavâsî, began to meditate treason against him. He extorted a great deal of money from his subjects, entered into an alliance with the Draviḍa king and other chiefs, and even endeavoured to foment sedition and treachery among Vikramâditya's troops. When the king heard of this, he made several attempts to dissuade his brother from his evil course, but they were of no avail ; and in a short time Jayasiṁha came with his numerous allies and his large army and encamped on the banks of the Kṛishṇâ. He plundered and burned the surrounding villages and took many prisoners, and considered success so certain that he sent insulting messages to Vikrama.[52] The king then marched against him at the head of his forces. As he approached the river he was harassed by the enemy's skirmishers, but driving them away he encamped on the banks.[53] He surveyed his brother's army and found it to be very large and strong. Then a battle ensued. At first the elephants of the enemy advanced and spread confusion in the ranks of Vikrama. All his elephants, horses, and men turned backwards ; but with remarkable bravery the king rushed forward on the back of his maddened elephant, dealing heavy blows right and left. The elephants of the enemy were driven back and the king killed a great many of his soldiers. The army was defeated and Jayasiṁha and his followers fled away. Vikrama did not pursue the enemy, but took the elephants, horses, women, and baggage left on the battle-field, and returned to his capital. After a time Jayasiṁha was caught skulking in a forest and brought to Vikramâ-

52 Bilhaṇa's Vikr. Ch., XIV., 1-13, 18, 49-56.

53 *Ib.*, XIV., 57, 70, 71.

Section XII.

ditya, who, however, is represented to have pardoned him.[54].

Invasion of Vikrama's dominions by Vishṇuvardhana.

In the latter part of Vikrama's reign his dominions were invaded by a prince of the Hoysaḷa branch of the Yâdava family reigning at Dvârasamudra, the modern Haḷebîḍ in Maisur; and with him were associated the kings of the Pâṇḍya country, Goa, and Konkan. This Hoysaḷa prince must have been Vishṇuvardhana, the younger brother of Ballâḷa and the grandson of Vinayâditya, who first brought the dynasty into prominence. For in the inscription of Vîra Ballâḷa, the grandson of Vishṇuvardhana, at Gaddaka, Vishṇuvardhana is represented to have overrun the whole country between his capital [87] and Belvoḷa and washed his horses with the waters of the Kṛishṇa-Veṇâ. It is also stated that "he was again and again reminded by his servants of the honour done to him by the king Paramardideva (Vikramâditya), who said, 'Know the Hoysaḷa alone among all princes to be unconquerable.' "[55] Vikramâditya despatched against these enemies a dependent chief of the name of Âcha or Âchagi, whose territory lay to the south. Âcha, who was "a very lion in war and shining like the hot-rayed sun, sounding his war-cry, pursued and prevailed against Poysaḷa, took Gove, put to flight Lakshma in war, valorously followed after Pâṇḍya, dispersed at all times the Malapas, and seized upon the Konkan."[56] Âcha must have fought several other battles for his

---

54 *Ib.*, XV., 23, 41-42, 55-71, 85-87.

55 Ind. Ant., Vol. II., p. 300. Dr. Fleet's translation of this verse is incorrect. The words are to be thus collocated :—नृपेषु असाध्यतया होयसलम् अवधारय इति परमर्दिदेवनृपतेः प्रत्युपचारं यः नियुक्तैः मुहुः आर्यते ।

56 Jour. B. B. R. A. S., Vol. XI., p. 244. Poysaḷa and Hoysaḷa are one and the same word.

master ; for he is represented to have made "the kings of Kaliṅga, Vaṅga, Maru, Gûrjara, Mâḷava, Chera, and Chola (subject) to his sovereign."[57] Vikramâditya himself had to take the field against the Chola prince, who had grown insubordinate. He was defeated and fled, and the king returned to his capital.[58] Vikramâditya II. constructed a large temple of Vishṇu and had a tank dug in front of it. In the vicinity he founded a town which was called Vikramapura.[59] He governed his subjects well and they were happy under his rule. The security they enjoyed was so great that, according to Bilhaṇa, "they did not care to close the doors of their houses at night, and instead of thieves the rays of the moon entered through the window openings." He was very liberal and bountiful to the poor and "gave the sixteen great gifts at each holy conjuncture."[60] That he was a patron of learning is shown by the fact of a Kâśmirian Paṇḍit like Bilhaṇa, who travelled over the whole of India in quest of support, having been raised by him to the dignity of Vidyâpati or chief Paṇḍit. Vijñâneśvara, the author of the Mitâksharâ, which is at present acknowledged over a large part of India, and especially in the Marâṭhâ country, as the chief authority on matters of civil and religious law, flourished in the reign of Vikramâditya and lived at Kalyâṇa. At the end of most manuscripts of that work there occur three stanzas, which may be translated as follows :[61]

Vikramâditya's patronage of learning.

Vijñâneśvara.

---

57 *Ib.*, p. 269.

58 Bilhaṇa's Vikr. Ch., XVII., 43-68.

59 *Ib.*, XVII., 15, 22, 29, and Jour. R. A. S., Vol. IV., p. 15.

60 Bilhaṇa's Vikr. Ch., XVII., 6, 36-37.

61 See Dr. Bühler's article on the subject in Jour. B. B. R. A. S., Vol. IX., p. 134.

Section XII.

"On the surface of the earth, there was not, there is not, and there will be not, a town like Kalyâṇa; never was a monarch like the prosperous Vikramârka seen or heard of; and—what more?—Vijñâneśvara, the Paṇḍit, does not bear comparison with any other[62] [88] (person). May this triad which is like a celestial creeper[63] exist to the end of the Kalpa!

"May the Lord of wisdom[64] live as long as the

---

62 Dr. Bühler's reading of the last two lines is विज्ञानेश्वरपण्डितो न भजते किं चान्यदस्योपमां कल्पस्थं स्थिरमस्तु कल्पलतिकाकल्पं तदेव त्रयम्। The Doctor connects कल्पस्थं with किं चान्यत् and translates "nothing else that exists in this Kalpa bears comparison with the learned Vijñânesvara." To mean "nothing else," किं चान्यत् must be किमप्यन्यत्; and in this construction पण्डितो, the nominative, has no verb, अन्यत् being taken as the nominative to the verb भजते. Again, it will not do to say "nothing that exists in this Kalpa bears comparison," &c., for one-half of this Kalpa only has passed away; the other half still remains, and what it *will* produce but *has not* yet produced cannot be spoken of as कल्पस्थम् or "existing in the Kalpa." The only proper reading with a slight alteration is that of the Bombay lithographed edition, which he has given in a footnote and which is किंवान्यदन्योपमामाकल्पं. Instead of वा, there must be चा here. And this is the reading of a manuscript of the Mitâksharâ, dated Saṁvat 1535 and Śaka 1401, purchased by me about ten years ago for the Bombay Government. The reading is to be translated as in the text.

63 Like the celestial creeper, in so far as the trial satisfies all desires.

64 Dr. Bühler reads तव विज्ञाननाथ and construes it as a vocative. The vocative does not look natural here. The Bombay lithographed edition and my manuscript have विज्ञाननाथः the nominative. Instead of तव the former has तथा and the latter तस्य. I have adopted this last. The author has here taken the name Vijnânesvara in its etymological sense and given to विज्ञान or "knowledge" the

sun and moon endure,—he who produces words which distil honey and than which nothing is more wonderful to the learned, gives wealth exceeding their wishes to a multitude of supplicants,[65] contemplates the form of the subjugator of Mura, and has conquered the enemies that are born with the body. **Section XII.**

"May the lord Vikramâditya protect this whole earth as long as the moon and the stars endure,—he whose feet are refulgent with the lustre of the crest jewels of prostrate kings from the bridge, which is the heap of the glory of the best scion of the Raghu race, to the lord of mountains, and from the Western Ocean, the waves[66] of which surge heavily with the nimble shoals of fishes, to the Eastern Ocean."

Though Sanskrit authors often indulge in hyperbolic expressions without sufficient basis and as mere conventionalities, still the [89] language and manner of these stanzas do show a really enthusiastic admiration in the mind of the writer for the city, its ruler, and the great Paṇḍit, who from the fact of the liberality attributed to him appears to have enjoyed the favour of the king and perhaps held

---

object तत्व or "truth," the whole meaning "the lord of the knowledge of truth."

65 Dr. Bühler's reading here is दातार्थिनामतिशययुजामर्थिसार्थार्थितायाः. Here र्थितायाः cannot make any sense; it ought to be र्थिंतायाः, which the lithographed edition and my manuscript have. The latter reads the whole line thus:— दातार्थिनामतिशयगुणामर्थिसार्थार्थिंना(ता)या[:]. There is another या after this, which is redundant.

66 The reading of the epithet of the "Western Ocean" is corrupt in all the three. I would improve that of the lithographed edition, which is चटुलतिमिकुलीपृक्षविंगलत्तरगात् to चटुलतिमिकुलोत्तुङ्गरिङ्गत्तरङ्गात् and of my manuscript to तुङ्गत्तरङ्गात्. The root रिङ्ग् is used in connection with waves (see B. & R.'s Lexicon *sub voce*).

Section XII. a high office. From this and from the description given by Bilhaṇa, as well as from Vikramâditya's inscriptions, of which we have about two hundred, it appears to be an undoubted fact that he was the greatest prince of this later Châlukya dynasty, and that during his reign the country enjoyed happiness and prosperity.

Someś-vara III. or Bhûloka-malla.

Vikramâditya II. was succeeded in Śaka 1048 and in the cyclic year *Parâbhava* (A.D. 1127) by his son Someśvara III., who assumed the title of Bhûloka-malla.[67] He had a short reign of about 11 years. He is represented to have "placed his feet on the heads of the kings of Andhra, Draviḷa, Magadha, Nepâḷa ; and to have been landed by all learned men."[68] This last praise does not seem to be undeserved ; for we have a work in Sanskrit written

Someśvara's Abhilashi-târtha Chintâmaṇi.

by Someśvara entitled Mânasollâsa or Abhilashi-târtha-Chintâmaṇi, in which a great deal of information on a variety of subjects is given. The book is divided into five parts. In the first are given the causes which lead to the acquisition of a kingdom ; in the second, those that enable one to retain it after he has acquired it ; in the third, the kinds of enjoyment which are open to a king after he has rendered his power firm ; in the fourth, the modes of diversion which give mental pleasure ; and in the fifth, sports or amusements. Each of these consists of twenty kinds. In the first are included such virtues as shunning lies, refraining from injury to others, continence, generosity, affability, faith in the gods, feeding and supporting the poor and helpless, friends and adherents, &c. Under the second head are described what are called the seven *aṅgas, i.e.*, the ideal king,

---

67 Jour. R. A. S., Vol. IV., p. 15. The current Śaka year corresponding to *Parâbhava* was 1049.

68 Jour. B. B. R. A. S., Vol. XI., p. 268.

Section XII.

his ministers including the priest and the astrologer, the treasury and the way of replenishing it, the army, &c. The enjoyments are—a beautiful palace, bathing, anointing, rich clothing, ornaments, &c. The diversions are—military practice, horsemanship, training elephants, wrestling, cockfights, bringing up of dogs, poetry, music, dancing, and others. The last class comprises sports in gardens and fields, or on mountains and sandbanks, games, enjoyment of the company of women, &c. In connection with these subjects there are few branches of learning or art in Sanskrit the main principles of which are not stated. We have polity, astronomy, astrology, dialectics, rhetoric, poetry, music, painting, architecture, medicine, training of horses, elephants, and dogs, &c. The king does appear to have been a man of learning, and it was on that account that he received the title of *Sarvajñabhûpa*[69] or the "all-knowing king." In the Mânasollâsa, in connection with the preparation of an almanac, the day used as an epoch from which to calculate the positions of certain heavenly bodies is stated as "Friday, the beginning of the month of Chaitra, [90] one thousand and fifty-one years of Saka having elapsed, the year of the cycle being *Saumya,* while the king Soma, the ornament of the Châlukya [race], who was the very sage Agastya to the ocean of the essences of all the Sâstras,[70] and whose enemies were destroyed, was ruling over the sea-begirt earth.[71] This work, there-

Date given in the Abhilashitârtha Chintâmaṇi.

---

69 *Ib.*, pp. 259 and 268.

70 That is, he drank the essences of all the Sâstras or sciences as the sage Agastya drank the whole ocean.

71 एकपञ्चाशदधिके सहस्रे शरदां गते ।
शकस्य सोमभूपाले सति चालुक्यमण्डने ॥

Section XII. fore, was written in the fourth year after his accession.

Someśvara III. or Bhûlokamalla was succeeded in the cyclic year *Kâlayukti*,[72] Śaka 1060 or A.D. 1138, by his son Jagadekamalla. Nothing particular is recorded of him. He reigned for 12 years and was succeeded by his brother Tailapa II., Nurmaḍi Taila or Trailokyamalla, in Śaka 1072, *Pramoda* Saṁvatsara.[73] During these two reigns the power of the Châlukyas rapidly declined, and some of the feudatory chiefs became powerful and arrogant. The opportunity was seized by a dependent chief named Vijjala or Vijjaṇa of the Kalachuri race, who held the office of Daṇḍanâyaka or minister of war under Tailapa. He conceived the design of usurping the throne of his master, and endeavoured to secure the sympathies and co-operation of some of the powerful

Jagadekamalla.

Tailapa II.

Ambitious designs of Vijjala.

समुद्ररसनामुर्वीं शासति चलविविचि ।
सर्वंशाखार्थसर्वस्वपाथोधिकलशोद्भवे ॥
सौम्यसंवत्सरे चैत्रमासाद्ये पक्षवासरे ।
परिशाधितसिद्धान्तशब्दाः सार्धं पक्का इमे ॥

72 The *Siddhârthin* Saṁvatsara is mentioned as the second of his reign, wherefore the preceding Kâlayukti (Śaka 1060) must have been the first. The current Śaka year was 1061. Ind. Ant., Vol. VI., p. 141. There are several inscriptions in which the name of Jagadekamalla occurs, but it is difficult to make out whether they belong to the reign of this king or Jayasiṁha-Jagadekamalla, since the cyclic year only is given in them. Sometimes the year of the king's reign is also given, but that even does not help in settling the point. For Jayasiṁha began to reign in Śaka 940, just 120 years or two complete cycles of 60 years each before Jagadekamalla II., and consequently the cyclic years and the years of their reigns are the same.

73 For the *Yuva* Saṁvatsara was the sixth of his reign and it fell next after Śaka 1077. In *Pramoda*, 1073 was the current Śaka year and 1072 years had expired; Pâli, Sans. and old Can. Ins. No. 181.

and semi-independent chiefs. Vijayârka, the Mahâmaṇḍaleśvara of Kolhâpur, was one of those who assisted him,[74] and Prolarâja of the Kâkateya dynasty of Tailaṅgaṇa, who is represented to have fought with Tailapa, did so probably to advance the same cause.[75] He kept his master Tailapa under complete subjection till Śaka 1079 or A.D. 1157, when Tailapa left Kalyâṇa and fled to Annigeri in the Dhârvâḍ district, which now became the capital of his kingdom greatly reduced in extent. There is an inscription dated Śaka 1079, in Vijjaṇa's name, the cyclic **Section XII.**

[91] year being *Iśvara ;* and the next Saṁvatsara, *Bahudhânya*, is spoken of as the second year of his reign.[76] He does not however seem to have assumed the titles of supreme sovereignty till Śaka 1084, when he marched against Tailapa II., who was at Annigeri, and proclaimed himself an independent monarch. Tailapa seems then to have gone further south and established himself at Banavâsî.[77] The latest year of his reign mentioned in the inscriptions is the fifteenth, the Saṁvatsara or cyclic year being *Pârthiva,* which was current next after Śaka 1087.[77] Assumption of supreme sovereignty by Vijjala.

For some time there was an interruption in the Châlukya power, and the Kalachuris seem to have held possession of the whole territory of that dynasty. But internal dissensions consequent on the rise of the Liṅgâyata creed and the assassination of Vijjaṇa considerably weakned the power of the Kalachuris, and

74 Grant of Bhoja II. of Kolhâpur, Trans. Bomb. Lit. Soc., Vol. III. See Section XVI.

75 He is said to have captured Tailapa and let him off through his devotion for him. He probably owed some allegiance to the Châlukya sovereign. Ins. of Rudradeva, Ind. Ant., Vol. XI., pp. 12-13, lines 27-30.

76 P. S. & O. C. Ins. Nos. 219 and 182.

77 Jour. R. A. S., Vol. IV., p. 16.

78 P. S. & O. C. Ins. No. 140.

Section XII.

Someś-
vara IV.

about the Śaka year 1104 Someśvara, the son of Nurmaḍi Taila, succeeded in wresting a considerable portion of the hereditary dominions of his family, and established himself at Annigeri. He owed his restoration to power to the valour and devoted attachment of a feudatory of his family named Brahma or Bomma, who fought several battles with the enemies of his master and is said to have conquered sixty elephants by means of a single one.[79] Bomma is represented in an inscription at Annigeri dated Śaka 1106 to have destroyed the Kalachuris and restored the Châlukyas to the throne.[80] But a short time after, the Yâdavas of the south rose under Vîra Ballâḷa and of the north under Bhillama. They both fought with Bomma ; but success at first attended the arms of Vîra Ballâla, who subdued the Châlukya general and put an end to the power of the dynasty.[81] We lose trace of Vîra Soma or Someśvara IV. after Śaka 1111.

Extinction of the Châlukya power.

A branch of the Châlukya family in Southern Konkan.

The Châlukya family must have thrown out several branches of petty chiefs. One such has been brought to light by a copper-plate grant dated Śaka 1182, *Raudra* Saṁvatsara, which was in the possession of the Khot of Teravaṇ, a village in the Râjâpur tâluka of the Ratnâgiri district.[82] The donor Keśava Mahâjani was the minister of a Mahâmaṇḍaleśvara or chief of the name of Kâṁvadeva, one of whose titles was "the sun that blows open the lotus bud in the shape of the Châlukya race." He is also called *Kalyáṇapuravarâdhîśvara* or "lord of Kalyâṇa the

79 Jour. R. A. S., Vol. IV., p. 16; Ind. Ant., Vol. II., p. 300, l. 29.

80 Jour. R. A. S., Vol. IV., p. 16.

81 Ind. Ant., Vol. II., p. 300, ll. 29-30.

82 Published in Jour. R. A. S., Vol. V., in Jour. B. B. R. A. S., Vol. IV., p. 105, and Memoir, Sâvantvâḍi State, Govt. Rec. No. X.

best of cities," which like several such titles of other chiefs[83] simply shows that he belonged to the family that once reigned with glory at Kalyâṇa. The village conveyed by the grant was Teravâṭaka, identified with Teravaṇ itself, from which it would appear that Kâṁvadeva was chief of that part of Konkan. There is an inscription in the temple of Ambâbâi at Kolhâpur in which is recorded the grant of a village by Somadeva who belonged to the Châlukya family and reigned at Saṁgameśvara, which is twelve *kos* to the north-east of Ratnâgiri. Somadeva was the son of Vetugideva and the father of the last was Karnadeva.[84] Probably the Kâṁvadeva of the Teravaṇ grant belonged to this branch of the family. There are still Marâṭhâ families of the name of Chaḷke reduced to poverty in the Saṁgameśvara Tâluka or in the vicinity.

---

83 See *infra*, Section XVI.

84 Jour. B. B. R. A. S., Vol. II., p. 263.

[93] SECTION XIII.

The Kalachuris.

Section XIII.

Original seat of the Kalachuri of Haihaya family.

The earliest mention of a family of this name that we have is in connection with Maṅgalîśa of the early Châlukya dynasty. Vinayâditya is represented in one of his inscriptions to have subdued the Haihayas and Vikramâditya II. married, as we have seen, two girls who were sisters belonging to the family.[1] The later Râshṭrakûṭa princes were also connected by marriage with the Haihayas. This family known also by the name of Kalachuri or Kulachuri[2] ruled over Chedi or the country about Jabalpur. The Kalachuris of Kalyâṇa must have been an offshoot of this family. One of the titles used by Vijjaṇa was *Kâlñjarapuravarâdhîśvara* "or Lord of the best city of Kâlañjara."[3] Kâlañjara was a stronghold belonging to the rulers of Chedi[4] and was probably their capital, though Tripura, the modern Tevur, is also known to have been the principal seat of the family. The title, therefore, connects the Kalyâṇa branch of the Kalachuris with the Chedi family. This branch was founded by Kṛishṇa, who in the Belgaum grant[5] is spoken of as "another Kṛishṇa," the incarnation of Vishṇu, and as "having done wonderful deeds even during his boyhood." He was succeeded by his son Jogama, and Jogama by his son Paramardin. Paramardin was the father of Vijjaṇa. Vijjaṇa before his usurpation called

1 *Supra*, Section X.

2 See grant published in Arch. Surv. West. Ind., No. 10.

3 Jour. B. B. R. A. S., Vol. IX., p. 330, No. 50.

4 Bilhaṇa's Vikr. Ch., XVIII., p. 93. Karṇa seems to be represented here to have conquered Kâlañjara.

5 Jour. B. B. R. A. S., Vol. XVIII., p. 270.

himself only a Mahâmaṇḍaleśvara or minor chief, and is first mentioned as a feudatory of Jagadekamalla, the successor of Someśvara III.[6] The manner in which he drove away Taila III. from Kalyâṇa, and having raised himself to the supreme power in the state gradually assumed the titles of a paramount sovereign, has already been described. But soon after, a religious revolution took place at Kalyâṇa, and Vijjaṇa and his family succumbed to it. **Section XIII.** **A religious revolution at Kalyâṇa.**

Its leader. The principal leader of that revolution was a person of the name of Basava. A work in Kanarese entitled Basava Purâṇa gives an account of Basava; but it is full of marvellous stories and relates the wonderful miracles wrought by him. The principal incidents, however, may be relied on as historical. On the other hand there is another work entitled Vijjalarâyacharita, written by a Jaina, which gives an account of the events from the opposite side, since the attacks of the Liṅgâyatas were chiefly directed against the Jainas, and these were their enemies.

Basava. Basava was the son of a Brâhmaṇ named Mâḍirâja, who lived at Bâgevâḍi in the Kalâdgi district. Baḷadeva, the prime minister of Vijjaṇa, was his maternal uncle and gave him his daughter in marriage.[7] After Baḷadeva's death the king appointed Basava his [94] prime minister as being closely related to Baḷadeva.[8] The Jainas, however, state that Basava had a beautiful sister named Padmâvatî, of whom the king became enamoured and whom he either married or made his mistress[9]; and it was on that account that he was raised to that office and

6 P. S. & O. C. Ins. No. 119.

7 Basava Purâṇa, Jour. B. B. R. A. S., Vol. VIII., p. 67.

8 Jour. B. B. R. A. S., Vol. VIII., p. 69.

9 *Ib.*, p. 97. Sir W. Elliot's paper, Jour. R. A. S., Vol. IV., p. 20.

Section XIII. became a man of influence. There must be some truth in this story; for the Basava Purâṇa narrates that the king gave his younger sister Nîlalochanâ in marriage to Basava, which looks as if it were a counter-story devised to throw discredit on the other which was so derogatory to Basava.[10] Basava had another sister named Nâgalâmbikâ, who had a son named Chenna-Basava or Basava the younger. In concert with him Basava began to propound a new doctrine and a new mode of worshipping Śiva, in which the Liṅga and the Nandin or bull were prominent. He speedily got a large number of followers, and ordained a great many priests, who were called Jaṅgamas. Basava had charge of the king's treasury, and out of it he spent large amounts in supporting and entertaining these Jaṅgamas, who led a profligate life. Vijjaṇa had another minister named Mañchaṇṇâ, who was the enemy of Basava, and informed the king of his rival's embezzlements.[11] In the course of time Vijjaṇa was completely alienated from Vasava and endeavoured to apprehend him. But he made his escape with a number of followers, whereupon the king sent some men in pursuit. These were easily dispersed by Basava, and then Vijjaṇa advanced in person. But a large number of followers now joined Basava, and the king was defeated and had to submit to his minister. Basava was allowed to return to Kalyâṇa and reinstated in his office.[12] There was, however, no possibility of a complete reconciliation, and after some time the leader of the new sect conceived the design of putting the king to death. The circumstances that immediately led to

Basava's rebellion.

10 Jour. B. B. R. A. S., Vol. VIII., p. 70.

11 *Ib.*, pp. 78 & 89.

12 Jour. R. A. S., Vol. IV., p. 21; Jour. B. B. R. A. S., Vol. VIII., p. 89.

the deed and the manner in which it was perpetrated are thus stated in the Basava Purâṇa.

Section XIII.

Basava plans the murder of the King.

Account of the event according to the Basava Purâṇa.

At Kalyâṇa there were two pious Liṅgâyatas named Halleyaga and Madhuveyya, who were the devout adherents of their master Basava. Vijjaṇa, listening to the calumnious accusations of their enemies, caused their eyes to be put out. All the disciples of Basava were highly indignant at this cruel treatment of these holy men, and assembled in their master's house. Basava ordered Jagaddeva to murder the king, pronounced a curse on Kalyâṇa, and left the town. Jagaddeva hesitated for a moment, but his mother spurred him on, and with two companions, Mallaya and Bommaya, went straight to the palace of the king ; and rushing through the throng of courtiers, counsellors, and princes, they drew their poignards and stabbed Vijjaṇa. Thence they went into the streets, and brandishing their weapons proclaimed the reason of their perpetrating the deed. Then arose dissensions in the city, men fought with men, horses with horses, and elephants with elephants ; the race of Vijjaṇa was extinct, Kalyâṇa was a heap of ruins, and the curse pronounced [95] by Basava was verified. Basava went in haste to his favourite shrine of Saṅgameśvara, situated on the confluence of the Malaprabhâ with the Kṛishṇa, and there in compliance with his prayers the god absorbed him in his body.[13]

Jaina account.

The account given by the Jainas is different. Vijjaṇa had gone on an expedition to Kolhâpur to reduce the Śilâhâra chief Bhoja II. to subjection. In the course of his march back to the capital he encamped at a certain place on the banks of the Bhîmâ, and, while reposing in his tent, Basava sent

13 Jour. B. B. R. A. S., Vol. VIII., p. 96; Wilson's Mackenzie MSS., pp. 309-310.

Section XIII.

to him a Jaṅgama disguised as a Jaina with a poisoned fruit. Vijjaṇa, who is said to have been a Jaina himself, unsuspectingly took the fruit from the hands of the seeming Jaina priest ; and as soon as he smelled it, he became senseless. His son Immadi Vijjaṇa and others hastened to the spot, but to no purpose. Vijjaṇa, however, somewhat recovered his senses for a short while ; and knowing who it was that had sent the poisoned fruit, enjoined his son to put Basava to death. Immadi Vijjaṇa gave orders that Basava should be arrested and all Jaṅgamas, wherever found, executed.[14] On hearing of this, Basava fled ; and being pursued went to the Malabar coast and took refuge at a place called Ulavi.[15] The town was closely invested and Basava in despair threw himself into a well and died, while his wife Nîlâmbâ put an end to her existence by drinking poison. When Vijjaṇa's son was pacified, Chenna-Basava surrendered all his uncle's property to him and was admitted into favour.[16] He now became the sole leader of the Liṅgâyatas ; but, even before, his position was in some respects superior to that of Basava. The religious portion of the movement was under his sole direction, and it was he who shaped the creed of the sect. In him the *Praṇava* or sacred syllable *Om* is said to have become incarnate to teach the doctrines of the Vîra Śaiva faith to Basava,[17] and, according to the Chenna-Basava Purâṇa, "Chenna-Basava was Śiva ; Basava, Vṛishabha (or Śiva's bull, the Nandin) ; Bijjala, the door-keeper ; Kalyâṇa, Kailâsa ; (and) Śiva worshippers (or

Chenna-Basava's leadership.

---

14 Wilson's Mackenzie MSS., p. 320.

15 Jour. R. A. S., Vol. IV., p. 22.

16 Wilson's Mackenzie MSS., p. 320.

17 *Ib.*, p. 311.

Lingâyatas), the Śiva host (or the troops of Śiva's attendants.)''[18]

Vijjaṇa's death took place in Śaka 1089 (1090 *current*), or A.D. 1167. He was succeeded by his son Soma, who is also called Sovideva or Someśvara. The Belgaum copper-plate charter was issued by him on the twelfth of the bright half of Kârttika in Śaka 1096, the cyclic year being *Jaya,* to confirm the grant of land to fourteen Brâhmaṇs and the god Someśvara made by one of his queens named Bâvaladevî. The king had given her his consent to make the grant as a reward for a beautiful song that she sang on an occasion when the most influential persons belonging to his own and other kingdoms had gathered together in his audience-hall. Soma reigned till Śaka 1100 and was followed by his brother Saṁkama, whose inscriptions come down to the cyclic year *Śubhakṛit.* In an [96] inscription at Baḷagâṁve the cyclic year *Vikârin* (Ś. 1101) is called the third of his reign,[19] while in another at the same place the same year is spoken of as the fifth.[20] In other inscriptions we have two names Saṁkama and Âhavamalla and the cyclic years *Śârvarin* (Ś. 1102) and *Plava* (Ś. 1103) are represented as the third year of his or their reign, which is possible, and *Śubhakṛit* (Ś. 1104) as the eighth.[21] About Śaka 1104 the Châlukya prince Someśvara IV. wrested some of the provinces of his ancestral dominions from the Kalachuris, and the rest must have been conquered by the Northern Yâdavas ; so that about this time the Kalachuri dynasty became extinct.

Sovideva.

Saṁkama.

Extinction of the Kalachuri dynasty.

---

18 Jour. B. B. R. A. S., Vol. VIII., p. 127.

19 P. S. & O. C. Ins. No. 183.

20 *Ib.* No. 189.

21 *Ib.* Nos. 190, 192 and 193.

Section XIII.

Religious and social condition of the people during the later Châlukya period.

During the period occupied by the later Châlukya dynasty and the Kalachuris (Śaka 895-1110 or A.D. 973-1188), the old state of things as regards the religious and social condition of the country may be said to have finally disappeared and the new ushered in. First, we have in this period what might be considered the last traces of Buddhism. In the reign

Buddhism.

of Tribhuvanamalla or Vikramâditya II., in the cyclic year *Yuvan*, and the nineteenth of his era (Śaka 1017), sixteen merchants of the Vaiśya caste constructed a Buddhistic *vihâra* or monastery and temple at Dharmavolal, the modern Dambal in the Dhârvâḍ district and assigned for its support and for the maintenance of another *vihâra* at Lokkiguṇḍi, the modern Lakkundi, a field and a certain amount of money to be raised by voluntary taxation.[22] In Śaka 1032 the Śilâhâra chief of Kolhâpur constructed a large tank and placed on its margin an idol of Buddha along with those of Śiva and Arhat, and

Jainism.

assigned lands for their support.[23] Jainism ceased in this period to be the conquering religion that it was, and about the end received an effectual check by the rise of the Liṇgâyata sect. This new creed spread widely among the trading classes, which before were the chief supporters of Jainism. There is a tradition in some parts of the country that some of the existing temples contained Jaina idols at one time and that afterwards they were thrown out and Brâhmaṇic ones placed instead. This points to a change of feeling with reference to Jainism, the origin of which must be referred to this period.

---

22 Ind. Ant., Vol. X., p. 185.

23 Jour. B. B. R. A. S., Vol. XIII., p. 4, and *infra*, Section XVI.

Section XIII.

Purâṇic religion. Codification of the civil and religious law.

The worship of the Purâṇic gods flourished ; and as in the times of the early Châlukyas the old sacrificial rites were reduced to a system, so during this period the endeavours of the Brâhmaṇs and their adherents were for the first time directed towards reducing the civil and the ordinary religious law to a system, or towards its codification, as it might be called. The texts or precepts on the subject were scattered in a great many Smṛitis and Purâṇas ; and often there were apparent inconsistencies and the law was doubtful. *Nibandhas* or digests, of which we have now so many, began to be written in this period, but the form which they first took, and which even now is one of the recognized forms, was that of commentaries on Smṛitis. Bhoja of Dhârâ, who belongs to the first part of this [97] period, must have written a treatise on the subject, since under the name of Dhâreśvara he is referred to by Vijñâneśvara in his work. He was followed by Vijñâneśvara, who, as we have seen, lived at Kalyâṇa in the reign of Vikramâditya II. Aparârka, another commentator on Yâjñavalkya, who calls his work a *nibandha* on the *Dharmaśâstra* or institutes of Yâjñavalkya, was a prince of the Śilâhâra family of northern Konkan and was on the throne in Śaka 1109 (A.D. 1187) and in the cyclic year *Parâbhava.*[24] Or, if he was the earlier prince of that name, he must have flourished about fifty years before. This movement was continued in the next or thirteenth century by Hemâdri, and by Sâyaṇa in the fourteenth.

---

24 Jour. B. B. R. A. S., Vol. XII., pp. 334-335.

Section XIII.

Genealogy of the Châlukya family between Vijayâditya and Tailapa as given in the Miraj grant of Jayasiṁha dated Śaka 946.

- Vijayâditya.
  - Vikramâditya II.
    - Kîrtivarman II.
  - Another son.
    - Kîrtivarman.
      - Tailapa.
        - Vikramâditya.
          - Ayyana, married the daughter of Kṛishṇa.
            - Vikramâditya, married Boṁthâdevî, the daughter of Lakshmaṇa, king of Chedi.
              - Tailapa.

Genealogy of the later Châlukyas.

1. Tailapa I. (Śaka 895-919. A.D. 973-997.)

2. Satyâśraya, Irivibhujaṅga. (Śaka 919-930. A.D. 997-1008.) — son of 1.

Daśavarman. — son of 1.

3. Vikramâditya I. (Śaka 930-940. A.D. 1008-1018.) — son of Daśavarman.

4. Jayasimha, Jagadekamalla I. (Śaka 940-962. A.D. 1018-1040.) — son of Daśavarman.

5. Someśvara I., Âhavamalla, Trailokyamalla I. (Śaka 962-991. A.D. 1040-1069.) — son of 4.

6. Someśvara II., Bhuvanaikamalla. (Śaka 991-998. A.D. 1069-1076.) — son of 5.

7. Vikramâditya II., Tribhuvanamalla. (Śaka 998-1048. A.D. 1076-1126.) — son of 5.

Jayasimha. — son of 5.

8. Someśvara III., Bhûlokamalla. (Śaka 1048-1060. A.D. 1126-1138.) — son of 7.

9. Jagadekamalla II. (Śaka 1060-1072. A.D. 1138-1150.) — son of 8.

10. Tailapa II., Nurmadi Taila, Trailokyamalla II. (Śaka 1074-1087 ? A.D. 1150-1165.) — son of 8.

11. Someśvara IV. (Śaka 1104-1111 ? A.D. 1182-1189.) — son of 10.

[98] SECTION XIV.

The Yâdavas of Devagiri.

Early History of the Family.

Section XIV.

Authorities

The genealogy of the Yâdavas is given in the introduction to the Vratakhaṇḍa attributed to or composed by Hemâdri who was a minister of Mahâdeva, one of the later princes of the dynasty. Some of the manuscripts of the work, however, do not contain it, and in others it begins with Bhillama, as it was he who acquired supreme power and raised the dynasty to importance. Others again contain an account of the family from the very beginning, the first person mentioned being the Moon who was churned out of the milky ocean. From the Moon the genealogy is carried down through all the Purâṇic or legendary ancestors to Mahâdeva. But it is not difficult from the account itself to determine where the legend ends and history begins. Besides, the names of most of the historical predecessors of Bhillama agree with those occurring in the copper-plate grant translated by Paṇḍit Bhagvânlâl Indraji.[1] He considered the Yâdava dynasty mentioned in his grant to be different from that of Devagiri and called it "A New Yâdava Dynasty," as, of course, in the absence of the information I now publish, he was justified in doing. But it is now perfectly clear that the princes mentioned in the grant were the ancestors of the Devagiri Yâdavas. The following early history of the family is based on the account given in the Vratakhaṇḍa[2] and on the grant published by the Paṇḍit.

---

1 Ind. Ant., Vol. XII., p. 119 *et seq.*

2 The edition of the Vratakhaṇḍa in the Bibliotheca Indica contains neither of these two very valuable and im-

The latter, however, brings down the genealogy only to [99] Seuṇachandra II. who was on the throne in 991 Śaka or 1069 A.D., and omits the names of some of the intermediate princes. Two other grants by princes of this dynasty found at Saṁgamner and Section XIV.

---

portant *Praśastis*. I have therefore had recourse to manuscripts. There is one manuscript only in the Government collections deposited in the Library of the Dekkan College and that is No. 234 of Collection A of 1881-82 which was made by me. It contains the shorter Praśasti beginning with the reign of Bhillama. There is another copy in the collection belonging to the old Sanskrit College of Poona, which contains the longer Praśasti. Unfortunately, however, the third and fourth leaves of the manuscript are missing; and the second ends with Parammadeva the successor of Seuṇachandra II., while the fifth begins with some of the last stanzas of the introduction referring to Hemâdri and his works. The valuable portion therefore was in leaves 3 and 4; but that is irretrievably lost. I therefore endeavoured to procure copies from the private collections in the city of Poona and obtained one from Khâsgivâle's library. It contains the shorter Praśasti only. My learned friend Gaṅgâdhar Śâstrî Dâtâr procured another. In it the two, the shorter one and the longer, are jumbled together. There are in the commencement the first seventeen stanzas of the shorter, and then the longer one begins; and after that is over, we have the remaining stanzas of the shorter. This is the only manuscript of the four now before me which contains the whole of the longer Praśasti, and the information it gives about the later princes of the dynasty known to us from the inscriptions is also valuable and new, but the manuscript is extremely incorrect. I therefore caused a search for other copies to be made at Nâsik, Kolhâpur, and Ahmedabad; but none was available at those places. I give the two Praśastis in Appendix C. [Since the first edition was published I have obtained and purchased another copy of the Vartakhaṇḍa for the Government collections. The introductory portion here is more correctly written, and I have used it in revising this section and the Praśasti in Appendix C.]

Section XIV. Kalas-Budruk of earlier dates[3] have been recently published, and these also have been compared.

Dṛiḍha-prahâra, the founder of the family.

Subâhu who belonged to the Yâdava race was a universal sovereign. He had four sons among whom he divided the whole earth ruled over by him. The second son Dṛiḍhaprahâra[4] became king in the south or Dekkan. The Yâdavas, it is stated, were at first lords of Mathurâ ; then from the time of Kṛishṇa they became sovereigns of Dvâravatî or Dvârakâ ; and came to be rulers of the south from the time of the son of Subâhu, *viz.*, Dṛiḍhaprahâra. His capital was Śrînagara according to the Vratakhaṇḍa, while from the grant it appears to have been a town of the name of Chandrâdityapura, which may have been the modern Châṁdor in the Nâsik district. He had a son of the name of Seuṇachandra who succeeded to the throne. The country over which he ruled was called Seuṇadeśa[5] after him, and he appears to have founded a town also of the name of Seuṇapura. Seuṇadeśa was the name of the region extending from Nâsik to Devagiri, the modern Daulatâbâd, since later on we are told that Devagiri was situated in Seuṇadeśa and that this latter was situated on the confines of Daṇḍakâraṇya.[6] This name seems to be preserved in the modern Khândeś. In a foot-note on

Seuṇa-chandra I. Seuṇadeśa.

---

[3] Mr. Cousen's impression of the first of these grants was seen by me before it was published by Prof. Kielhorn in Epigraphia Indica, Vol. II., p. 212 *et seq.*, and its contents embodied in the copy of this work revised for this second edition. I have, however, since availed myself of one or two points made out by Prof. Kielhorn and not noticed by me. The second grant is published in Ind. Ant., Vol. XVII., p. 120, *et seq.*

[4] He is called Dṛiḍhaprahâri (nom. sing.) in the MSS.; stanza 20, Appendix C. I.

[5] Stanza 22, Appendix C. I.

[6] Stanza 19, Appendix C. II.

Section XIV.

the opening page of the Khândeś Volume, the Editor of the "Bombay Gazetteer" observes that the name of the country was older than Musalman times, and it was afterwards changed by them to suit the title of Khân given to the Fâruki kings by Ahmed I. of Gujarât. Seuṇadeśa, therefore, was very likely the original name and it was changed to Khândeś, which name soon came into general use on account of its close resemblance in sound to Seuṇadeśa. The country however extended farther southwards than the present district of Khândeś, since it included Devagiri or Daulatâbâd, and probably it did not include the portion north of the Tâpî.

Seuṇachandra's successors.

Seuṇachandra's son Dhâḍiyappa[7] became king after him and he was succeeded by his son Bhillama. After Bhillama, his son Śrîrâja according to the grants, or Râjugi according to the other authority, came to the throne, and he was succeeded[8] by his son Vaddiga or Vâdugi. Vaddiga is in the Saṁgamner grant represented as a follower of Kṛishṇarâja who was probably Kṛishṇa III. of the Râshṭrakûṭa dynasty, and to have married Voddiyavvâ,

---

7 Called Dhâḍiyasa in the MSS.; Appendix C. I., stanza 23.

8 *Ibid.* Pandit Bhagvânlâl translates the words *arvâk tasya* (see note 10 below) occurring in the Yâdava grant as "before him," and placing Vaddiga before Śrîrâja, conjectures that he was Bhillama's son and that Śrîrâja his uncle deposed him and usurped the throne; (Ind. Ant., Vol. XII., pp. 125*a* and 128*b*). But *arvâk tasya* can never mean "before him," and must mean "after him," and hence the conjectures are groundless. I have never seen a *preceding* prince mentioned in the grants after his successor, with such an introductory expression as "*before him* so and so became king." By the occurrence of the word भजनिष in stanza 23, line 2, Appendix C. I., it appears Râjagi was the son of Bhillama I.

Section XIV. daughter of a [100] prince of the name of Dhorappa. Then came Dhâḍiyasa,[9] who was the son of Vâdugi according to the Vratakhaṇḍa. Two of the grants omit his name, probably because he was only a collateral and not an ancestor of the grantor in the direct line, and the third has a line or two missing here. Dhâḍiyasa was succeeded by Bhillama, who was the son of Vaddiga or Vâdugi and consequently his

Bhillama II. brother.[10] Bhillama married according to the grants

---

9 Appendix C. I. stanza 24. If he had been mentioned in the grant, he would probably have been called Dhâḍiyappa.

10 *Ibid.* Paṇḍit Bhagvânlâl omits this prince though he is mentioned in his grant. The last two lines of the fourth stanza in this are :—

प्राग्गास्य बभूव भूतलहरिः श्रीवड्डिगाख्यो नृपः
तस्माच्छ्रीवरभिल्लमक्षितिपतेः प्रत्यक्षधर्मोऽभवत् ॥

The Paṇḍit translates this :—"Before him was the illustrious king Vaddiga, a Hari on earth; and therefore he was exactly like the illustrious good Bhillama in his actions." I have already remarked that instead of "before him," we should have "after him" here. The word तस्मात् is translated by "therefore." "Wherefore?" I would ask. No reason is given in the first of these lines for his being *exactly like* Bhillama; and therefore, it will not do to translate तस्मात् by "therefore." Again, the Paṇḍit's interpretation of प्रत्यक्षधर्मा as "exactly like in actions" is farfetched and unnatural. The thing is, the genitive or ablative क्षितिपते cannot be connected with any word in the line, and is therefore one of the innumerable mistakes which we have in this grant and most of which have been pointed out by the Paṇḍit himself. What is wanted here is the nominative क्षितिपतिः for क्षितिपतेः and then the whole is appropriate, and तस्मात् will have its proper sense of "after him," or "from him." The correct translation then is *"After him* was a king of the name of Vaddiga the prosperous, who was a Hari on earth, and *after him* or *of him* (*i.e.* Vaddiga) came the prosperous, great Bhillama in whom Virtue became

Lakshmî or Lachchiyavvâ,[11] the daughter of Jhañjha, who was probably the Śilahâra prince of Ṭhânâ of that name. Lachchiyavvâ sprang on her mother's side from the Râshṭrakûṭa family, and through her son became "the upholder of the race of Yadu;"[12]

---

incarnate." In this way we have here another king Bhillama, as mentioned in the Praśasti in the Vratakhaṇḍa in the passage cited above.

11 This lady, according to my translation, becomes the wife of Bhillama, who is the king mentioned immediately before, and not of his father Vaddiga as the Paṇḍit makes out.

12 Here there is another difficulty arising from a mistake in the grant which Paṇḍit Bhagvânlâl has in my opinion not succeeded in solving; and he bases upon that mistake conjectures which are rather too far-reaching (p. 125*a*, Ind. Ant., Vol. XII.). The stanza is:—

भार्या यस्य च झंझराजतनया श्रीलच्छियव्वाह्वया
धर्मत्यागविवेकशुद्धिसगुणा राष्ट्रकूटान्वया।
या जाता नवबालभाजसमये यदन्वयाधारिता
सप्तांगीयतराज्यभारधरणाद्रायत्रयार्घ्या ततः॥

The Paṇḍit's translation is:—"Whose wife was the daughter of king Jhañjha Lasthiyavvâ by name, possessed of the (three) good qualities of virtue, liberality, and hospitality, who was of the Râshṭrakûṭa race, *as being adopted (by them) at the time of the rule of the young prince (during his minority)* and who therefore by reason of bearing the burden of the kingdoms, with its seven aṅgas, was an object of reverence to the three kingdoms."

I agree with the Paṇḍit in reading श्री before राष्ट्रकूटान्वया and taking रायत्रय as राज्यत्रय, and, generally, in his translation of the first two and the fourth lines. But the translation of the third line, that is, the portion italicised in the above, is very objectionable. The Paṇḍit reads राज from भाज and says that the य in यदन्वया० ought to be long for the metre, but would make no sense. Now, in seeking the true solution of the difficulty here, we must bear in mind that in the fourth line the lady is spoken of as "an object of reverence to the three kingdoms." Which are the three

Section XIV. so that she was connected with three ruling dynasties and flourishing kingdoms. The Saṁgamner grant appears to have been issued by this Bhillama in the Śaka year 922, *i.e.* 1000 A.D., and the prince mentioned in [101] the grant as having struck a blow against the power of Muñja and rendered the sovereign authority of Raṇaraṅgabhîma firm seems also to be he himself. Raṇaraṅgabhîma was probably

---

kingdoms? First evidently, that of Jhañjha, her father, who is spoken of in the first line; and secondly, that of the Râshṭrakûṭas from whose race she is spoken of as having sprung in the second line. Now, we must expect some allusion to the third kingdom in the third line. The third kingdom was clearly that of the Yâdavas into whose family she had been married. I, therefore, read यद्वन्वया० for यदन्वया० and thus the difficulty about the metre is removed, the य becoming prosodially long in consequence of the following द्व. In the same manner I think बालजाज is a mistake for बालजान. The word जान the writer must have taken from his vernacular and considered it a Sanskrit word; or probably not knowing Sanskrit well, he must have formed it from the root जन् on the analogy of माद from मद्, साद from सद्, मान from मन् &c. Or बालजाज may be considered as a mistake for बालजन्म, the sense being the same, viz. "birth of a child." The compound यद्वन्वयाधारिता is to be dissolved as आधारितः यद्वन्वयः यया। आधारित being made the second member according to Pâṇini II. 2, 37. Or, the line may be read as या याता नवबालजन्मसमये यद्वन्वयाधारतां, the dot over ता being omitted by mistake, and याता written as जाता in consequence of the usual confusion between य् and ज्. The translation of the line, therefore, is "who became the upholder of the race of Yadu on the occasion of the birth of a new child," *i.e.* through her child she became the upholder of the Yâdava race. In this manner the supposition of her being adopted by the Râshṭrakûṭas during the young prince's minority becomes groundless. She must have belonged to the *Râshṭrakûṭa* race on her mother's side.

Section XIV.

Tailapa, and thus it follows that the Yâdava prince Bhillama II. assisted Tailapa in his war with Muñja which we have already noticed. Vaddiga was a follower of Kṛishṇa III. of the Râshṭrakûṭa family, whose latest known date is 881 Śaka, and Bhillama II. of Tailapa. The date 922 Śaka of Bhillama's grant is consistent with these facts. The Yâdavas appear thus to have transferred their allegiance from the old to the new dynasty of paramount sovereigns as soon as it rose to power. The next king was Vesugi[13] called in Paṇḍit Bhagvânlâl's grant Tesuka, which is a mistake or misreading for Vesuka or Vesuga. He married Nâyaladevî, the daughter of Gogi, who is styled a feudatory of the Châlukya family,[14] and was perhaps the same as the successor of the Ṭhânâ prince Jhañjha. The Râshṭrakûṭas must have been overthrown by the Châlukyas about the end of Jhañjha's reign, and thus his successor became a feudatory of the Châlukyas.

Bhillama III., son-in-law of Jayasiṁha.

[102] The Vratakhaṇḍa places Arjuna after Vesugi,[15] but the two grants omit his name; and perhaps the former mentions Arjuna not as a Yâdava prince, but Arjuna the Pâṇḍava, meaning to compare Vesugi with him and his enemies to Bhîshma. The next king was Bhillama[16] who according to the Kalas-Budruk grant was Vesugi's son. He married Hammâ, the daughter of Jayasiṁha and sister of Âhavamalla, the Châlukya emperor, under whose standard he

13 Stanza 24, Appendix C. I.

14 The expression चालुक्यान्वयमण्डलीक in the grant admits of being taken in the manner I have done, मण्डलीक being a mistake for माण्डलिक. The Paṇḍit understands Gogirâja as belonging to the Châlukya race. I consider my interpretation to be more probable.

15 Stanza 24, Appendix C. I. 16 Stanza 26, *Ibid.*

Section XIV.

fought several battles.[17] The Kalas-Budruk charter was issued by this prince in 948 Śaka. The cyclic year being Krodhana, 948 Śaka must have been the current year, corresponding to 1025 A.D. Paṇḍit Bhagvâanlâl's grant then proceeds at once to the donor, the reigning prince Seuṇa, who is spoken of in general terms as "having sprung from the race" of the last-mentioned king, and is represented to have defeated several kings and freed his kingdom from enemies after "the death of Bhillama." This Bhillama was his immediate predecessor, but he was a different person from the brother-in-law of Âhavamalla, since Seuṇa, is spoken of not as the son of the latter or any such near relation but simply as "having sprung from his race." The Vratakhaṇḍa supplies the names of the intermediate princes. The elder Bhillama was succeeded by Vâdugi,[18] his son, "whose praise was sung by poets in melodious words." After him Vesugi[19] became king, but how he was related to Vâdugi we are not told. He humbled a number of subordinate chiefs who had grown troublesome.

Seuṇa-chandra II. the ally of Vikram-âditya II.

Then came Bhillama, and after him Seuṇa[20] who issued the charter translated by Paṇḍit Bhagvânlâl. What relationship the last three princes bore to each other is not stated. Seuṇa is represented to have saved Paramardideva, that is, Vikramâditya II., who is styled the "luminary of the Châlukya family" from a coalition of his enemies, and to have placed him on the throne of Kalyâṇa.[21] This appears to be a reference to the coalition between the Veṅgi prince and Vikramâditya's brother Someśvara. The Yâdava

---

17 This appears to me to be the general sense of stanza 8 and not that he fought with Âhavamalla as Paṇḍit Bhagvânlâl understands. I need not discuss the matter in detail.

18 Stanza 26, Appendix C. I.

19 Stanza 27, *Ibid.*

20 Stanza 28, *Ib.*

21 Stanza 29, *Ib.*

prince Seuṇa was thus a close ally of the Châlukya monarch and their dates also are consistent with the fact. Seuṇachandra's grant is dated Śaka 991 *Saumya Saṁvatsara,* while Vikramâditya II. got possession of the Châlukya throne in Śaka 998 *Nala.* The grant mentions the relations of previous Yâdava princes to the Châlukyas of Kalyâṇa, while the important service rendered by Seuṇachandra to Vikramâditya is not recorded, and he is spoken of only in general terms as having vanquished "all kings." This itself shows that in all likelihood the fact mentioned in the Vratakhaṇḍa of Seuṇachandra's having delivered that prince from his enemies and placed him on the throne took place after Śaka 991, and we know it as a matter of fact that Vikramâditya became king in Śaka 998. **Section XIV.**

Successors of Seuṇachandra II.

[103] Seuṇachandra was succeeded by Parammadeva who was probably his son, and after him came Siṁharâja[22] or "King Siṁha," whose full name was Siṅghaṇa[23] and who appears to have been his brother. He is said to have brought an elephant of the name of Karpûratilaka from Lañjîpura and thus did a piece of service to Paramardin, who appears to be Vikramâditya II. of the Châlukya dynasty.[24] He was succeeded by his son Mallugi, who took a town of the name of Parṇakheṭa from his enemies, and while residing there carried away by force the troop of elephants belonging to the king of Utkala or Orissa.[25] Then followed his son Amaragâṅgeya[26] whose name is mentioned in a copper-plate grant issued in the reign of a subsequent king.[27] After him came

---

22 Stanzas 30 and 31, Appendix C. I.

23 Ind. Ant., Vol. XIV., p. 315.

24 Stanza 32, Appendix C. I.

25 Stanzas 33 and 34, *Ibid.*

26 Stanza 35, *Ibid.*

27 Jour. B. B. R. A. S., Vol, XV., p. 386.

Section XIV.

Bhillama V., the founder of the Yâdava Empire.

Govindarâja who was probably his son. Govindarâja was succeeded by Amaramallagi, a son of Mallugi, and he by Kâliya Ballâḷa. This prince was in all likelihood the son of Amaramallagi, though it is not expressly stated. Ballâḷa's sons were set aside and the sovereignty of the Yâdava family fell into the hands of his uncle Bhillama,[28] who was possessed of superior abilities. Bhillama being represented as the uncle of Ballâḷa must have been another son of Mallugi, and he is so spoken of in the grant referred to above.[29] He got possession of the throne after two of his brothers and their sons, wherefore he must have been a very old man at the time. Hence it is that he reigned only for a short time, having come to the throne in Śaka 1109 and died in 1113. It was this Bhillama who acquired for his family the empire that was ruled over by the Châlukyas.

Seuṇachandra of Añjaneri.

Paṇḍit Bhagvânlâl has published a stone-inscrip-

---

28 Stanzas 35-37, Appendix C. I.

29 In an inscription at Gadag published by Dr. Kielhorn (Epigraphia Indica, Vol. III., p. 219) Bhillama is represented as the son of Karṇa, who is said to be a brother of Amaragâṅgeya. In the many inscriptions of the Yâdava dynasty and in the Praśastis given in several books the name Karṇa does not occur even once. The Gadag inscription makes Mallugi the son of Sevaṇadeva, while in the Vratakhaṇḍa and the Paiṭhan plates he is represented as the son of Singhaṇa, who according to the former authority was one of the successors of Seuṇachandra and was probably his younger son. The inscription is here opposed to two authorities which agree with each other. Hence this must be a mistake; and that makes it probable that the other is also a mistake. These suppositions are strengthened by the fact that the composer of the Gadag inscription does not mention a single particular fact with reference to any one of the princes, thus showing that he had no accurate knowledge of them. Such a merely conventional description is characteristic of a forged charter. I am, for these reasons, inclined to think that the Gadag grant published by Dr. Kielhorn is a forgery.

Section XIV.

tion[30] existing in a ruined temple at Añjaneri near Nâsik, in which a chief of the Yâdava family, named Seuṇadeva, is represented to have made some grant in the Śaka year 1063[31] to a Jaina temple. From the account given above, it will be seen that there were two princes only of the name of Seuṇa in the Yâdava family, and that the later of the two was an ally of Vikramâditya II., and consequently reigned about the end of the tenth and the beginning of the eleventh century of the Śaka [**104**] era. The Seuṇadeva of the Añjaneri inscription therefore cannot be this individual, and no other prince of that name is mentioned in the Vratakhaṇḍa. Besides Seuṇdeva calls himself pointedly a *Mahâsâmanta* or chief only; while about 1063 Śaka, when the Châlukya power had begun to decline, it does not appear likely that the Yâdava of Seuṇadeśa should give themselves such an inferior title. It therefore appears to me that the Seuṇadeva of Añjaneri belonged to a minor branch of the Yâdava family dependent on the main branch, and that the branch ruled over a small district of which Añjaneri was the chief city.

Approximate date of the foundation of the Yâdava family.

The number of princes who reigned from Dṛiḍhaprahâra to Bhillama V. inclusive is 22. There are in the list a good many who belonged to the same generation as their predecessors and consequently these twenty-two do not represent so many different generations. Allowing, therefore, the usual average, in such cases of 18 years to each reign, the period that must have elapsed between the accession of Dṛiḍhaprahâra and the death of Bhillama V. is 396 years. The dynasty, therefore, was founded about

30 Ind. Ant., Vol. XII., p. 126.

31 The correct year has been shown to be 1064 Śaka by Prof. Kielhorn, Ind. Ant., Vol. XX., p. 422.

Section XIV.

717 Śaka or 795 A.D., that is, about the time of Govind III. of the Râshṭrakûṭa race. Possibly considering that Vaddiga I. was contemporary of Kṛishṇa III., one might say that the dynasty was founded in the latter part of the reign of Amoghavarsha I.

Genealogy of the early Yâdavas or the Yâdavas of Seuṇadeśa.

- Dṛiḍhaprahâra.
  - Seuṇachandra I.
    - Dhâḍiyappa I.
      - Bhillama I.
        - Râjagi or Śrîrâja.
          - Vâdugi or Vaddiga I.
            - Dhâḍiyappa II.
            - Bhillama II. Śaka 922.
              - Vesugi I.
                - Bhillama III. Śaka 948.
                  - Vâdugi II.
                    - Vesugi II.*
                      - Bhillama IV.*
                        - Seuṇchandra II.* Śaka 991 or A.D. 1069.
                          - Parammadeva.
                          - Singhaṇa.
                            - Mallugi.
                              - Amaragâṅgeya.
                                - Govindarâja.
                              - Amaramallagi.
                                - Ballâḷa.
                              - BHILLAMA V. or I. died Śaka 1113 or A.D. 1191.

---

* The relations of those whose names are marked with an asterisk to their predecessors are not clearly stated.

[105] SECTION XV.

The Yâdavas of Devagiri.

Later History.

Section XV.

Ambitious projects of the Hoysaḷa Yâdavas.

We have seen that the Hoysaḷa Yâdavas of Haḷebiḍ in Maiṣur were becoming powerful in the time of Tribhuvanamalla or Vikramâditya II. and aspiring to the supreme sovereignty of the Dekkan, and Vishṇuvardhana, the reigning prince of the family at that period, actually invaded the Châlukya territory and encamped on the banks of the Kṛishṇâ-Veṇâ. But those times were not favourable for the realization of their ambitious projects. The Châlukya prince was a man of great ability, the power of the family was firmly established over the country, its resources were large, and the dependent chiefs and noblemen were obedient. But the state of things had now changed. Weaker princes had succeeded, the Châlukya power had been broken by their dependents the Kalachuris, and these in their turn had succumbed to the internal troubles and dissensions consequent on the rise of the Liṅgâyata sect. At this time the occupant of the Hoysaḷa throne was Vîra Ballâḷa, the grandson of Vishṇuvardhana. He fought with Brâhma or Bomma, the general of the last Châlukya prince Somesvara IV., and putting down his elephants by means of his horses defeated him and acquired the provinces which the general had won back from Vijjaṇa.[1]

Vîra Ballâḷa.

Rise of Bhillama.

The Yâdavas of the north were not slow to take advantage of the unsettled condition of the country to extend their power and territory. Mallugi seems to have been engaged in a war with Vijjaṇa. A

[1] Ind. Ant., Vol. II., p. 300.

Section XV. person of the name of Dâdâ was commander of his troops of elephants and is represented to have gained some advantages over the army of the Kalachuri prince. He had four sons of the names of Mahîdhara, Jahla, Sâmba, and Gaṅgâdhara. Of these Mahîdhara succeeded his father and is spoken of as having defeated the forces of Vijjaṇa.[2] But the acquisition of the empire of the Châlukyas was [**106**] completed by Mallugi's son Bhillama. He captured a town of the name of Śrivardhana from a king who is called Antala, vanquished in battle the king of Pratyaṇḍaka, put to death the ruler of Maṅgalaveshṭaka, (Maṅgaḷ-veḍheṁ), of the name of Villaṇa, and having obtained the sovereignty of Kalyâṇa, put to death the lord of Hosala who was probably the Hoysala Yâdava Narasiṁha, the father of Vîra Ballâḷa.[3] The commander of his elephants was Jahla, the brother of Mahîdhara, and he is represented to have rendered Bhillama's power firm. He led a maddened elephant skilfully into the army of the Gûrjara king, struck terror into the heart of Malla, frightened the forces

---

2 Introduction to Jahlâṇ's Sûktimuktavali, now brought to notice for the first time :

तस्यान्वयेऽभूत्करिवृन्दनाथो दादा: सदादानविदानभूत: ।
यस्येभवाजिव्रजभूपसैन्यं दैन्यं गतं संयति विक्रमेण ॥ ५ ॥
चत्वारस्तस्य संजातास्तनया नयशालिन: ।
भुजा इव हरे: मन्त्रविक्रमश्रीविभूषिता: ॥ ६ ॥
चतुर्भुजमुखोद्गीर्णनिगमा इव ते बभु: ।
ख्याता महीधरो जल्ह: साम्बो गङ्गाधरस्तथा ॥ ७ ॥
उपायैरिव तै: कान्तै चतुर्भि: सुप्रयोजितै: ।
मै (सै) सुगिभूमिपालस्य राज्यं जातं सदोन्नतम् ॥ ८ ॥
विज्जणबलजलराशिं विमथ्य भुजमन्दरेण य: कृतवान् ।
कीर्तिश्रियमनवद्यां स न कस्य महीधर: स्तुत्य: ॥ ९ ॥

The full introduction will be published elsewhere.

3 Appendix C. I., stanza 38. Maṅgaḷvedheṁ is near Panḍharpur. It was probably the capital of a minor chief.

Section XV.

of Mallugi, and put an end to the victorious career of Muñja and Anna.[4] When in this manner Bhillama made himself master of the whole country to the north of the Krishṇâ, he founded the city of Devagiri[5] and having got himself crowned, made that city his capital. This took place about the Śaka year 1109.

Foundation of Devagiri.

Contests between the rivals.

Bhillama then endeavoured to extend his territory farther southwards, but he was opposed by Vîra Ballâḷa, who, as we have seen, had been pushing his conquests northwards. It was a contest for the possession of an empire and was consequently arduous and determined. Several battles took place between the two rivals, and eventually a decisive engagement was fought at Lokkiguṇḍi, now Lakkuṇḍi, in the Dhârvâḍ District, in which Jaitrasiṁha, who is compared to "the right arm of Bhillama" and must have been his son, was defeated and Vîra Ballâḷa became sovereign of Kuntala. The inscription in which this is recorded bears the date Śaka 1114 or A.D. 1192;[6] and Vira Ballâḷa who made the grant recorded in it was at that time encamped with his victorious army at Lokkiguṇḍi, from which

---

4 Intr. Jahl. Sukt. :—

विजित्य विश्वमर्थं याति सुरलोकं मल्लीश्वरे ।
तिनाय भिल्लमं मल्ली राजतां चयवर्जिताम् ॥ ११ ॥
गूर्जरभूभृत्कटके कण्टकविषमेऽतिदुर्गमे येन ।
भगदत्तकीर्तिभाजा दुष्टगजःखेलया नीतः ॥ १२ ॥
मल्लः पल्लवितोरुभीतिरभितश्चलत्स्फुलो मैल्लुगि-
र्मुञ्जः पिच्छितविक्रमस्त्रिभुवनश्लाघ्या चिरं प्रापकः ।
यस्मै गुरुपराक्रमो विधुतभूर्भूरवप्राप्तधी
धीमाकारि मुरारिविक्रमभृता किं किं न तत्कीर्तितम् ॥ १३ ॥

The Mallugi mentioned here must have been one of the enemies of Bhillama. He probably belonged to a minor branch of the Yâdava family.

5 Appendix C. I., st. 39.

6 Ind Ant., Vol. II., p. 300.

Section XV. it would appear that the battle had taken place but a short time before. The northern Yâdavas had to put off the conquest of Kuntala or the Southern Marâṭhâ Country for a generation.

Jaitrapâla. Bhillama was succeeded in 1113 Śaka by his son Jaitrapâla or Jaitugi. He took an active part in his father's battles. "He assumed [107] the sacrificial vow on the holy ground of the battle-field and throwing a great many kings into the fire of his prowess by means of the ladles of his weapons, performed a human sacrifice by immolating a victim in the shape of the fierce Rudra, the lord of the Tailaṅgas, and vanquished the three worlds."[7] This same fact is alluded to in the Paiṭhaṇ grant, in which Jaitugi is represented to have killed the king of the Trikaliṅgas in battle. He is there spoken of also as having released Gaṇapati from prison and to have placed him on the throne.[8] The Rudra therefore whom he is thus represented to have killed on the field of battle must have been the Rudradeva of the Kâkatîya dynasty whose inscription we have at Anamkoṇḍ near Woraṅgaḷ, and the Gaṇpati, his nephew[9] who was probably placed in confinement by Rudradeva. In other places also his war with the king of the Andhras or Tailaṅgas and his having

---

7 Appendix C. I., st. 41. Just as the fruit of a horse sacrifice is the conquest of the whole world, the fruit of a man-sacrifice is supposed here to be the conquest of the three worlds. Jaitrapâla performed metaphorically such a sacrifice; and that is considered to be the reason, as it were, of his having obtained victories everywhere, *i.e.* in the usual hyperbolic language, of his having succeeded in vanquishing the three worlds.

8 Ind. Ant., Vol. XIV., p. 316.

9 Ind. Ant., Vol. XXI., p. 197.

Section XV.

raised Gaṇapati to the throne are alluded[10] to, and he is represented to have deprived the Andhra ladies of the happiness arising from having their husbands living.[11] Lakshmîdhara, the son of the celebrated mathematician and astronomer Bhâskarâcharya, was in the service of Jaitrapâla and was placed by him at the head of all learned Paṇḍits. He knew the Vedas and was versed in the Tarkaśâstra and Mîmâṁsâ.[12]

Singhana.

Jaitrapâla's son and successor was Siṅghaṇa, under whom the power and territory of the family greatly increased. He ascended the throne in 1132 Śaka.[13] He defeated a king of the name of Jajjalla and brought away his elephants. He deprived a monarch named Kakkûla of his sovereignty, destroyed Arjuna who was probably the sovereign of Mâlvâ, and made Bhoja a prisoner. Janârdana, the son of Gaṅgâdhara, who was Jahla's brother, is said to have taught Siṅghaṇa the art of managing elephants which enabled him to vanquish Arjuna.[14] He had succeeded to the office of commander of elephants held by Jahla and after him by Gaṅgâdhara. "King Laksh-
[108] mîdhara, the lion of Bhambhâgiri, was reduced, the ruler of Dhârâ was besieged by means of troops of horses, and the whole of the country in

---

10 Jour. B. B. R. A. S., Vol. XV., p. 386, and Epigraphia Indica, Vol. III., p. 113.

11 Jour. R. A. S., Vol. I., N. S., p. 414.

12 *Ib.* p. 415.

13 Jour. R. A. S., Vol. IV., p. 5.

14 Intr. Jahl. Sukt. :—

आसीद्गङ्गाधरस्तस्य भ्राता गङ्गाधरोपमः ।
एकाम्बवन्ध यो व्यालाम्बुधीचैकाम्बहस्तया ॥ १६ ॥
तस्याभवत्सुतस्तूनसत्त्वो जनार्दनाख्यः शिवाङ्घ्रिलीनः ।
समुद्रवद्यो भुवनं बभार सह श्रिया चित्रमभीक्ष्णमेतत् ॥ १८ ॥
सिंहोऽप्यध्यापितस्तेन गजशिक्षां तदद्भुतम् ।
यजार्जुनं ससंपन्नं समूलमुदमूलयत् ॥ २० ॥

Section XV. the possession of Ballâḷa was taken. All this was but a child's play to King Siṅghaṇa."[15] Jajjalla must have been a prince belonging to the eastern branch of the Chedi dynasty that ruled over the province of Chhattisgarh, for that name occurs in the genealogy of that dynasty.[16] The name Kakkûla I would identify with Kokkala which was borne by some princes of the western branch of the family, the capital of which was Tripura or Tevur. The kings of Mathurâ and Kâśî were killed by him in battle, and Hammîra was vanquished by but a boy-general of Siṅghaṇa.[17] In an inscription also at Tiḷivaḷḷi in the Dhârvâḍ District, he is represented to have defeated Jajalladeva, conquered Ballâḷa the Hoysaḷa king, subdued Bhoja of Panhâḷâ, and humbled the sovereign of Mâlava.[18] He is also spoken of as "the goad of the elephant in the shape of the Gûrjara king."[19] We have an inscription of his at Gaddaka dated 1135 Śaka, which shows that Vîra Ballâḷa must have been deprived of the southern part of the country before that time.[20] Siṅghaṇa is represented as reigning at his capital Devagiri.[21]

The Bhoja of Panhâlâ spoken of above was a prince of the Śilâhâra dynasty, and after his defeat the Kolhâpur kingdom appears to have been annexed by the Yâdavas to their dominions. They put an end to this branch of the family as later on they did

---

15 Appendix C. I., st. 43 and 44. Ind. Ant., Vol. XIV., p. 316.

16 General Cunningham's Arch. Reports, Vol. XVII., pp. 75, 76 and 79.

17 Jour. R. A. S., Vol. I., N. S., p. 414.

18 Jour. B. B. R. A. S., Vol. IX., p. 326.

19 Major Graham's Report on Kolhapur, Ins. No. 13.

20 Ind. Ant., Vol. II., p. 297.

21 Major Graham's Report, Ins., No. 10

Section XV.

to another which ruled over Northern Konkan. From this time forward the Kolhâpur inscriptions contain the names of the Yâdava princes with those of the governors appointed by them to rule over the district. An inscription of Siṅghaṇa at Khedrâpur in that district records the grant of a village to the temple of Koppeśvara in the year 1136 Śaka.

Siṅghaṇa's invasions of Gujarât.

Siṅghaṇa seems to have invaded Gujarât several times. In an inscription at Âṁbeṁ a Brâhmaṇ chief of the name of Kholeśvara of the Mudgala Gotra is spoken of as a very brave general in the service of the Yâdava sovereign. He humbled the pride of the Gûrjara prince, crushed the Mâlava, destroyed the race of the king of the Âbhîras, and being like "wild fire to the enemies" of his master, left nothing for Siṅghaṇa to be anxious about. His son Râma succeeded him, and a large expedition under his command was again sent to Gujarât. Râma advanced up to the Narmadâ, where a battle was fought, in which he slew numbers of Gûrjara soldiers, but he himself lost his life.[22] From this it would appear that Gujarât was invaded by Siṅghaṇa on two occasions at least, if not more ; and this is borne out by what we find stated in the authorities [109] for the history of Gujarât. Somadeva, the author of the Kîrtti-kaumudî, which gives an account of the minister Vastupâla and his masters the princes of the Vâghelâ branch of the Châlukya family, describes an invasion of Gujarât by Siṅghaṇa in the time of Lavaṇaprasâda and his son Vîradhavala. "The capital of Gujarât trembled with fear when the advance of Siṅghaṇa's army was reported. Being afraid of this foreign invasion no one among the subjects of the Gûrjara king began the construction of a new house or stored grain, and the minds of all

First Invasion.

22 Arch. Surv. of W. I., Vol. III., p. 85.

Section XV. were restless. Neglecting to secure the grain in their fields they showed a particular solicitude to procure carts, and as the army of the enemy approached nearer and nearer, the people with their fears greatly excited removed farther and farther. When Lavaṇa-prasâda heard of the rapid advance of the innumerable host of the Yâdava prince, he knit his brow in anger ; and though he had but a small army, proceeded with it to meet that of the enemy, which was vastly superior. When the forces of Siṅghaṇa arrived on the banks of the Tâpî he rapidly advanced to the Mahî. Seeing, on the one hand, the vast army of the enemy and, on the other, the indomitable prowess of the Châlukya force, the people were full of doubt and could not foresee the result. The enemy burnt villages on their way, and the volume of smoke that rose up in the air showed the position of their camp to the terrified people and enabled them to direot their movements accordingly. The Yâdavas overran the country about Bharoch while the plentiful crops were still standing in the fields ; but the king of Gujarât did not consider them unconquerable."[23] In the meanwhile, however, four kings of Mârvâḍ rose against Lavaṇaprasâda and his son Vîradhavala, and the chiefs of Godhrâ and Lâṭa, who had united their forces with theirs, abandoned them and joined the Mârvâḍ princes. In these circumstances Lavaṇaprasâda suddenly stopped his march and turned backwards.[24] The Yâdava army, however, did not, according to Someśvara, advance farther ; but he gives no reason whatever, observing only that "deer do not follow a lion's path even when he has left it."[25] But if the invasion spread such terror over the country as Someśvara

---

23 Kirttikaumudî IV., stanzas 43-53.

24 *Ib.*, st. 55-60.

25 *Ib.*, st. 63.

Section XV.

himself represents, and the army of Siṅghaṇa was so large, it is impossible to conceive how it could have ceased to advance when the Gûrjara prince retreated, unless he had agreed to pay a tribute or satisfied the Yâdava commander in some other way. In a manuscript discovered some years ago of a work containing forms of letters, deeds, patents, &c., there is a specimen of a treaty with the names of Siṃhaṇa and Lavaṇaprasâda as parties to it, from which it appears that a treaty of that nature must actually have been concluded between them.[26] The result of the expedi-

---

[26] This work is entitled Lekhapañchâśikâ, and the manuscript was purchased by me for Government in 1883. The first leaf is wanting and the colophon does not contain the name of the author. The manuscript, however, is more than four hundred years old, being transcribed in 1536 of the Vikrama Saṁvat. For the variable terms in the forms given by the author, he often uses the usual expression *amuka*, meaning "some one" or "such a one." This general expression, however, is not used to indicate the date, and we have in all the forms one date, *viz.* 15 Sudi of Vaiśâkha, in the year of Vikrama 1288, except in one case where it is the 3rd Sudi. This probably was the date when the author wrote. Similarly, when giving the form of a grant inscribed on copper-plates, the author in order probably to make the form clear, uses real and specific names. He gives the genealogy of the Châlukya kings of Anahila-pattana from Mûlarâja to Bhîma II. and then introduces Lavaṇaprasâda, whom he calls Lavaṇyaprasâda and styles a Mahâmaṇḍaleśvara, as the prince making the grant. Similarly, in giving the form of a treaty of alliance called *yamalapattra,* the persons who are introduced as parties to it are Siṁhaṇa and Lâvayṇaprasâda and the form runs thus :—

संवत् १२८८ वर्षे वैशाखशुदि १५ सोमेऽद्येह श्रीमद्विजयकटके महा-राजाधिराजश्रीमत्सिंहणदेवस्य महामण्डलेश्वरराणकश्रीलावण्यप्रसादस्य च। संराज (साम्राज्य or सम्राट्) कुलश्रीश्रीमतिसिंहणदेवेन महामण्डलेश्वरराण-श्रीलावण्यप्रसादेन पूर्वरूढात्मीय २ (i.e., आत्मीय again) देशेषु रहणीयं। केनापि कस्यापि भूमी नाक्रमणीया।

Section XV. tion, [**110**] therefore, was that Lavaṇaprasâda had to submit and conclude a treaty of alliance with Siṅghaṇa.

Second Invasion.

This invasion of Gujarât must have been one of the earlier ones alluded to in the Âṁbeṁ inscription, and Kholeśvara himself must have been the commander of the Yâdava army on the occasion. For Lavaṇaprasâda is said to have declared himself independent of his original master Bhîma II. of Anahilapattana about the year 1276 Vikrama,[27] corresponding to 1141 Śaka, which was about the ninth or tenth year of Siṅghaṇa's reign, and the work in which the treaty mentioned above occurs was composed in 1288 Vikrama, *i.e.* 1153 Śaka. But the expedition under the command of Râma, the son of Kholeśvara, must have been sent a short time before

"On this day the 15th Sudi of Vaiśâkha, in the year Saṁvat 1288, in the Camp of Victory, [a treaty] between the paramount king of kings, the prosperous Siṁhaṇa and the Mahâmaṇḍalesvara Râṇaka, the prosperous Lâvaṇyaprasâda Siṁhaṇa whose patrimony is paramount sovereignty, and the Mahâmaṇḍaleśvara Râṇâ the prosperous Lâvaṇyaprasâda should according to former usage confine themselves, each to his own country; neither should invade the country of the other."

The treaty then provides that when either of them is taken up by an enemy, the armies of both should march to his release; that if a prince from either country ran away into the other with some valuable things, he should not be allowed quarter, &c. Now, it is extremely unlikely that the author of the work should introduce these persons in his form unless he had seen or heard of such a treaty between them. Siṁhaṇa is but another form of Siṅghaṇa, and he is spoken of as a paramount sovereign. The treaty, it will be seen, was concluded in the "victorious camp," which is a clear reference to the invasion described by Someśvara.

In रहवीदं we have, I think, the vernacular root रह् "to remain," "to live." For further details see my Report on the search for manuscripts during 1882-83, pp. 39 and 225.

27 Ind. Ant., Vol. VI., p. 190.

Section XV.

Śaka 1160, the date of the Aṁbeṁ inscription. For Râma's son is represented to have been a minor under the guardianship of that chief's sister Lakshmî, who governed the principality in the name of the boy. Râma, therefore, had not died so many years before Śaka 1160 as to allow of his boy having attained his majority by that time. On the occasion of this expedition Vîsaladeva, the son of Vîradhavala, was the sovereign of Gujarât. For in an inscription of his he boasts [111] of his having been "the submarine fire that dried up the ocean of Siṅghaṇa's army,"[28] and he must have succeeded his father about the year 1292 Vikrama corresponding to Śaka 1157,[29] though he obtained possession of the throne at Anahilapattana in Vîkrama 1302, corresponding to Śaka 1167 and 1246 A.D. The foundation of his boast was probably the fact of Râma's having been killed in the battle. What the ultimate result was, however, the inscription does not inform us.

Conquests in the South.

Siṅghaṇa appointed one Bîchaṇa or Bîcha, the son of Chikka and younger brother of Malla, to be governor of the southern provinces and his viceroy there. He fought with his master's enemies in the south as Kholeśvara did in the north and kept them in check. Bîchaṇa is represented to have humbled the Raṭṭas who were petty feudatories in the Southern Marâṭhâ Country, the Kadambas of Konkan, *i.e.* of Goa, the Guttas sprung from the ancient Guptas, who held a principality in the south, the Pâṇḍyas, the Hoysaḷas, and the chiefs of other southern provinces, and to have erected a triumphal

28 Ind. Ant., Vol. VI. pp. 191 and 212.

29 Vîradhavala, it is said, died not long before Vastupâla. The death of the latter took place in Vikrama 1297. Vastupâla was minister to Vîsaladeva also for some time. We might, therefore, refer the accession of the latter to Vikrama 1292. Ind. Ant., Vol. VI., p. 190.

Section XV.

column on the banks of the Kâverî.[30] The date of the grant in which all this is recorded is Śaka 1160 or A.D. 1238.

Siṅghaṇa's titles.

It thus appears that the Yâdava empire became in the time of Siṅghaṇa as extensive as that ruled over by the ablest monarchs of the preceding dynasties. The full title of a paramount sovereign are given to Siṅghaṇa in his inscriptions, such as "the support of the whole world," "the lover of the earth (*Pṛithvîvallabha*)," and "king of kings." Since Kṛishṇá, the eighth incarnation of Vishṇu, is represented in the Purâṇas to have belonged to the Yâdava family, the princes of Devagiri called themselves *Vishṇuvaṁśodbhava* ;[31] and as Kṛishṇa and his immediate descendants reigned at Dvârakâ, they assumed the title of *Dvâravatîpuravarâdhîśvara,* "the supreme lord of Dvâravatî, the best of cities."[32] In the reign of Siṅghaṇa as well as of his two predecessors the office of chief secretary or *Śrîkaraṇâdhipa,* which in a subsequent reign was conferred on Hemâdri, was held by a man of the name of Soḍhala. He was the son of Bhâskara, a native of Kaśmîr who had settled in the Dekkan. Soḍhala's son Śaṅgadhara wrote in this reign a treatise on music entitled Saṁgîtaratnâkara which is extant.[33] There is a com-

---

[30] Jour. B. B. R. A. S., Vol. XV., pp. 386-7, and Vol. XII., p. 43.

[31] *i.e.* "of the race of Vishṇu."

[32] Graham's Report, Ins. No. 10, and Jour. B. B. R. A. S., Vol. XII., p. 7.

[33] तस्याभूत्तनयः प्रभूतविनयः श्रीसोढलः प्रौढधीर्येन श्रीकरणप्रबन्धविभवं भूपश्रमं भिल्लमम् । आराध्याखिललोकशोकशमनी कीर्त्तिः समासादिता जैत्रे जैत्रपदं व्यधायि महती श्रीसिंहणे श्रीरपि ॥ Then follows one verse in praise of Siṅghaṇa, and two in praise of Soḍhala in which he is represented to have pleased Siṅghaṇa by his merits and to have conferred benefits on all through the wealth and influence thus acquired; and then we have

Section XV.

mentary [112] on this work attributed to a king of the name of Siṅga who is represented as a paramount sovereign of the Andhra circle. This Siṅga appears in all likelihood to be Siṅghaṇa ; and the commentary was either written by him or dedicated to him by a dependant, as is often the case.[34] Châṅgadeva, the grandson of Bhâskarâchârya and son of Lakshmîdhara, was chief astrologer to Siṅghaṇa ; and also Anantadeva, the grandson of Bhâskarâchârya's brother Śrîpati and son of Gaṇapati. Châṅgadeva founded a Maṭha or college for the study of his grandfather's Siddhântaśiromaṇi and other works at Pâṭṇâ in the Châlisgaṁv division of the Khândeś district, and Anantadeva built a temple at a village in the same division and dedicated it to Bhavânî on the 1st of Chaitra in the Śaka year 1144 *expired.*[35]

Jaitrapâla, Siṅghaṇa's son, died before him.

Siṅghaṇa's son was Jaitugi or Jaitrapâla, who "was the abode of all arts, and was thus the very moon in opposition, full of all the digits, that had come down to the earth, to protect it. He was death to hostile kings and firm in unequal fights."[36] But if he protected the earth at all he must have done so during the lifetime of his father as *Yuvarâja,* for the latest date of Siṅghaṇa is Śaka 1169, and in a copper-plate inscription of his grandson and Jaitugi's son Kṛishṇa, Śaka 1175, *Pramâdi-Saṁvatsara,* is stated to be the seventh of his reign, so that Kṛishṇa began

---

तस्मादुग्धाम्बुधेर्जातः शार्ङ्गदेवः सुधाकरः । उपर्युपरि सर्वाम्बः सदोदारः स्फुरत्करः ॥ Introduction to Saṁgîtaratnâkara, No. 979, Collection of 1887—91, Dekk. Coll. इति श्रीमदनविनोदश्रीकरणाधिपतिश्रीसोढलनन्दननिःशङ्कश्रीशार्ङ्गदेवविरचिते संगीतरत्नाकरे प्रकीर्णकाध्यायस्तृतीयः समाप्तः fol. 122*a*.

[34] My Report on MSS. for 1882-83, pp. 37, 38 and 222.

[35] Jour. R. A. S., Vol. I., N. S., p. 415, and Epigraphia Indica, Vol. III., p. 113.

[36] Appendix C. II., st. 7.

Section XV. to reign in Śaka 1169 corresponding to 1247 A.D.[37] And in the longer of the two historical introductions to the Vratakhaṇḍa, Jaitugi is not mentioned at all.

Kṛishṇa. After Siṅghaṇa, we are told that his grandsons Kṛishṇa and Mahâdeva came to the throne, of whom the elder Kṛishṇa reigned first.[38] Kṛishṇa's Prâkṛit name was Kanhâra, Kanhara, or Kandhâra. He is represented to have been the terror of the kings of Mâlava, Gujarât, and Konkan, to have "established the king of Teluṅga," and to have been the sovereign of the country of the Chola king.[39] In the Vratakhaṇḍa also he is said to have destroyed the army of Vîsala, who we know was sovereign of Gujarât at this time and who had been at war with Siṅghaṇa, and, in general terms, to have "conquered a great many enemies in bloody battles in which numbers of horses and elephants were engaged, reduced some to captivity and compelled others to seek refuge in forests, and, having thus finished the work of vanquishing the series of earthly kings, to have marched to the heavenly world to conquer Indra."[40] Lakshmîdeva, son of Janârdana, is represented by his wise counsels to have helped Kṛishṇa to consolidate his power and to have by his sword subdued his enemies.[41] Kṛishṇa performed a great many sacrifices

[113]

37 Jour. B. B. R. A. S., Vol. XII., p. 42.

38 Appendix C. I., st. 45.

39 Jour. B. B. R. A. S., Vol. XII., p. 38.

40 That is, "left this world," "died," Appendix C. II., st. 11.

41 Intr. Jahl. Sukt. :—

विश्वासैकपरायणः स्फुरदुरुप्रज्ञाचिंतार्थिव्रज-
साम्राज्याद्भुतविक्रमः समभवल्लक्ष्मीधिदेवः सुधीः ।
मन्त्रैर्निर्जितदेवमन्त्रिविषयैर्जायन्नयप्रक्रमे
राज्यं कृष्णमहीपतेरविकलं दत्वा स्थिरं योऽभ्यधात् ॥ २१ ॥
अगस्त्य इव यस्यासिर्व्यथितक्षितिभृद्भवौ ।
चित्रं सोऽप्यकरोन्नृत्यद्रक्तवन्यसमरार्णवम् ॥ २२ ॥

and thus "brought fresh strength to the Vedic ceremonial religion which in the course of time had lost its hold over the people." In a copper-plate grant dated Śaka 1171, found in the Belgaum Tâluka, Malla or Mallisetti is spoken of as the elder brother of Bîcha or Bîchaṇa, the viceroy of Siṅghaṇa in the south, and was himself governor of the province of Kuhuṇḍ. He lived at Mudugala, probably the modern Mudgala, and gave, by the consent of Kṛishṇa, his sovereign, lands in the village of Bâgevâḍi to thirty-two Brâhmaṇs of different Gotras.[42] Among the family names of these it is interesting to observe some borne by modern Mahârâshṭra Brâhmaṇs, such as *Paṭavardhana* and *Ghaisâsa*, prevalent among Chitpâvanas, and *Ghaḷisâsa*, *Ghaḷisa*, and *Pâṭhaka*, among Deśasthas. The name *Trivâḍi* also occurs; but there is no trace of it among Marâṭhâ Brâhmaṇs, while it is borne by Brâhmaṇs in Gujarât and Upper Hindustan. In another grant, Chauṇḍa the son of Bîchaṇa, who succeeded to the office and title of his father, is represented to have personally solicited king Kṛishṇa at Devagiri to permit him to grant the village mentioned therein.[43] Jahlaṇa, son of Lakshmîdeva who had succeeded his father, assisted Kṛishṇa diligently by his counsels in conjunction with his younger brother. He was commander of the troops of elephants and as such fought with Kṛishṇa's enemies. He compiled an anthology of select verses from Sanskrit poets, called Sûktimuktâvali, which is

---

42 Jour. B. B. R. A. S., Vol. XIII., p. 27. Ind. Ant., Vol. VII., 304. Kuhuṇḍi corresponds to a part of the modern Belgaum district.

43 Jour. B. B. R. A. S., Vol. XII., p. 43.

Section XV. extant.[44] The Vedântakalpataru, which is a commentary on Vâchaspatimiśra's Bhâmatî [114] which itself is a commentary on Śaṁkarâchârya's Vedânta-sûtrabhâshya, was written by Amalânanda in the reign of Kṛishṇa.[45]

Mahâdeva.

Kṛishṇa was succeeded by his brother Mahâdeva in 1182 Śaka or 1260 A. D. "He was a tempestuous wind that blew away the heap of cotton in the shape of the king of the Tailaṅga country, the prowess of his arm was like a thunderbolt that shattered the mountain in the shape of the pride of the swaggering Gûrjara, he destroyed the king of Konkan with ease, and reduced the arrogant sovereigns of Karṇâta and Lâṭa to mockery."[46] The Gûrjara here mentioned must be Vîsaladeva noticed above, as Mahâdeva is represented in the Paiṭhaṇ grant to have vanquished him ;[47] and the king of Karṇâta was probably a Hoysaḷa Yâdava of Haḷebîd. "King Mahâdeva never killed a woman, a child, or one who submitted to him ; knowing this and being greatly afraid of him, the Andhras placed a woman on the throne ;

---

[44] Intr. Jahl. Sukt. :—

तस्यास्ते वनधी नवीदधिविधुर्बन्धुर्बुधानां सुधीः
सारासारविचारचारु चतुरः श्रीजल्हणाख्यः क्षितौ ॥ २६ ॥
मत्पित्रा ह्यन्तमस्मै प्रतिकृतनवयङ्केपि सर्गोपसर्गे
राज्यं प्राज्यप्रभावप्रथितभुजभता जयराजाय भक्त्या ।
तन्निर्वाह्यं भवीति त्रिगुणितविषयाप्रतिभक्तिर्विधत्ते
सर्वं यः स्वामि (मि) कार्यं क्षितसमयहता भावुकीभागुणेन ॥ २७ ॥
भुवं यस्याक्षि ह्रस्वाभं महाम्भा करिवाहिनी ।
दानोदकप्रवाहेण हस्त्यति कायमन्यथा ॥ २८ ॥
तेनेयं क्रियते वीक्ष्य सत्सुभाषितसंग्रहान् ।
सूक्तिमुक्तावलीकण्ठकन्दलीभूषणं सताम् ॥ २८ ॥

[45] Transactions Ninth Congress of Orientalists, Vol. I., p 423.

[46] Appendix C. I., st. 48, and II., st. 13.

[47] Ind. Ant., Vol. XIV., p. 316.

Section XV.

and the king of Mâlava also for the same reason installed a child in his position, and forthwith renouncing all his possessions practised false penance for a long time. He took away in battle the elephants and the five musical instruments of the ruler of Tailaṇgaṇa, but left the ruler Rudramâ as he refrained from killing a woman."[48] In a work on Poetics called Pratâparudrîya by Vidyânatha there occurs a specimen of a dramatic play in which Gaṇapati of the Kâkatîya dynasty, the same prince who is represented in the Paiṭhaṇ grant to have been released from confinement by Jaitugi, is mentioned as having left his throne to his daughter, whom, however, he called his son and named Rudra, and who is spoken of as "a king" and not queen. She adopted Pratâparudra, the son of her daughter, as her heir. This, therefore, was the woman spoken of above as Rudramâ and as having been placed on the throne by the Andhras.[49] "Soma, the lord of Konkan, though skilled in swimming in the sea, was together with his forces drowned in the rivers formed by the humour trickling from the temples of Mahâdeva's maddened elephants." "Mahâdeva deprived Someśvara of his kingdom and his life.[50] We have seen that Kṛishṇa fought with the king of Konkan, but it appears he did not subjugate the country thoroughly. His successor Mahâdeva, however, again invaded it with an army consisting of a large number of elephants. [115] Soma or

Conquest of Northern Konkan.

---

48 Appendix C. I., st. 52, and II., st. 14 and 15.

49 एवमेतत्। अन्यथा कथमीश्वरप्रसादादृते निरङ्कुशं स्त्रीव्यक्ति-विशेषस्य लोकाधिपत्यम्। एवं मातुपन्मुना गणपतिमहाराजेनाभ्यन्तर-स्यानुभावस्य सदृशमेव पुत्र इति व्यवहारः कृतश्चादगुणा च रुद्र इत्याख्या। Poona lithographed edition of Śaka 1771, fol. 29. See also Dr. Hultzsch's paper, Ind. Ant., Vol. XXI., pp. 198, 199.

50 Appendix C. I., st. 49, 50, and II., st. 17.

Section XV. Someśvara was completely defeated on land and his power broken, whereupon he appears to have betaken himself to his ships. There somehow he met with his death,[51] probably by being drowned, for it is said that "even the sea did not protect him" and that "he betook himself to the submarine fire," thinking the fire of Mahâdeva's prowess to be more unbearable.[52] Konkan was thereupon annexed to the territories of the Yâdavas. Hence it is that the country was governed by a viceroy appointed by the Devagiri king during the time of Mahâdeva's successor, as we find from the Ṭhânâ plates published by Mr. Wathen.[53] The Someśvara whom Mahâdeva subdued belonged to the Śilâhâra dynasty of Ṭhânâ that had been ruling over that part of Konkan for a considerable period. He is the last prince of the dynasty whose inscriptions are found in the district, and his dates are Śaka 1171 and 1182.[54] Mahâdeva like his predecessors reigned at Devagiri, which is represented as the capital of the dynasty to which he belonged and as situated in the country called Seuṇa on the borders of Daṇḍakâraṇya. "It was the abode of the essence of the beauty of the three worlds and its houses rivalled the peaks of the mountain tenanted by gods, and the Seuṇa country deserved all the sweet and ornamental epithets that might be applied to it."[55] At Paṇḍharpur there is an inscription dated 1192 Śaka, *Pramoda Saṁvatsara,* in which Mahâdeva is represented to have

[51] Appendix C. I., st. 49.

[52] *Ib.* I., st. 51, and II., st. 18.

[53] Jour. R. A. S. (old series), Vol. V., p. 177.

[54] Bombay Gazetteer, Vol. XIII., Part II.; p. 422.

[55] Appendix C. II., st. 19 and 20. "The mountain tenanted by gods" may be the Himâlaya or Meru. In this epithet there is a reference to the etymology of Devagiri which means "a mountain of or having gods."

Section XV.

been reigning at the time. He is there called *Prauḍhapratâpa Chakravartin,* or "Paramount sovereign possessing great valour." The inscription records the performance of an *Aptoryâma* sacrifice by a Brâhmaṇ chief of the name of Keśava belonging to the Kaśyapa Gotra.

Râmachandra or Râmadeva.

The immediate successor of Mahâdeva was Âmaṇa[56] who appears to have been his son ; but the sovereign power was soon wrested from his hands by the rightful heir Râmachandra, son of Kṛishṇ, who ascended the throne in 1193 Śaka or 1271 A.D. He is called Râmadeva or Râmarâja also. In the Ṭhânâ copper-plate grants he is spoken of as "a lion to the proud elephant in the shape of the lord of Mâlava," from which it would appear that he was at war with that country. He is also called "the elephant that tore up by the root the tree in the shape of the Tailaṅga king." This must be an allusion to his wars with Pratâparudra the successor of Rudramâ, which are mentioned in the work noticed above. Several other epithets occur in the grants ; but they are given as mere *birudas* or titles which were inherited by Râmachandra from his predecessors, and do not point to any specific events in his reign. His inscriptions are found as far to the south as the confines of Maisur, so that the empire [116] he ruled over was as large as it ever was. There is in the Dekkan College Library a manuscript of the Amarakośa written in Konkan on Tâla leaves during his reign in the year 4398 of the Kaliyuga corresponding to Śaka 1219 and A.D. 1297. His viceroy in Konkan in Śaka 1212 was a Brâhmaṇa named Kṛishṇa belonging to the Bhâradvâja Gotra, whose grandfather Padmanâbha first acquired royal

56 Paiṭhaṇ grant, Ind. Ant., Vol. XIV., p. 317.

Section XV.

favour and rose into importance in the reign of Siṅghaṇa. One of the Ṭhânâ grants was issued by him, and the other dated 1194 Śaka by Achyuta Nâyaka, who was also a Brâhmaṇ and who appears to have been a petty chief and held some office which is not stated. Where he resided is also not clear. By the Paiṭhaṇ copper-plate charter, which was issued in Śaka 1193, Râmachandra assigned three villages to fifty-seven Brâhmaṇs on conditions some of which are rather interesting. The Brâhmaṇs and their descendants were to live in those villages, not to mortgage the land, allow no prostitutes to settle there, prevent gambling, use no weapons, and spend their time in doing good deeds.[57]

Hemâdri, the minister of Mahâdeva and Râmadeva.

Hemâdri, the celebrated author, principally of works on Dharmaśâstra, flourished during the reigns of Mahâdeva and Râmachandra and was minister to both. In the introduction to his works on Dharmaśâstra he is called Mahâdeva's *Śrîkaraṇâdhipa* or *Śrîkaraṇaprabhu*. In the Ṭhânâ copper-plate of 1194 Śaka also, he is said to have taken upon himself the *âdhipatya* or controllership of all *karaṇa*. This office seems to have been that of chief secretary or one who wrote and issued all orders on behalf of his master and kept the state record. Hemâdri is also called *Mantrin* or counsellor generally. In his other works and in the Ṭhânâ plate Râmarâja instead of Mahâdeva is represented as his master. Mahâdeva's genealogy and his own are given at the beginning of his works on Dharma. Sometimes the former begins with Siṅghaṇa, sometimes with Bhillama, while in the Dânakhaṇḍa the exploits of Mahâdeva alone are enumerated. The description of the several princes is often couched in general

---

57 Ind. Ant., Vol. XIV., p. 319.

terms and consists of nothing but eulogy. But the Vratakhaṇḍa, which was the first work composed by Hemâdri, contains, as we have seen, a very valuable account of the dynasty from the very beginning, and by far the greater portion of it is undoubtedly historical.

Hemâdri's Works.

Hemâdri was a Brâhmaṇ of the Vatsa Gotra. His father's name was Kâmadeva, grandfather's, Vâsudeva, and great-grandfather's, Vâmana.[58] He is described in terms of extravagant praise ; and the historical truth that may be gleaned from it appears to be this. Hemâdri was very liberal to Brâhmaṇs and fed numbers of them every day. He was a man of learning himself, and learned men found a generous patron in him. He is represented to be religious and pious, and at the same time very brave. He evidently possessed a great deal of influence. Whether the voluminous works attributed to him were really written by him may well be questioned ; but the [117] idea at least of reducing the religious practices and observances that had descended from times immemorial to a system must certainly have been his, and must have been carried out under his supervision.

Chaturvarga Chintâmaṇi.

His great work is called the *Chaturvarga Chintâmaṇi,* which is divided into four parts, viz., (1) *Vratakhaṇḍa,* containing an exposition of the religious fasts and observances ; (2) *Dânakhaṇḍa,* in which the several gifts to which great religious importance is attached are explained ; (3) *Tîrthakhaṇḍa,* which treats of pilgrimages to holy places ; and (4) *Mokshakhaṇḍa,* in which the way to final deliverance is set forth. There is a fifth *Khaṇḍa* or part which is called *Pariśeshakhaṇḍa* or appendix, which contains voluminous treatises on (1) the deities

58 Pariśeshakhaṇḍa, Ed. Bib. Ind., pp. 4-5.

Section XV.

that should be worshipped, (2) on *Śrâddhas* or offerings to the manes, (3) on the determination of the proper times and seasons for the performance of religious rites, and (4) on *Prâyaśchitta* or atonement. All these works are replete with a great deal of information and innumerable quotations. They are held in great estimation, and future writers on the same subjects draw largely from them. A commentary called *Âyurvedarasâyana* on a medical treatise by Vâgbhaṭa and another on Bopadeva's *Muktâphala,* a work expounding Vaishṇava doctrines, are also attributed to him.

Other works.

Bopadeva.

This Bopadeva was one of Hemâdri's protegees and the author of the work mentioned above and another entitled Harilîlâ, which contains an abstract of the Bhâgavata. Both of these were written at the request of Hemâdri as the author himself tells us.[59] Bopadeva was the son of a physician named Keśava and the pupil of Dhaneśa. His father as well as a teacher lived at a place called Sârtha situated on the banks of the Varadâ. Bopadeva, therefore, was a native of Berâr. Bopadeva, the author of a treatise on grammar called *Mugdhabodha,* appears to be the same person as this, since the names of the father and the teacher there mentioned are the same as those we find in these works. A few medical treatises also, written by Bopadeva, have come down to us.

Hemâḍpant of the Marâṭhâs.

Hemâdri has not yet been forgotten in the Marâṭhâ country. He is popularly known by the name of Hemâḍpant and old temples throughout the

---

59 विद्वद्धनेशशिष्येण भिषक्केशवसूनुना । हेमाद्रिर्बोपदेवेन मुक्ताफलमचीकरत् ॥ श्रीमद्भागवतस्कन्धाध्यायार्थादि निरूप्यते । विदुषा बोपदेवेन मन्त्रिहेमाद्रितुष्टये ॥ Dr. Râjendralâl's notices of Skr. MSS., Vol. II., pp. 48 and 200.

country of a certain structure are attributed to him. He is said to have introduced the moḍî or the current form of writing and is believed to have brought it from Lankâ or Ceylon. As chief secretary he had to superintend the writing of official papers and records, and it is possible he may have introduced some improvements in the mode of writing.

Section XV.

Jñâneśvara, the Marâṭhâ sâdhu.

The great Marâṭhâ *sâdhu* or saint Jñâneśvara or Dnyâneśvara as his name is ordinarily pronounced, flourished during the reign of [118] Râmachandra. At the end of his Marâṭhî commentary on the Bhagavadgîtâ he tells us: "In the Kali age, in the country of Mahârâshṭra and on the southern bank of the Godâvarî, there is a sacred place five *kos* in circuit, the holiest in the three worlds, where exists Mahâlayâ, who is the thread that sustains the life of the world. There, king Râmachandra, a scion of the Yadu race and the abode of all arts, dispenses justice, and there a vernacular garb was prepared for the Gîtâ by Jñânadeva, the son of Nivṛittinâtha, sprung from the family of Maheśa."[60] The date of the completion of the work is given as Śaka 1212 or A.D. 1290, when we know Râmachandra was on the throne.

Conquest of the country by the Mussalmans.

Râmachandra was the last of the independent Hindu sovereigns of the Dekkan. The Mussalmans

60 ऐसें युगीं परि कळीं । आणि महाराष्ट्रमंडळीं ।
श्रीगोदावरीच्या कूळीं । दक्षिणकळीं ॥ १ ॥
त्रिभुवनैकपवित्र । अनादि पंचक्रोशक्षेत्र ।
जेथ जगाचें जीवनसूत्र । श्रीमहालया असे ॥ २ ॥
तेथ यदुवंशविलास । जो सकळकळानिवास ।
न्यायातें पोषी क्षितीश । श्रीरामचंद्र ॥ ३ ॥
तेथ महेशान्वयसंभूतें । श्रीनिवृत्तिनाथसुतें ।
केलें ज्ञानदेवें गीते । देशीकार लेणें ॥ ४ ॥

Section XV. had been firmly established at Delhi for about a century, and though they had not yet turned their attention to the Dekkan it was not possible they should refrain from doing so for a long time. Alla-ud-din Khiliji, the nephew of the reigning king, who had been appointed governor of Karra, was a person of a bold and adventurous spirit. In the year 1294 A.D. or Śaka 1216 he collected a small army of 8000 men and marched straight to the south till he reached Ellichpur, and then suddenly turning to the west appeared in a short time before Devagiri. The king never expected such an attack and was consequently unprepared to resist it. According to one account he was even absent from his capital. He hastily collected about 4000 troops, and threw himself between the city and invading army. But being aware he could not hold out for a long time, he took measures for provisioning the fort and retired into it. The city was then taken by the Mahomedans and plundered, and the fort was closely invested. Alla-ud-din had taken care to spread a report that his troops were but the advanced guard of the army of the king which was on its way to the Dekkan. Râmachandra, therefore, despairing of a successful resistance, began to treat for peace. Alla-ud-din, who was conscious of his own weakness, received his proposals with gladness and agreed to raise the siege and retire on condition of receiving from the king a large quantity of gold. In the meantime, Râmachandra's son Śaṁkara collected a large army and was marching to the relief of the fort, when Alla-ud-din left about a thousand men to continue the siege and proceeded [119] with the rest to a short distance from the town and gave battle to Śaṁkara's forces. The Hindus were numerically superior and forced the Mahomedans to fall back ;

but the detachment left to observe the movements of the garrison joined them at this time, and Śaṁkara's followers thinking it to be the main army that was on its way from Delhi were seized with a panic, and a confusion ensued which resulted in the complete defeat of the Hindus.

Râmachandra or Râmadeva then continued the negotiations, but Alla-ud-din raised his demands. The Hindu king's allies were preparing to march to his assistance, but in the meanwhile Râmachandra discovered that the sacks of grain that had been hastily thrown into the fort really contained salt; and since the provisions had been well nigh exhausted he was anxious to hasten the conclusion of peace. It was therefore agreed that he should pay to Alla-ud-din "600 maunds of pearls, two of jewels, 1000 of silver, 4000 pieces of silk, and other precious things," cede Ellichpur and its dependencies, and send an annual tribute to Delhi. On the receipt of the valuable treasure given to him by the Devagiri prince Alla-ud-din retired.

Some time after, Alla-ud-din assassinated his aged uncle and usurped the throne. King Râmachandra did not send the tribute for several years, and to punish him the Delhi monarch despatched an expedition of 30,000 horse under the command of Malik Kafur, a slave who had risen high in his favour. Malik Kafur accomplished the long and difficult march "over stones and hills without drawing rein," and arrived at Devagiri in March 1307 A.D., or about end of Śaka 1228. A fight ensued in which the Hindus were defeated and Râmadeva was taken prisoner.[61] According to another account, Malik

61 Elliot's History of India, Vol. III., p. 77.

Section XV. Kafur came laying waste the country about Devagiri, and the Hindu king observing the futility of resistance surrendered himself. Râmachandra was sent to Delhi, where he was detained for six months and afterwards released with all honour. Thenceforward he sent the tribute regularly and remained faithful to the Mahomedans. In Śaka 1231 or A.D. 1309, Malik Kafur was again sent to the Dekkan to subdue Tailaṅgaṇa. On the way he stopped at Devagiri, where he was hospitably entertained by the king.

Râmadeva died this year and was succeeded by his son Śaṁkara. He discontinued sending the annual tribute to Delhi and Malik Kafur was again sent to the Dekkan in Śaka 1234 or A.D. 1312 to reduce him to submission. He put Śaṁkara to death, laid waste his kingdom, and fixed his residence at Devagiri.

In the latter years of Alla-ud-din his nobles, disgusted with the overwhelming influence which Malik Kafur had acquired over him, revolted. In the meantime Alla-ud-din died and was succeeded by his third son Mubarik. The opportunity was seized [120] by Harapâla, the son-in-law of Râmachandra, who raised an insurrection and drove away some of the Mahomedan governors. In 1240 Śaka or A.D. 1318 Mubarik marched to the Dekkan in person to suppress the revolt. He took Harapâla prisoner and inhumanly flayed him alive.

Thus ended the last Hindu or Marâṭhâ monarchy of the Dekkan, and the country became a province of the Mahomedan empire.

Genealogy of the later Yâdavas or the Yâdavas of Devagiri. **Section XV.**

Mallugi.

1. BHILLAMA
(Śaka 1109-1113 or A.D. 1187-1191.)

2. JAITRAPÂLA or Jaitugi.
(Śaka 1113-1132 or A.D. 1191-1210.)

3. SINGHAṆA
(Śaka 1132-1169 or A.D. 1210-1247.)

Jaitrapâla or Jaitugi.

4. KṚISHṆA, Kanhâra or Kandhâra.
(Śaka 1169-1182 or A.D. 1247-1260.)

6. RÂMACHANDRA or Râmadeva.
(Śaka 1193-1231 or A.D. 1271-1309.)

7. ŚAMKARA (Śaka 1231-1234 or A.D. 1309-1312.)

Brother-in-law, Harapâla, killed in Śaka 1240 or A.D. 1318.

5. MAHÂDEVA
(Śaka 1182-1193 or A.D. 1260-1271.)

Âmaṇa.

[121] SECTION XVI.

The Silâhâras of Kolhâpur.

Section XVI.

Three branches of the Silâhâra family.

Three distinct families of chiefs or minor princes with the name of Silâra or Silâhâra ruled over different parts of the country. They all traced their origin to Jîmûtavâhana the son of Jîmûtaketu, who was the king of a certain class of demigods called Vidyâdharas, and who saved the life of a serpent named Sankhachûḍa by offering himself as a victim to Garuḍa in his place.[1] One of the titles borne by the princes of all the three families was *Tagarapuravarâdhîśvara* or "lords of Tagara, the best of cities," which fact has a historical significance. We have seen that Kâṁvadeva, the donor of the Râjâpur grant who was a Châlukya, called himself *Kalyâṇapuravarâdhîśvara*, and one of the titles of the later Kadambas after they had been reduced to vassalage and of the rulers of Goa was *Banavâsîpuravarâdhîśvara*. As these titles signify that the bearers of them belonged to the families that once held supreme power at Kalyâṇa and Banavâsî, so does

Tagara, the original seat of the family.

Tagarapuravarâdhîśvara show that the Silâhâras who bore the title belonged to a family that once possessed supreme sovereignty and reigned at Tagara. In one Silâhâra grant it is expressly stated that "the race known by the name of Silâhâra was that of the kings who were masters of Tagara."[2] As mentioned in a former section, Tagara was a famous town in the early centuries of the Christian

---

1 This story has been dramatized in the Sanskrit play Nâgânanda attributed to Srî-Harsha.

2 Grant translated by Dr. Taylor and published in the Transactions of the Literary Society of Bombay, Vol. III. शिलाहाराख्यवंशोयं तगरेश्वरभूभृताम् ।

Section XVI.

era and retained its importance till a very late period, but unfortunately the town has not yet been identified, nor have we found any trace of the Śilâhâra kingdom with Tagara as its capital. Perhaps it existed between the close of the Andhrabhṛitya period and the foundation of the Châlukya power.

The North Konkan branch.

The three Śilâhâra dynasties of Mahâmaṇḍaleśvaras or dependent princes which we have been considering were founded in the times of the Râshṭrakûṭas. One of them ruled over Northern Konkan, which was composed of fourteen hundred villages, the chief of them being Purî, which probably was at one time the capital of the province. As represented in an inscription at Kânheri noticed before, Konkan was assigned to Pullaśakti by Amoghavarsha a few years before Śaka 775.

The South Konkan branch.

Another Śilâhâra family established itself in Southern Konkan. The founder or first chief named Śaṇaphulla enjoying the favour of Kṛishṇarâja acquired the territory between the sea-coast and the Sahya range.[3] There were three Râshṭrakûṭa princes of the name of Kṛishṇarâja but the one meant here must be the first prince of that name who reigned in the last quarter of the seventh century of the Śaka era [122] or between 753 and 775 A.D.[4] The genealogy

3 Khârepâṭan plates, Jour. B. B. R. A. S., Vol. I., p. 217. The name of the first chief is read "Jhallaphulla" by Bâl Gangâdhara Śâstrî; but the first letter looks like स though there is some difference. That difference, however, brings it nearer to श. The letter which was read by him as झ is clearly ण. For दैवसंभावनो I find दैवसंवावनो on the plates.

4 From Śaṇaphulla the first chief to Raṭṭa the last three are ten generations. Somehow each succeeding chief in this line happens to be the son of the preceding. Though in a line of princes some of whom bear to others the relation of brother or uncle, the average duration of each reign is

Section XVI.

of this dynasty is given in the Khârepâṭaṇ grant, the last prince mentioned in which was on the throne in Śaka 930 while the Châlukya king Satyâśraya was reigning. The capital must have been situated somewhere near Khârepâṭaṇ.

The Kolhâpur branch.

The third Śilâhâra family the history of which falls within the scope of this paper ruled over the districts of Kolhâpur, Miraj, and Karhâḍ, and in later times Southern Konkan was added to its territory. This dynasty was the latest of the three and was founded about the time of the downfall of the Râshṭrakûṭa empire, as will be hereafter shown. The first prince of the family was Jatiga, who was succeeded by his son Nâyimma or Nâyivarman.

---

from 19 to 21 years; the average duration of a generation is always much longer, and varies from 26 to 28 years. One can verify this by taking any line of princes or chiefs in the world. Raṭṭa was on the throne in Śaka 930, and supposing him to have begun to reign about that time, nine generations or about 27×9 years must have passed away from the date of the foundation of the family to Śaka 930. Subtracting 27×9=243 from 930, we have Śaka 687 as the approximate date of Śaṇaphulla. If we take the average to be 26, we shall have 696 as the date. In either case we are brought to the reign of Kṛishṇa I. The dates of Kṛishṇa II. range from Śaka 797 to 833 and of Kṛishṇa III. from Śaka 862 to 881, and therefore neither of these will do. Even if we take the other average of a reign in the present case and subtract 19×9=171 from 930, we get Śaka 759, which will not take us to the reign of Kṛishṇa II. whose earliet date is Śaka 797. The Khârepâṭaṇ family therefore was the oldest of the three, and was founded in the reign of Kṛishṇa I.

Bâl Śâstrî read the name of the last chief in the grant as Rahu; but the second syllable of the name is certainly not ट्ट the form of which in the grant itself is different. It looks exactly like the ट्ट in the word परमभट्टारक and भाषट्टगाणि which occur elsewhere in the grant.

Section XVI.

Jatiga, the founder.

Nâyimma was followed by his son Chandrarâja, and Chandrarâja by his son Jatiga, who is called "the lion of the hill-fortress of Panhâḷâ."[5] Jatiga's son and successor was Goṁka, otherwise called Goṁkala or Gokalla. He is represented to have been the ruler of the districts of Karahâṭa-Kuṇḍi[6] and Mairiñja and to have harassed Konkan. He had three brothers named Gûvala, Kîrtirâja, and Chandrâditya, of whom the first at least appears to have succeeded him. Then followed Mârasiṁha the son of Goṁka, whose grant first published by Wathen is dated Śaka 980. He is represented to have constructed temples ; and to have been reigning at his capital, the fort of Khiḷigiḷi, which probably was another name of Panhâḷâ in the Kolhâpur districts. Mârasiṁha was succeeded by his son Gûvala and he by his brother Bhoja I. Bhoja's two brothers Ballâḷa and Gaṇḍarâditya governed the principality after him in succession.

An inscription at Kolhâpur mentions another brother named Gañgadeva and the order in which the brothers are spoken of is Gûvala [123] Gañga, Ballâḷa, Bhoja, and Gaṇḍarâditya.[7] But the grants of Gaṇḍarâditya and Bhoja II. agree in representing Bhoja as the elder and Ballâḷa as the younger brother, and in omitting Gañga.

Gaṇḍarâditya.

Of all these brothers the youngest Gaṇḍarâditya seems to have been the most famous. He is the

---

5 See the grant of Gaṇḍarâditya published by Paṇḍit Bhagvânlâl Indraji in Jour. B. B. R. A. S., Vol. XIII., p. 2, of Mârasiṁha in Jour. R. A. S., Vol. IV., p. 280, and Arch. Surv. W.I., No. 10, p. 102, and of Bhoja II. in Trans. Lit. Soc. Bom., Vol. III.

6 Mârasiṁha's grant. Kuṇḍi or Kuhuṇḍi was some part of the Belgaum district, as stated before. Mairiñja is Miraj.

7 Inscription No. 4, Major Graham's Report.

Section XVI. donor, as indicated above, in the grant published by Paṇḍit Bhagvânlâl Indraji,[8] and in others recorded on stone at Kolhâpur and in the districts. His dates are Śaka 1032, 1040, 1058.[9] He ruled over the country of Miriñja along with the seven Khollas and over Konkan, which thus seems to have been subjugated by the Kolhâpur Śilâhâras before 1032. Probably it was added to their dominions in the time of Gonka or soon after. From the grant of Bhoja II. it appears that the part of Konkan ruled over by the Dekkan Śilâhâras was the same as that which was in the possession of the family mentioned in the Khârepâṭaṇ grant,[10] wherefore it follows that the Śilâhâras of southern Konkan were uprooted by their kinsmen of the Kolhâpur districts. Gaṇḍarâditya fed a hundred thousand Brâhmans at Prayâga. This must be the place of that name which is situated near Kolhâpur ; and not the modern Allahâbâd. He built a Jaina temple at Âjaram, a village in the Kolhâpur districts,[11] and constructed a large tank, called after him *Gaṇḍasamudra* or "the sea of Gaṇḍa," at Irukuḍi in the Miraj district, and on its margin placed idols of Îśvara or Śiva, Buddha, and Arhat (Jina), for the maintenance of each of which he assigned a piece of land. Several other charities of his, in which the Jainas also had their share, are mentioned, and his bountiful nature as well as good

---

8 In *loc. cit.*

9 Bhagvânlâl's plates, and Inscriptions Nos. 1, 2, and 3, Major Graham's Report. The Śaka in Bhagvânlâl's grant and No. 1 of Major Graham's inscriptions is the same, *i.e.* 1032, though in the translation of the latter it is erroneously given as 1037, but the cyclic years are different. As to this see Appendix B.

10 For the village granted is Kaśeḷî, which is near Jaitâpur and Khârepâṭaṇ.

11 Ind. Ant., Vol. X., p. 76, note.

Section XVI.

and just government are extolled.[12] He first resided at a place called Tiravâḍa and afterwards at Valavâṭa, which has been identified with the present Valavdeṁ[13]

Vijayârka.

Gaṇḍarâditya was succeeded by his son Vijayârka, who was on the throne in Śaka 1065 and 1073.[14] He restored the chiefs of the territory about Ṭhânâ to their principality which they had lost, and replaced the princes of Goa on the throne and fortified their position which had become shaky.[15] He assisted Vijjaṇa[16] in his revolt against his masters, the Châlukyas of Kalyâṇa, and enabled him to acquire supreme sovereignty. This event, as we have seen, took place about 1079 Śaka.

Bhoja II.

[**124**] After Vijayârka, his son Bhoja II. became Mahâmaṇḍaleśvara and reigned in the fort of Panhâḷâ. His dates are Śaka 1101, 1109, 1112, 1113, 1114, and 1127.[17] He granted the village of Kaśeḷî in Konkan near Khârepâṭaṇ on the application of his son Gaṇḍarâditya for feeding Brâhmaṇs regularly ;[18] and gave lands for Hindu and Jaina

---

12 His grant in *loc. cit.*

13 Bhagvânlâl's plates and Major Graham's Ins. No. 2.

14 Ins. Nos. 4 and 5, Major Graham's Report.

15 Grant of Bhoja II. in *loc. cit.*

16 In the transcript of the inscription in Vol. IV. Trans. Lit. Soc. Bom. we have Vîkshaṇa for Vîjjaṇa. There is no question this must be a mistake of the reader of the inscription or of the engraver. For the Kalachuri usurper at Kalyâṇa is called both Vijjala or Vijjaṇa in his inscriptions, and there was none who about the date of Vijayârka obtained the position of a Chakravartin or paramount sovereign, as stated in the inscription.

17 Major Graham's Ins. Nos. 6, 7, 8, the grant, and Ind. Ant., Vol. X., p. 76, note.

18 There are, however, some mistakes here in the transcript of the grant and the sense is not clear, though it appears pretty certain that it was the village that was granted and not a field in it or anything else, from the fact that the boundaries of the village are given.

Section XVI. temples in other places also. Two of the grantees in one case at Kolhâpur are called Karahâṭakas, which shows that the caste of Karhâḍe Brâhmaṇs had come to be recognized in those days ; and two others bore the family name of *Ghaisâsa,* which is now found among Chitpâvan Brâhmaṇs.[19] In the reign of Bhoja II. a Jaina Paṇḍit of the name of Somadeva composed in Śaka 1127 a commentary entitled *Śabdârṇavachandrikâ*[20] on Pûjyapâda's Sanskrit Grammar. The Kolhâpur chiefs enjoyed a sort of semi-independence. Vijjaṇa, the new sovereign at Kalyâṇa, however, endeavoured probably to establish his authority over Bhoja. But that chief was not content to be his feudatory, and to reduce him to subjection Vijjaṇa marched against Kolhâpur a little before his assassination in Śaka 1089.[21] On the establishment of the power of the Devagiri Yâdavas, Bhoja seems similarly to have assumed independence ; but Siṅghaṇa subdued him completely, and annexed the principality to the Yâdava empire.[22]

Approximate date of the foundation of the Kolhâpur branch.

The number of generations from Jatiga, the founder of the dynasty, to Gaṇḍarâditya is seven. The latest date of the latter is Śaka 1058 and the earliest of his successor Vijayârka is 1065 ; so that if we suppose Gaṇḍarâditya to have died in 1060 and allow about 27 years to each generation, we shall arrive at Śaka 871 as the approximate date of the foundation of the family. At that time the reigning Râshṭrakûṭa sovereign was Kṛishṇa III., the uncle of Kakkala the last prince.

One of the many titles used by the Śilâhâras was

19 Ins. No. 8, Major Graham's Report.

20 Ind. Ant., Vol. X., p. 76, note. The manuscript here mentioned is in the Dekkan College library and I have seen in it the colophon given in the note.

21 Vijalarâya Charitra in Wilson's Mackenzie MSS. p. 320.

22 Sec. XV.

Section XVI.

Religion of the Kolhâpur Śilâhâras.

Śrîman-Mahâlakshmî-labdha-vara-prasâda, i.e. "one who has obtained the favour of a boon from the glorious Mahâlakshmî." Mahâlakshmî was thus their tutelary deity, and they were clearly the followers of the Purâṇic and Vedic religion ; but they patronized both Brâhmaṇs and Jainas alike ; and their impartiality is strikingly displayed by the fact noticed above of Gaṇḍarâditya's having placed an idol of Buddha, whose religion had well nigh become extinct, along with those of the gods worshipped by the other two sects, on the margin of the tank dug by him.

There are at the present day many Marâṭhâ families of the name of Selâra reduced to poverty, and the name Selâravâḍi of a station [126] on the railway from Khaṇḍâlâ to Poona is also, I believe, to be traced to the family name of the sovereigns of Tagara.

Genealogy of the Silâhâras of Kolhâpur.

- Jatiga I.
  - Nâyimma.
    - Chandrarâja.
      - Jatiga II.
        - Gomka.
          - Mârasimha, Śaka 980 or A.D. 1058.
            - Gûvala II.
            - Bhoja I.
            - Ballâḷa,
            - Gaṇḍâraditya, Śaka 1032, 1040, 1058, or A.D. 1110, 1118, 1136.
              - Vijayârka, Śaka 1065, 1073, or A.D. 1143, 1151.
                - Bhoja II, Śaka 1101, 1109, 1112, 1113, 1114, 1127, or A.D. 1179, 1187, 1190, 1191, 1192, 1205.
        - Gûvala I.
        - Kirtirâja.
        - Chandrâditya.

[126] APPENDIX A.

Note on the Gupta Era.

Appendix A.

In order to render the chronologies of the different dynasties that ruled over western and northern India in the early centuries of the Christian era mutually consistent, it is necessary to discuss the initial date of the Gupta era. Albiruni, who accompanied Mahmud of Ghizni in his invasion of Gujarât in the early part of the eleventh century, states that that era was posterior to the Śaka by 241 years, and that it was the epoch of the extermination of the Guptas. He mentions another era named after Balaba, the initial date of which was the same as that of the Guptas.

Now in some of the inscriptions of the Gupta kings and their dependent chiefs the dates are referred to *Guptakâla* or the Gupta era, wherefore Albiruni's statement that it was the epoch of their extermination cannot be true. This error is regarded as throwing discredit on his other statement, *viz.*, that the era was posterior to the Śaka by 241 years. But it has nothing whatever to do with it. Albiruni must have derived his knowledge of the initial date from contemporary evidence, since the era of the Guptas was, as stated by him, one of those ordinarily used in the country in his time, and as his statements regarding the initial dates of the Vikrama and the Śaka eras are true, so must that with reference to the Gupta era be true. On the other hand, his information as regards the event which the Gupta era memorialized must have been based upon the tradition current among the Hindu astronomers of the day, who were his informants. Such traditions are often erroneous, as has been proved in many a case.

Albiruni was also informed that the Śaka era was the epoch of the defeat of the Śaka king by Vikramâditya. This was the tradition as to its origin among Indian astronomers, though it has now given place to another. For Soḍhala in his commentary on Bhâskarâchârya's Karaṇakutûhala, a manuscript of which more than four hundred years old exists in the collection made by me for Government during 1882-83, tells us that "the epoch when Vikramâditya killed Mlechchhas of the name of Śakas is ordinarily known as the Śaka era." But we know that in Maṅgalîśa's inscription at Bâdâmî it is spoken of as the era of the "coronation of the Śaka king", that Ravikîrti in the inscription at Aihole describes it as the era of the Śaka kings and that it is similarly represented in many other places. Albiruni's error therefore as regards the origin of the Gupta era no more invalidates his statement as to its initial date than his error about the origin of the Śaka era does his statement about the initial date of that era. The only reasonable course for us under the circumstances is to reject the statement as to the era being an epoch of the extermination of the Guptas and accept that about the initial date of the era. But some antiquarians reject both these statements and accept what simply hangs on them and what must fall with them, *viz.*, that the Guptas were exterminated in Śaka 242, and make elaborate endeavours to find an earlier initial date for the era. If the inscriptions show that the era was not posthumous but contemporaneous, we should rather believe that the Guptas rose to power in Śaka 242, assigning its due value to the statement of Albiruni, which must have been based on contemporary evidence, that the era began in that year. But if instead of that we declare that they cease to reign in Śaka 242, we in

Appendix A. effect reject contemporary evidence and accept a mere tradition which in so far as it represents the era to be posthumous has been proved to be erroneous.

Again, Albiruni's statement that the initial date of the Gupta era and of the Valabhî era was the same seems to some not "at all probable." To [127] my mind the improbability is not so great as to render valueless what clearly is contemporary evidence. We all know that the date occuring in a grant of one of the sons of the founder of the dynasty is 207, and we have a large number of grants of subsequent kings with dates posterior to this and in harmony with it. So that it is clear that these dates cannot refer to an era dating from the foundation of the dynasty. Such a long time as 207 years cannot be considered to have elapsed between the father who founded the dynasty and his son, even supposing him to have been a posthumous son. The dates, therefore, are understood to refer to the Gupta era. What, then, could have been the Valabhî era, if it was never used by the Valabhî princes during the 275 years or thereabouts of the existence of their dynasty? An era cannot receive the name of a certain line of princes unless used by those princes, at least on a few occasions, and enforced. The era used by the Valabhî princes must be the Valabhî era. One certainly would expect that it should be so. The only supposition, therefore, on which the whole becomes intelligible is that the era introduced by the Valabhîs in Surâshṭra and used by them was called the Valabhî era by their subjects, and not one dating from the foundation of the dynasty ; for such a one, we see, was not used by the Valabhî princes themselves. The era introduced and used by the Valabhîs was that of the Guptas, whose dependents they were in the beginning, and hence Albiruni's statement that the initial date of the Gupta and Valabhî eras was the same is true. From an inscription at Somanâth discovered by Colonel Tod, we gather that Śaka 242 was the first year of the Valabhî era. Hence, therefore, the initial date of the Gupta era was 242 Śaka, as stated by Albiruni. **Appendix A.**

The question in this way is, I think, plain enough. Still since astronomical calculations have been resorted to to prove the incorrectness of the date given by Albiruni and to arrive at an earlier one so as to place the extinction of the Gupta dynasty in Śaka 242, it is necessary to go into the question further. The following tests may be used and have been used to determine the correctness of a proposed initial date:—

1. The date of Budha Gupta's pillar inscription at Eran, which is Thursday, the 12th of Âshâḍha, in the Gupta year 165.
2. Râjâ Hastin's inscription dated 156 Gupta, the year of the 12-year cycle of Jupiter being Mahâvaiśâka.
3. Râjâ Hastin's inscription dated 173 Gupta, the year of the 12-year cycle being Mahâśvayuja.
4. Râjâ Hastin's inscription dated 191 Gupta, the year of the 12-year cycle being Mahâchaitra.
5. Râjâ Saṁkshobha's inscription dated 209 Gupta, the year of the 12-year cycle being Mahâśvayuja.
6. An eclipse of the sun mentioned in the Morvi copper-plate grant dated 5th Phâlguna Sudi 585 of the Gupta era.

Before applying these tests to the initial date given by Albiruni, it must be premised that according to the Arabic author the Gupta era was 241

Appendix A. years posterior to the Śaka. To convert a Śaka date into a Valabhî date, or which is the same thing, into a Gupta date, he tells us to deduct from it the cube of 6 and the square of 5, that is, 241. And proceeding to give actual instances, he says 953 Śaka corresponds to 712 Valabhî or Gupta. We have thus to add 241 to a Gupta date to arrive at the corresponding Śaka date. Again, as I shall show in Appendix B, in inscriptions the numerical date indicates, in a large number of instances, the number of years of an era that have elapsed, that is, the *past* year and in about a third of the instances, the *current* year. The year of the cycle, however, whenever it occurs, is as a rule the current year, though in rare cases that also is the past year. If, therefore, a past Gupta year is to be converted into [128] the current Śaka year, we shall have to add 242 to the former ; while if both are current or both past, the difference between them is only 241.

Now, as to the first of the above tests, Gupta 165+241=406 Śaka. If Albiruni is correct, the 12th Âshâḍha Sudi of this year should be a Thursday. I asked my friend Professor Keru Lakshmaṇ Chhatre to make the calculation for me, and he tells me that it *was* a Thursday. Since our astronomical methods are based on the past Śaka year, and even our present Śaka year 1805 really represents, as I shall show in the next Appendix, the years that have elapsed, the current year being really 1806, Gupta 165 was a past year, as well as Śaka 406. Hence only 241 has to be added. Śaka 406 corresponds to 484 A.D. General Cunningham takes the Gupta 165 to correspond to 483 A.D., adding 240+78 =318 to it, and of course arrives at the result that "the 12th day of Âshâḍha Sudi was a Friday instead of a Thursday." If, however, he had added

241+78=319 and taken 484 A.D. to correspond to Gupta 165, he would have arrived at the correct result. Appendix A.

Then as to the dates in years of the 12-year cycle, General Cunningham himself has placed before us the means of verifying them. In the tables published by him in Volume X. of the Archæological Reports, the cyclic year corresponding to the *current* Christian year is given, and if we subtract 78 from the number representing the year, we shall arrive at the *current* Ŝaka year. Now, if we take the Gupta figured dates to represent the years that had elapsed before the cyclic year commenced, (and this way of marking the dates is, as remarked above, the one we usually find), then 173 Gupta, the third date in the above, corresponds to 414 Ŝaka *past* and 415 *current*, 241 being added in the first case, and 242 in the second. If we add 78 to 415 we shall get the *current* Christian year, which is 493. Now in General Cunningham's tables we do find the year *Mahâŝvayuja* given as corresponding to 493 A.D. In the same way, 191 Gupta *past*+242=433 Ŝaka *current*, +78=511 A.D. *current*. In the tables we find 511 put down under *Mahâchaitra*. Similarly 209 Gupta *past*+242=451 Ŝaka *current*, +78=529 A.D. *current* which was *Mahâŝvayuja*.

Now, as to the first of the dates in the 12-year cycle, 156 Gupta+242+78 is equal to 476 A.D., which however is Mahâchaitra instead of Mahâvaiŝâkha. Here there is a discrepancy of one year; but such discrepancies do sometimes occur even in Ŝaka dates and the years of the 60-years' cycle given along with them, and some of them will be noticed in the note forming the next Appendix. They are probably due to the fact that the frequent use of the past or expired year and also of the

Appendix A. current year led sometimes the *past* year to be mistaken for the *current* year, just as we *now* mistake the year 1805 Śaka for the current year, though it really is the completed or past year. Thus the completed year 157 must, in the case before us, have come to be mistaken by the writer of the inscription for the current year, and he thought 156 to be the past year and thus gave that instead of 157. Now 157 Gupta + 242 + 78 = 477 A.D., which is *Mahâvaiśâkha,* according to the tables.*

[129] The eclipse mentioned in the Morvî plate occurred, according to my friend Professor Keru Lakshmaṇ, on the 30th of Vaiśâkha, Śaka 827. The Gupta year given in the plate is 585. If 827 is in the astronomical calculation the *current* year, it must correspond to 585 Gupta *past*; for 585 + 242 = 827. It is by no means necessary to suppose that the eclipse occured on the new-moon day inmediately previous to the 5th of Phâlguna Sudi mentioned in the grant. For it is perfectly possible that the actual religious ceremoney with reference to the grant was made in Vaiśâkha and the deed executed in Phâlguna.†

---

* Though by using General Cunningham's table, I arrive at the desired result in three cases, still I now find that his current Christian year is derived by adding 78 to the past Śaka, while I have added 79; *i.e.*, the cyclic year given in the dates is true not of the Gupta year in the date as a past year but of the Gupta year + 1 as a past year. And the third date 173 Gupta is a correction of General Cunningham's, the actual date in the inscription being 163. I have, however, allowed the paragraphs to remain, as I am by no means quite satisfied that the question of these cyclic dates is settled beyond dispute (1894).

† There was an eclipse also in Śaka 826 the new-moon day of Kârttika; so that Gupta 585 *past* + 241 = 826 Śaka. This is evidently the eclipse mentioned in the grant and not that mentioned in the text. On the whole question

I have thus shown that Albiruni's initial date for the Gupta era stands all these tests. It may even be said that it stands them better than 167 A.D. and 190 A.D. proposed by General Cunningham and Sir E. Clive Bayley respectively. But I am loath to decide such questions simply on astronomical grounds; for there are several very confusing elements involved, and a modern astronomer cannot know them all and make allowance for them.

It now remains to notice the last point relied on by the opponents of Albiruni. The date on a copper-plate grant by the last Śîlâditya of Valabhî hitherto known is 447. This Śîlâditya is also styled Dhrûbhaṭa in the grant and has been identified with the Tu-lu-va-po-tou or Dhruvabhaṭa of Hwan Thsang who visited Valabhî in 640 A.D. The date 447 is understood as referring to the Gupta era, and, 319 being added it, corresponds to 766 A.D. It has therefore been argued that an earlier initial date must be assigned to the Gupta era so as to bring this Śîlâditya or Dhrûbhaṭa nearer to the date of Hwan Thsang's visit. But the identification of the last Śîlâditya with Hwan Thsang's Dhruvabhaṭa cannot stand. In the Si-yu-ki the Chinese writer does not speak of *a king* but of *kings*, and says they were nephews of Śîlâditya of Mâlvâ and the younger of them named Dhruvabhaṭa was son-in-law to the son of Harshavardhana. If they were nephews of the king of Mâlvâ they were brothers and both of them kings. Now, the predecessor of the last Śîlâditya of Valabhî was his father, and among the kings of Valabhî we do not find brothers reigning in succession at this period. There were two brothers who occupied the throne before this period, one of them

see my paper on the epoch of the Gupta era, Jour. B. B. R. A. S., Vol. XVII., p. 80.

Appendix A.

being named Dharasena and the other Dhruvasena. They were the sons of Kharagraha, and the younger of them was the father and predecessor of Dharasena IV. This younger brother or Dhruvasena must have been Hwan Thsang's Dhruvabhaṭa. Nothing important is involved in the suffix *Bhaṭa*. It was a mere title or honorific termination as Pant and Râv are among us the Marâṭhâs. Sena, Siṁha, and Bhaṭa were the Valabhî honorific endings and they could be used promiscuously. The king spoken of in the plates as Dhruvasena may have been called Dhruvabhaṭa by ordinary people, from whom Hwan Thsang must have got the name. Now, a copper-plate grant of Dhruvasena bears the date 310, and the earliest date of his successor Dharasena IV. is 326. The first corresponds to 629 A.D. (310+241+78 =629), and the second to 645 (326+241+78=645). It is quite possible, therefore, that Dhruvasena was on the throne in 640 A.D. at the time when Hwan Thsang visited Valabhî.

[130] The initial date mentioned by Albiruni is thus consistent with everything with which it has been thought to be not consistent. I have shown that the statement of the Arabic writer is in itself entitled to our confidence, being based, as it must have been, on contemporary evidence, as his statements about the Śaka and Vikrama eras were. I will now show that the date mentioned by him is alone consistent with the information we possess as regards the relations of the several dynasties that ruled over Gujarât and Kâṭhiâwâḍ in the early centuries of the Christian era, and the dates proposed by General Cunningham and Sir E. Clive Bayley are not. We know that the Guptas succeeded the Satraps, and the Valabhîs were at first dependents of the Guptas and afterwards attained independence.

Chandragupta II. must have been the Gupta prince who overthrew the Satraps, since he is the first prince of that dynasty whose silver coins are a close imitation of those of the Satraps. The latest date of that monarch is 93. This corresponds to 260 A.D. and 283 A.D. on the supposition that the Gupta era took its start in 167 A.D. and 190 A.D. respectively. Now, the latest date of the Satrap dynasty is 304. If the era to which it refers is the Śaka, it corresponds to 382 A.D., that is, we shall have to suppose one of the princes of the dynasty to have reigned about a hundred years after the dynasty had been put an end to by Chandragupta II. The Śaka era will therefore not do. Supposing the Satrap dates refer to the Vikrama era, 304 corresponds to 48 A.D., which of course is consistent with Chandragupta's date 260 A.D. or 283 A.D. If then the Satrap dates refer to the era of Vikrama, Rudradâman's 72 must correspond to 16 A.D. Rudradâman's grandfather Chashṭana will have to be placed about B.C. 4. But Ptolemy, writing after 150 A.D., tells us that Ujjayinî was ruled over about the time when he wrote by Tiastenes, who has been very reasonably identified with Chashṭana. Ptolemy's information cannot certainly be 150 years old. It has, however, been argued that Ptolemy does not state that Tiastenes reigned about the time when he lived, and that he and Siro Polemios were contemporaries. For, he gives the information in the form of two short notes, "Ozone, the royal residence of Tiastenes," and "Baithana, the royal residence of Siro Polemios." Such notes it is possible that one should write even if the princes reigned several hundred years before him, as a modern geographer *may* mention Berlin as "the capital of Frederick the Great," or Ghizni as "the capital of Mahmud." As to this I have to observe

Appendix A. that the analogy does not hold good. A modern geographer and his readers are very well acquainted with past history, while neither Ptolemy nor those for whom he wrote could have known the past history of India. A modern geographer knows which of the princes that ruled over a certain country in past times was the ablest or most powerful, and selects him out of a number and mentions his name in connection with a certain place. It is extremely improbable or almost impossible that Ptolemy should have known many Indian princes who reigned before he lived, along with their achievements, and should have chosen the ablest of them for being mentioned. And, as a matter of fact, we know that one at least of the rulers mentioned by him could be a person of no importance. For Baleocuros who according to him held power in Hippocura was, as we have seen, but a Viceroy or dependent of Puḷumâyi and Gotamîputra Yajña Śrî, since as Viḷivâyakura his name occurs along with those of the two princes on the Kolhâpur coins. Again, Ptolemy must have derived his information from merchants carrying on trade with India and these from the natives of the country. And we know that natives of India care very little for past history and [131] soon forget their kings. Hence the information derived by the merchants cannot have reference to princes who reigned long before the time of Ptolemy. It is possible that Indians may remember a celebrated prince for a century or two. But, as stated above, one of the rulers mentioned by Ptolemy was but a dependent sovereign and could not have been a man of note. The only other supposition that our opponents may resort to, is that Ptolemy's statements were based on those of previous geographers whose contemporaries the princes mentioned by him were. No ground whatever has however been adduced in support of such a supposition. In the Periplus which was written before Ptolemy, Paithana and Ozene are mentioned, but Polemios and Tiastenes are not. On the contrary, the author of that work says that Ozene was "formerly the capital wherein the king resided." If Tiastenes lived before him, and Ptolemy's mention of the former was due to his having been a prince of note like Frederick the Great and Mahmud of Ghizni in modern times, we should expect the author of the Periplus to have noticed him, especially when he does allude to the kings of Ozene. Tiastenes, Polemios and Baleocuros must thus have reigned about the time of Ptolemy. The last two were, we know, contemporaries, and so also must the third have been.

In this manner the Vikrama era will not do for the Satrap dates. Besides, no trace whatever has hitherto been discovered of the use of that era in the early centuries of Christ. Since, then, the use of no other era at the time has been well authenticated, the Satraps must be supposed to have employed the Śaka era. The circumstances of the country at that period render, as I have shown, the establishment of this era by the Śakas who ruled over the country in every way probable. The latest Satrap date will thus correspond to 382 A.D., and Chandragupta, the conqueror of the Satraps, can be rendered posterior to this only by taking 242 Śaka *current* or 319-320 A.D. as the first *current* year of the Gupta era ; for his 93 *past* will then correspond to 412-413 A.D. And in this way Rudradâman's 72 will correspond to 150 A.D. ; and Chashṭana's date will be about 130 A.D., *i.e.* anterior to the date of Ptolemy's geography by about 25 years.

Appendix A. Thus, then, the evidence in favour of Albiruni's initial date for the Gupta era appears to me to be simply overwhelming.

[132] APPENDIX B.

Note on the Śaka dates and the years of the Bârhaspatya cycle, occurring in the Inscriptions.

There are certain difficulties with reference to the Śaka dates and the cyclic years or *Samvatsaras* occurring in the inscriptions which require to be cleared up. The current Śaka year (A.D. 1883-84) in the Bombay Presidency is 1805, and the year of the sixty years' cycle, *Subhânu.* In the southern provinces and the Madras Presidency the current Śaka year is 1806, the cyclic year being the same. The first question, then, is, "Do the dates in the inscriptions conform to the Bombay reckoning or the Madras reckoning?" and the next, "What is the cause of this difference of a year?"* We have also to consider whether the Śaka dates in the inscriptions represent the number of years *that have expired* before the event recorded in them or the *current* year in which the event took place. **Appendix B.**

* It will be obvious to any careful reader that the manner in which the question here proposed for solution is stated, is based upon the ordinary view that Śaka 1805 was the current year in 1883-84. I have no right to assume in the beginning of my inquiry that the ordinary view is mistaken, and it would be unscientific to do so. But having stated the question in that manner, I come at the end of my inquiry to the conclusion that the ordinary view is incorrect, and that 1805 Śaka was not *current* in 1883-84 A.D. but *past,* and that the Madras way of understanding the matter alone is correct. In the previous note also I have stated that "we *now* mistake the year 1805 Śaka for the *current* year" (in 1883-84); so that there is no possibility whatever of anybody misunderstanding my meaning.

Appendix B.

Mr. Robert Sewell of the Madras Civil Service gives in the first column of the Chronological Tables compiled by him the number of the Śaka years that have expired before the beginning of the cyclic year set against it in the same line in the third column. The current Śaka year corresponding to that cyclic year is the one given in the next line in the first column. Thus against Śaka 855, the date of the Sâṅgalî grant of Govind IV. of the Râshṭrakûṭa dynasty, we have in the third column the cyclic year *Vijaya* which shows that 855 years of the Śaka era ***had expired*** before the *Vijaya* year began, while the *current* Śaka year corresponding to *Vijaya* was that given in the next line, *viz.* 856. Mr. Sewell follows the Madras reckoning. If we interpret the tables according to the Bombay mode, the Śaka year appearing in the first column will be the current year corresponding to the cyclic year in the same line in the third column, while the number in the line immediately above will represent the years that have expired before the beginning of that cyclic year. Thus against 1805, the current Śaka year on this side of the country, we have in the third column the current cyclic year *Subhânu,* while 1804 in the line above shows the number of years that have expired. By comparing the Śaka dates and cyclic years occurring in the inscriptions with those in the tables we shall be able to determine the points raised above.

In the analysis of Pâli, Sanskrit, and old Kânarese inscriptions published by Dr. Fleet and Dr. Burgess there are 97 cases in which the Śaka date as well as the cyclic year are distinctly given. On comparing these with the tables I observe that in 58 out of these the given Śaka date occurs in the same line with the cyclic year mentioned in the inscription. These are :—

[133] Nos. 18, 20, 21, 23, 24, 25, 28, 29, 35, 36, 37, 38, 52, 70, 87, 88, 90, 92, 98, 99, 101, 102, 109, 114, 123, 125, 126, 127, 128, 129, 131, 134, 136, 141, 148, 149, 150, 154, 155, 156, 157, 158, 159, 160, 161, 183, 189, 201, 214, 215, 219, 229, 230 (first part), 240, 241, 243, 283, 286.

Thus in inscription No. 20, the date given is 1200, and the cyclic year the *Bahudhânya*, both of which occur in the same line set against each other in the tables.

In 28 cases the Śaka date given in the inscription occurs in the tables in the line below that in which the given cyclic year occurs. These are :—

Nos. 19, 22, 26, 33, 34, 47, 72, 89, 91, 95, 96 (first part), 96 (second part), 100, 110, 111, 112, 118 (first part), 118 (second part), 146, 151, 194, 227, 230 (second part), 231, 234, 236, 237, 281.

In No. 19, for instance, the Śaka date is 1184 and the cyclic year *Durmati*. In the tables, *Durmati* occurs in the upper line set against 1183, and 1184 is in the line below, and *Dundubhi* is the year marked against it.

Now on the supposition that the inscriptions conform to the Madras reckoning, in the first 58 cases the Śaka date represents the number of Śaka years that *had expired* before the current cyclic year of the inscription and in 28 it shows the *current* year of that era. If we suppose the Bombay reckoning to have been in use, the dates in the first 58 cases will represent the current year and those in the next 28, the *future* year and not the *past*. But since it is almost absurd to suppose that the immediately next year should be stated in the inscriptions, it follows that the Madras mode of reckoning was the one in use. The objection, however, may be obviated by supposing that these 28 cases conform

Appendix B.

to the Madras reckoning and give the current year, while the first 58 follow the Bombay mode. But this supposition is not reasonable or probable, since these groups are not confined to particular provinces, and often one of the former exists in the same district or even place with one of the latter. We thus see that though in the majority of cases the inscriptions give the *past* Śaka year, there is a large number in which the *current* year is given and not the *past*.

I have also compared other dates with the tables, and the result I give below:—

	Śaka date.	Cyclic year.	What the Śaka date represents.
Kânarese grant of Govinda III. Râshṭrakûṭa	726	Subhânu	Current year.
Râdhânpur grant of Govinda III. ...	730	Sarvajit	Do.
Kṛishṇa II. or Akâlavarsha, completion of the Jaina Purâṇa ...	820	Piṅgala	Do.
Do., in a Jaina temple by Chîkârya ...	824	Dundubhi	Years elapsed.
Govinda IV., Sâṅgalî grant	855	Vijaya	Do.
Kakkala, Karḍâ grant	894	Aṅgiras	Do.
Tailapa's accession ...	895	Śrîmukha	Do.
Satyâśraya, Khârepâtaṇ plates of Raṭṭa ...	930	Kîlaka	Do.
Jayasiṁha Jagadekamalla, Miraj grant ...	946	Raktâkshi	Do.
Mârasiṁha Śilâhâra of Kolhâpur, grant ...	980	Vilambin	Do.
Gaṇḍarâditya Śilâhâra of Kolhâpur, Ins. No. 1	1032	Vikṛiti	Do.
Gaṇḍarâditya Śilâhâra grant translated by Paṇḍit Bhagvânlâl ...	1032	Virodhin	Current year.
Do. Kolhâpur Ins. No. 2	1040	Vilambin	Years elapsed.
Vijayârka do. do. No. 4	1065	Dundubhi	Current year.
Someśvara III. Bhûlokamalla, Abhilashita Chintâmaṇi ...	1051	Saumya	Years elapsed.

	Śaka date.	Cyclic year.	What the Śaka date represents.
Bhojadeva II., Kolhâpur Ins. No. 6 ...	1101	Vilambin	Current year.
Bhojadeva II., Kolhâpur Ins. No. 8 ...	1112	Sâdhârana	Years elapsed.
Bhojadeva II., Dr. Taylor's grant	1113	Virodhin	Do.
Bhojadeva II., Kolhâpur Ins. No. 8 ...	1114	Paridhâvin	Do.
Singhaṇa Yâdava, Khedrâpur Ins. ...	1136	Śrîmukha	Current year.
Kâmvadeva Châlukya	1182	Raudra	Years elapsed.
Mahâdeva Yâdava, Paṇḍharpur Ins. ...	1192	Pramoda	Do.
Râmachandra Yâdava, Ṭhânâ	1194	Aṅgiras	Do.
Râmachandra Yâdava, Ṭhânâ	1212	Virodhin	Current year.

Out of these 24 dates, eight give the current year and the rest the years that had expired, the proportion being the same as in the other case, *viz.* 1 to 2. In all cases in which the cyclic year is given it is possible to determine whether the date represents the current or past year, but not in others. The inscriptions of the early Châlukyas do not give it, and hence the exact date remains doubtful.

Now the Bombay mode of reckoning, which is one year behind that prevalent in Madras, is, I believe, due to a mistake. We have seen it was more usual in recording a date to mark the years that had expired than the current year. A word expressive of that sense such as *gateshu*, "having elapsed," was used after the number, and another such as *pravartamâne*, "being current," was used in connection with the name of the cyclic year. These words were, for brevity's sake, afterwards dropped; and in the course of time the sense, to express which

Appendix B. they were used, was also forgotten, and the number came to be regarded as denoting the current year. So that what we do on this side of the country is that we use the *past* or *expired* year without knowing that it is the *past* year. And there are in the inscriptions instances of mistakes due to the circumstance that the real *past* year came to be regarded as the current year. Thus in No. 86 of the Pâli, Sanskrit, and old Kânarese inscriptions, Śaka 911 is given along with the cyclic year Vikṛiti. Now, according to the tables, the number of years that had expired before Vikṛiti was 912 and the current year was 913. This discrepancy is to be explained by the supposition that Śaka 912 which represented the years that had expired came to be thought of as the current year, just as we, on this side of the country, consider 1805 as the current year now, though it indicates the past year, and the writer of the inscription wishing to give the years that had expired before his current year, put them as 911. The same is the case with Nos. 27, 67, 115, 130, 224, and 284, the Śaka dates in which are 1444, 1084, 1430, 1453, 1114, and 1128, respectively, and are two years behind the current year as determined by the cyclic years given along with them. In some cases the Śaka dates are in advance of the *Samvatsara* or cyclic year by one year. Thus in the Vaṇi-Diṇḍori grant of Govinda III. the Śaka date is 730 and the Saṁvatsara *Vyaya,* and in the Kânheri inscription of Amoghavarsha we have Śaka 775 and the *Prajâpati* Saṁvatsara. [135] Now the Śaka years immediately preceding Vyaya and Prajâpati were 728 and 773, while the current years were 729 and 774 respectively. This difference might be accounted for on the supposition that the *current* years 729 and 774 were from the usual custom understood to be *past* years and the writers of the documents desirous of giving the *current* years added 1 and put them down as 730 and 775. The date in No. 79 of Pâli, Sanskrit, and old Kânarese inscriptions is three years behind the current Saṁvatsara, and that in No. 228, four years ; No. 221 has 1113 for 1121 ; and No. 246, 1492 for 1485. These must be considered to be mistakes. Appendix B.

The Śaka dates given in the preceding pages represent in *most* cases the years that had expired before the particular occurrences mentioned. Thus "in 855" means *after 855 years of the Śaka era had expired*.

[136] APPENDIX C.

Introduction to Hemâdri's Vratakhaṇḍa.

Appendix C.

In the critical notes D. represents the MS. in the Dekkan College Library, No. 234 of A. 1881-82; D 2. another recently added to the collection; S. the MS. belonging to the old Sanskrit College, No. 657; Kh. the MS. belonging to Khâsgivâle, and G. the MS. procured by Gaṅgâdhar Śâstrî Dâtâr. See Section XIV., first page, note 2.

* श्रीगोपालमपारवैभवभवत्स्वच्छन्दलीलामयं
सान्द्रस्निग्धतमालकोमलदलश्यामाभिरामाकृतिम्।
कूजत्कोकिलकामिनीकलरवप्रोल्लासिगोपाङ्गना-
गीतस्फीतपवित्रचित्रचरितप्रान्तं नमस्कुर्महे ॥ १ ॥
उन्मीलत्कमनीयकान्तिसरसीमध्ये विशुद्धप्रभं
सारासारविचारचारुमनसा हंसेन संसेवितम्।
नित्यानन्दपरागसङ्गसुभगं वन्दारुमन्दारक-
१ २
श्रेणीभक्तमनङ्गवैरिचरणाम्भोजद्वयं पातु वः ॥ २ ॥

* These two stanzas exist only in a mutilated form in S. and D 2, but they occur fully in D. and Kh. which contain the shorter Praśasti. In G., which contains both the Praśastis mixed together, they occur at the head of the shorter one, so that they appear to belong to the latter rather than to the other.

१ सङ्ग for भक्त D. Kh. २ नः for वः D. Kh.

Râjapraśasti I.

१
जीयाद्भूतभूतसर्गसमयाविर्भावसंभावना-
२
तुष्यत्तल्पभुजङ्गपुङ्गवशिरःश्रेणीश्रितैर्बिम्बितः।
कल्पान्तोपरमेषु नाभिकमलप्रोद्दामसामस्वर-
स्वैरोच्चारविचारचालितविधिव्याधूतनिद्रो हरिः ॥ १ ॥

१ जायाद्भू॰ S. जीवद्भू॰ G. २ ॰तल्प॰ S. तुल्य. G.

अस्ति प्रशस्तं पुरुषोत्तमस्य शय्यातलं क्षीरमयः पयोधिः।
यदीयपीयूषरसायनेन स्वर्लोकभाजामजरामरत्वम् ॥ २ ॥
संतानचिन्तामणिकामधेनुकल्पद्रुमश्रीजननैकहेतोः।
सिन्धोरमुष्मादुदभूदमन्दनिस्यन्दमाना[1]मृतबिन्दुरिन्दुः ॥ ३ ॥
ततस्तनूजं विबुधप्रधानं[2] बुधं सुधादीधितिरप्यसूत।
बभूव तस्मादथ चक्रवर्ती पुरूरवाः पुण्यपथा[3]नुवर्ती ॥ ४ ॥
अभजत[4] जनिमस्मादायुरायुः प्रजानां
मनुजपदनिदानं ज्योतिरासीत्ततोपि।
[137] नृपतिरथ ययातिः ख्यातिमानप्यमुष्मा-
द्यदमपि यदुमूर्तिं[5] कीर्तिमाविश्चकार ॥ ५ ॥
यदोरदोषविशदैर्यशोभिरभिशोभितः
अन्ववायः स एवायमवाप यदुवंशताम् ॥ ६ ॥
ततः क्रोष्टा तस्मादजनि वृजिनीवानपि नृप-
स्ततो जज्ञे राज्ञः क्षितिपतिविरिष्टः स्वाहित[6] इति।
नृपस्तुषद्गुस्तत्पुत्रः समभवदथो चित्ररथ इ-
त्यतो जातः ख्यातः स किल शशबिन्दुर्नरपतिः ॥ ७ ॥
ततः पृथुश्रवा वीरस्तदनन्तरमन्तरः।
ततः सुयज्ञ उशनाः सितेयुरिति च क्रमात् ॥ ८ ॥
सुतस्तस्य मरुत्त इत्यनुपमः प्रोद्दामदोर्विक्रम-
स्तस्मा[7]त्कम्बलबर्हिरुल्बणयशःप्रक्षालितक्ष्मातलः।
एतस्मादुदियाय रुक्मकवचस्तस्मात्पराजिन्नृप-
स्तस्माद् रिपुरंगमे[8]धसुज्ञातो राजाजनि ज्यामघः ॥ ९ ॥
ततो विदर्भः क्रथकुन्तिवृष्णिनिवृत्तिसंज्ञाः परतो दशार्हः।
व्योमा[9] च जीमूत इति क्रमेण जाता नरेन्द्रा विकृतिश्च वीरः ॥ १० ॥
तदनु भीमरथः पृथिवीपतिर्नवरथश्च ततो रथिनां वरः।
दशरथः शकुनिश्च करम्भिरित्युपदिशन्ति पुराणपरायणाः ॥ ११ ॥

---

१ ०मानो G. मानी S. २ प्रतापं for प्रधानं G. ३ र था० for पथा० S. D2. ४ जम S. D2. अस्ति G. for अजि. ५ मूर्तिः S. D2. मूर्तिं G. ६ स्वाहित S. स्वाहित G. ७ यशा: S. G. ८ मेधि S. G. ९ व्योमाह S. व्योमाय G. व्योमाह D 2.

देवराजस्तत:[1] श्रीमान्देवक्षेत्रस्ततो मधु: ।
तत: कुरुवशो राजा[2] पुरुहोत्र: क्रमादभूत् ॥ १२ ॥

अथायुरासीदथ सात्वतो[3]भूदथान्धकोऽस्माद्भजमान[4]संज्ञ: ।
विदूरथस्तत्परतोपि शूरराज्ञि[5]: प्रतिक्षत्र इति क्षितीश: ॥ १३ ॥

बभूवाथ स्वयंभोजस्ततोपि हृदिकोभवत् ।
असूत सोपि धर्मात्मा राजानं देवमीढुषम् ॥ १४ ॥

निखिलमनि:शेषितवैरिपूरस्तत: क्षितिं पालयति स्म शूर: ।
ततोपि राजा वसुदेवनामा यो विश्वहेतोरपि हेतुरासीत् ॥ १५ ॥

वृन्दारवृन्दारकवृन्दमालिमन्दारमालासुरभी कृताङ्घ्रि: ।
आसीदमुष्मात्सुरापतारभारापहाराय पुरा मुरारि:[6] ॥ १६ ॥

[138] बभूव प्रद्युम्न: किल कुसुमधन्वा मधुरिपो-
स्त्रिलोकीवीरोसौ तनयमनिरुद्धं प्रसुषुवे ।
ततोभूत्स्वपक्षक्षपणनिपुणेनैव[7] महसा
परिस्फुर्जन्वज्र:[8] प्रतनखसत्त्व: प्रादुरभवत् ॥ १७ ॥

वज्रस्य सूनु: प्रतिबाहुरासीद्ग्रासीकृतव्याप्तविपक्षबाध: ।
ततोपि तस्मादभवत्सुबाहु:[9] प्रासूत सोयं चतुरस्तनूजान् ॥ १८ ॥

तेन ते सार्वभौमेन तनया विनयान्विता: ।
विभज्य वसुधाचक्रं चक्रिरे पृथिवीश्वरा: ॥ १९ ॥

यथाविभागं वसुधामशेषां तेषां तदा पालयतां[10] चतुर्णां ।
हठप्रहारी द्विषि दर्पितेष्वा प्रभुर्बभूव प्रथमात्कनीयान् ॥ २० ॥

---

१ देवरात: D 2. २ नाम for राजा G. ३ सत्वतो D 2. ४ ०न्धकाख्या० G. S. ५ So both MSS., also D 2. But there must be a mistake. The name of Śûra's son शिनि is disguised as राज्ञि. Perhaps the reading is शूरशीनी. ६ पुरा मुरारि: S. पुरारि: D 2. ७ स for एव D 2. ८ परिस्फुर्ज्जन्वज्र: S.; G. totally incorrect and there is a lacuna. D 2. has वज्रु: for वज्र of S. 9. The Purâṇic genealogy ends here. Subâhu, however, is there called Suchâru १० द्रावयतां D 2.

सर्वेऽपि पूर्वं मथुराधिनाथा: कृष्णादितो द्वारवतीश्वरास्ते ।
सुबाहुसूनोस्तु दक्षिणाशाप्रवासिनो यादववंशवीरा: ॥ २१ ॥

तत: स राजा निजराजधानीमधिष्ठित: श्रीनगरं गरीय: ।
लेभे सुतं सेउणचन्द्रसंज्ञं यत्संज्ञया सेउणदेशमाहु: ॥ २२ ॥

अथ धाडियसो महीपतिस्तनयस्तस्य बभूव भिल्लम: ।
अजनिष्ट ततोऽपि राजगिस्तदनु[1] प्रादुरभूत्स वाडुगि:[2] ॥ २३ ॥

जज्ञे धाडियमस्तत:[3] प्रतिभटक्ष्मापालकालानल-
स्तस्मादाविरभूत्प्रभूतविभवो भर्ता भुवो भिल्लम: ।
एतस्मान्महसां महानिधिरसौ श्रीवेसुगिर्लब्धवान्
कन्या[4] श्रीचभुजोजसामसुहृदां तस्मादभूदर्जुन: ॥ २४ ॥
अजस्रमाविष्कृतदानवारि: प्रभूतहस्तार्पितदानवारि: ।
तत: स राजा विरराज राजश्रियो विलासैर्जितराजराज: ॥२५॥ ॥

आसीद्विलासी नृपतेरमुष्मात्स भिल्लम: पल्लवितोरुकीर्ति: ।
स वाडुगि: स्वादुगिरां कवीनां स्तोत्रैकपात्रं[5] भवति स्म तस्मात् ॥२६॥

ततो महीं महीपाल:[6] पालयामास वेसुगि: ।
संहृत[7]प्रोद्यदुद्दामधामसामन्तसंतति: ॥ २७ ॥

ततोऽपि नृपभिल्लम: समरसीमभीमक्रिया-
निरर्गलभुजार्गलायुगलकालकेलिलय: ।
[139] तत: समदमेदिनीपतिपतङ्गभङ्गव्रत:
प्रतापशिखिलङ्घित[8]त्रिजगदङ्गण: सेउण: ॥ २८ ॥

समुद्धृतो[9] येन महाभुजेन श्रियो विमर्दात्परमर्दिदेव: ।
आख्यापि चालुक्यकुलप्रदीप: कल्याणराजोऽपि स एव येन ॥ २९ ॥

---

१ राजुगिस्तदनु D 2. २ स वाडुगि S. सुबाहुदुव: G. ३ This is the reading of S., D 2 and G. probably for धाडियस. But the name according to Paṇḍit Bhagvânlâl's grant was धाडियप्प. ४ S. and G. have a wrongand unintelligible reading here. ५ पात्र S. पात्रे G. for पात्रं ६ The vîsarga is dropped in S. and G. ७ संहत D 2. ८ S. G. have लंघित: त्रिजग० ९ समुद्धतो D 2.

परमर्द्दिव: स ततो बभूव विपक्षभूमीपघनाम्बुवृष्टी[१] ।

प(ऐ) रम्बर्द्दिनैव यथा यदीन यस्य प्रतापेन चिरं[२] व्यराजि ॥ २० ॥

तस्मादनन्तरमनल्पभुजप्रताप:[३] क्षोणीपति: समभवत्[४] स सिंहराज: ।

तस्मात्तु जयादनु भूवलयं[५] बलीयानजायत त्रिजगतीविजयी स राजा ॥ २१ ॥

काञ्चीपुरात्समानीय कर्पूरतिलकं गजम् ।

स कर्पूरव्रतं पूर्णमकरोत्परमर्द्दिन:[६] ॥ २२ ॥

तस्मादप्रतिम[७]श्रीमून्मक्कनिर्वर्म्म: क्षिते: ।

उदजृम्भत जम्भारिर्भूरिदोर्दण्डविक्रमा ॥ २३ ॥

यासाय[८] सद्य: स्वनिवासहेतो: श्रीपर्वखेटे नगरं रिपुभ्य: ।

अकारि[९] येनोत्कलभूमिपालादुपुष्करमालघटा कटेन ॥ २४ ॥

तस्मादमरगाङ्गेय: संबभूव भुव: पति: ।

यथाविन्दत गोविन्दराज: साम्राज्यसंपदम् ॥ २५ ॥

ततो मल्लगि[१०]पुर्वीभृत्पालोमर[११]मल्लगि: ।

अथ कालीयवल्लाल: पालयामास मेदिनीम् ॥ २६ ॥

मल्लोपतेस्तस्य विभाय पुत्रान् गुणानुरक्ता यदुवंशलक्ष्मी: ।

श्रीभिल्लमं तस्य तत: पितृव्यमवाजराजद्गुणमाजगाम ॥ २७ ॥

य:[१२] श्रीवर्धनमाससाद नगरं क्षोणीपतेरंतलात्[१३]

य: प्रत्यण्डकभूभृतं च समरे दुष्टं व्यजेष्ट क्षणात् ।

---

१ प्रता for घना S. G. २ Here S. ends, and the following is based on G. and D 2, of which the former is, as I have already observed, an extremely incorrect manuscript. ३ प्रतापं G. ४ सहि सिंहि G. ५ This word in G. must be some mistake as it has no significance here. D 2. has गुयामु which also is a mistake. ६ मन्दिर: for मर्दिन: G. ७ G. has मुक्तगि० ८ स्वनिवास is सनिवाह in G. ९ आकारि D 2. १० मुल्लगि D 2. ११ ०लोपर० D 2. १२ स D 2. for य: १३ रंसलात् for रंतलात् G

यो वा मल्लुगिवेष्टकं क्षितिपतिं श्रीविज्जणं[1] जिग्निवान्

कल्याणश्रियमप्यवाप्य विदधे यो भीमसीमं व्यसुं[2] ॥ ३८ ॥

[140] स दक्षिणामण्डलमण्डयितीमकम्पसंपत्प्रभवैर्विलासैः ।

चक्रे पुरं देवगिरिं गिरीशप्रसादसं[3]सादितदिव्यशक्तिः ॥ ३९ ॥

तदनु मदनमूर्तिः कार्त्तिकीचन्द्रसान्द्र-

द्युतिविशदयशोभिः शोभिताशावकाशः[4] ।

अभवदवनिपालो जैत्रपालः करालः

प्रखरखरखरक्लगुरुदुगुणःखड्गः ॥ ४० ॥

दीक्षित्वा[5] रणरङ्गदेवयजने प्रोद्दामशस्त्रस्रुचः

श्रेणीभिर्जगतीभुजस्तवता येन प्रतापानले ।

तैलङ्गा[6]धिपतेः पशोर्विशसनं रौद्रस्य[7] रौद्राकृतेः

कृत्वा पुरुषमेधयज्ञविधिना लब्धश्रीलोकोजयः ॥ ४१ ॥

तस्मादभूदभिनवस्मरचारुमूर्त्तिः[8]

कीर्त्तेः पदं स किल सिंघणदेवभूपः ।

उद्दण्डदोर्युगलगर्वितवैरिवीर-

सीमन्तिनी[9]वदनकैरवचण्डभानुः ॥ ४२ ॥

येनानीयत मत्तवारणघटा जज्जल्लभूभृतः

कक्कूलादवनीपतेरपहृता येनाधिराजश्रियः ।

येन श्रीणीभृदर्जुनोपि बलिना नीतः कथाशेषतां

येनोद्दामभुजेन भोजनृपतिः काराकुटुम्बीकृतः ॥ ४३ ॥

यद्रम्भा[10]गिरिकेसरी विनिहतो[11] लक्ष्मीधरः क्ष्मापति-

र्येनाज्ञावलिभिः प्रसह्य ररुधे धाराधराधीश्वरः ।

---

१ वज्जिणं for विज्जणं G. २ G. has वसु and D 2. व्यसं for व्यसुं. ३ In the MSS. we have प्रसादमासादित०. ४ G. has विकाश for वकाशः. ५ रणरंगसत्संगदुत्तग. D 2. ६ तल्लिंग in G. ७ रौद्रस्य ought to be रुद्रस्य, unless the son of Rudradeva is meant. ८ कीर्त्तिः for मूर्तिः D. 2. ९ This line is thus written in G. सीमंतविनोदनकैरवचन्द्रभासान्; also in D 2. except त् for last न्. १० यद्दंगारिग G. ११ विनिहतो G.

Appendix C.

यश्चालक्षितिपालपालित[1]भुवां सर्वोपकारश्च यः

श्रीसिंहस्य महीपतेर्विजयते तद्बाल[2]लीलायितम् ॥ ४४ ॥

कृष्णो महादेव इति प्रतीतौ जातौ ततः सिंहनृपस्य पौत्रौ ।
तयोस्तु पूर्वप्रभवः पुरस्तात् कृष्णोतिविख्यातमतिर्नृपोभूत् ॥ ४५ ॥

येनाकारि विशालवीसलचमूर्मण्डावकालानलो
हेलोन्मूलितमूलराजसमरे निर्वीरमुर्वीतलम् ।
येनानेकमहाफलक्रतुकृता संवर्धमानोनिशं
चौथः[3] कालवशात्पुनस्तदच्यतां धर्मोपि संप्रापितः ॥ ४६ ॥

[141] ततः कृष्णे राजन्यमरतरुणीचामरमरु-
त्तरङ्गैस्तुङ्गं दिवि किमपि तेजः श्रितवति ।
परित्राता भूमेः समजनि जगज्जित्वरमहा[4]
महादेवः सेवारसिकसकलक्ष्माभृन्नुतः ॥ ४७ ॥

तिलङ्गक्षितिपालतूल[5]निचयप्रक्षेपचण्डानिलो
गर्जद्गूर्जरगर्वपर्वतभिदादम्भोलिदोर्विक्रमः ।
हेलोन्मूलितकौङ्कणक्षितिपतिः कर्णाटलाटोद्भट-
चोळोपालविडम्बनः स हि महादेवः कथं वर्ण्यते ॥ ४८ ॥

यो भोजदेवान्नृपतेः प्रतापी जयाय याते मदमन्दसत्त्वः[6] ।
साधं जनन्या सहजीवितेन सोमेश्वरस्यापि जहार राज्यम्[7] ॥ ४९ ॥

---

१ लालित for पालित G. २. यद्बाल० G. ३ चौथे G. This ४ महा is omitted in the MSS. since it is followed by another महा, and the copyists mistook the one for the other. The compound is to be dissolved as जगतो जित्वरं जगज्जित्वरम्। जगज्जित्वरं महो यस्य स जगज्जित्वरमहाः. ५ चूल for तूल D 2. ६ मदमन्दसत्त्वः which is also the reading of D. 2, as an epithet of Mahâdeva, involves censure instead of praise. The correct form of the word is, probably, मदमन्दसत्त्वात्, in which case it would be an epithet of Bhojadeva. 4 After this follow stanzas 14 and 19 of the next Praśasti in D 2.

यदीयगन्धद्विपगण्डशालीनिष्ठ्यूतदानाम्बुतरङ्गिणीषु ।
स्नात: समुद्रत्वपेयुषापि ममज्ज सैन्यै: सह कुरुवेश: ॥ ५० ॥
सामाजिकेननेव यस्य जगतां संहार इत्युच्यते
क्रुद्धे वज्रधरेपि य: क्षितिभृतं मैनाकमत्रायत ।
क्षा.रं सारममुष्य दु:सहमह:संदोहदावानलं
तेनाम्भोनिधिनापि कुङ्कणपतिर्नीरचि कुक्षिस्थित ॥ ५१ ॥
बाहानामपि यस्य वैरिविषयेष्वातन्वता धन्विना (ता?)
मातङ्गिन्नृपाङ्गणादनुदिनं बाष्पादिलीलाभवत् ।
यस्तस्यैव रणे जहार करिणस्तत्पञ्चशब्दादिकान्
यस्तत्याज वधूवधादुपरतस्सद्भुजं रुद्रनाम् ॥ ५२ ॥

Râjapraśasti II.

वंशो हिमांशोर्जयति प्रसिद्धो यस्मिन्स राजा यदुराविरासीत् ।
बभूव यस्मिन्नसुरावतारभारापहाराय पुरा मुरारि: ॥ ३ ॥
वंशे तस्मिन्कंसविध्वंसनस्य क्षोणीपालो भिल्लम: प्रादुरासीत् ।
नित्यं नाथं वैरिभूभृत्पतङ्गान्यस्यानेकद्वीपदीप: प्रताप: ॥ ४ ॥
[142]नम्रीभवत्सकलराजसमाजमौलीमालाविकस्वरदीधितिविबोधितपादपद्म: ।
उद्दामदर्परिपुसर्पविहङ्गराज: श्रीभिल्लमादवनिपोजनि जैत्रपाल: ॥ ५ ॥
तस्मादभूदभिनवस्मरचारुमूर्ति: कीर्ते: पदं जगति सिंहणदेवभूप: ।
उद्दण्डदो[1]र्युगलगर्वितवैरिवर्गसीमन्तिनीवदनकैरव[2]चण्डभानु: ॥ ६ ॥
अथ सकलकलानामालय: पालनाय क्षितितलमवतीर्ण: पौर्णमासीशशीव ॥
अभवदवनिपालो जैतुगिर्नाम तस्मादसमसमरधीरद्वेषिभूपालकाल: ॥ ७ ॥
स भूमिपालो जनयांबभूव कृष्णं महादेवमहीपतिं च ।
हिताय लोकस्य यथा पयोधिश्चिन्तामणिं कौस्तुभमप्युदारम् ॥ ८ ॥
जन्मान्तरोत्थं परिवर्तयन्तौ ज्येष्ठावरत्वं किल कौतुकेन
कृतावतारौ यदुराजवंशे प्रीत्या पुनस्ताविव रामकृष्णौ ॥ ९ ॥
धर्मार्थाविव तौ साक्षात्पालयन्तौ वसुंधराम् ।
विलोक्य लोक: सस्मार राजानौ रामलक्ष्मणौ ॥ १० ॥
हस्त्यश्वारूढवाजिवारवारणक्षोणीषु जित्वा बहून् ।
दासीकृत्य तथापरान्विहितवानन्यानरथ्यौ ऋण: ।
इत्थं पार्थिवराजराजिविजयव्यापारपारंगत-
सखी शक्रजयाय कृष्णनृपति: [3]स्वर्लोकयात्रागतम् ॥ ११ ॥

---

१ युगल Kh. २ चन्द्रभानु: D. & Kh. चण्डभात: G. ३ यात्रा गत: Kh.

अथ प्रतापातिशयेन लब्धं विभज्य श्रीकन्तलाधिपत्यम् ।
त्रिविष्टपं शासति जम्भभेदि भुवं महादेवनृपः प्रशास्ति ॥ १२ ॥

४ ५ ६
तैलङ्गक्षितिपालतूलनिचयप्रक्षेपझञ्झानिलो
मत्तं हूणं रमर्दपर्वतभिदादम्भोलिदोर्विक्रमः ।
७
हेलोन्मूलितकौलवक्षितिपतिः कर्णाटलाटोद्भट-
योधोपात्तविजृम्भणः स हि महादेवः कथं वर्ण्यते ॥ १३ ॥

यस्य त्रिपुरुषोत्तमागतानां कृत्ता महादेवनृपो न जातु ।
८
इत्थं विनिश्चित्य सतीतिभीतैरङ्गैः पुरन्ध्री निहिता नृपत्वे ॥ १४ ॥

९
अत एव हि मालवेश्वरः श्रियमेव सपदि न्यवेशयत् ।
१०
स्वयमाशु विहाय संपदं कपटेनैव चिरं तपस्यति ॥ १५ ॥

११
विषमसमरकर्तुः प्रश्रयो यस्य पाणौ
प्रलयदहनधूमश्यामधामातिभीमम् ।
पृथुतरकरवालव्यालमालोकयन्ती
भय शरणमितीमं मन्त्रमुच्चारयन्ति ॥ १६ ॥

[143] यदीयगन्धद्विपगण्डपालीनिष्ठ्यूतदानाम्बुतरङ्गिणीषु
१२
सोमः समुद्रत्रयपीतलोऽपि ममज्ज सैन्यैः सह कुङ्कणेशः ॥ १७ ॥

१३
एतत्प्रतापी वहिरम्बुराशेर्गोर्वान्तरिष्यसि कुतः प्रयासि ।
चिरं विमृश्येति यदीयवैरी सोमेश्वरो वाडवमेव यातः ॥ १८ ॥

---

४ तरिलंग Kh. & G. ५ प्रोत्क्षेप Kh. चोक्षेप G. ६ चंडानिलो Kh. & G. ७ °लाटोद्भवयोधौ° Kh. °लाटोद्भवः. योधो G. ८ इत्थं विनिश्चिन्त्य यती विभितैरङ्गैः Kh. विनिश्चित्य D. ९ हिमाचलेश्वरं G. ८ न पश्यति for तपस्यति G. ९ पाणौ: Kh. १० सौन्यैः G. ११ °राशेरन्तः पुरोऽष्यसि कुतः प्रयामि D. प्रयासि Kh.

आस्ते महिततदक्षकापरिसरः श्रीसेउणाख्यः[३] परं
देशः पेशलवेशभूषणवधूमाधुर्यधुर्याकृतिः ।
तस्मिन्देवगिरिः पुरी विजयते त्रैलोक्यसारश्रिया
विभ्रान्तिः सुरसालिमौलिशिखरस्पर्धिष्णु[४]सौधावलिः ॥ १९ ॥
जगत्त्रयीगीतगुणप्रशस्तिः प्राप्ता समस्तावनिमण्डलस्य ।
श्रीमानिमामन्वयाराजधानीं सोयं महादेवनृपो बिभर्ति ॥ २० ॥
कुर्वन्विभूतिविस्तारैरिलाहतसमश्रियम ।
अधितिष्ठति हेमाद्रिरिमां विबुधबान्धवः ॥ २१ ॥
सा संपत्तदिदं यशो बलमिदं सोयं प्रतापो महा-
मेकैकं पृथिवीभृतो भुवि महादेवस्य लोकोत्तरम् ।
यस्य[५] श्रीकरणाधिपः स्वयमयं[६] हेमाद्रिसूरिः पुरः
प्रौढप्रातिभवर्यमानविभवस्तस्यो भूर्ज्ज श्रीभति ॥ २१ ॥

इति राजप्रशस्तिः ॥

---

३ सेवणाख्यः D. सेवणाख्याः Kh. The middle letter of the name in G. looks somewhat like ठ, but there is little question that the copyist had ण before him and made it appear like ठ by producing the nether curve and making its end touch the knot of ण. ४ स्पर्धालु D. ५ तस्य D 2. ६ चार्य for वर्य D 2.

NOTES

ADDITIONS AND FURTHER CORRECTIONS

By Prof. D. R. Bhandarkar, M.A., Ph.D.

Pp. 1-2. For a further discussion about Dakshiṇâpatha, see P. V. Kane, *Jour. B. B. R. A. S.*, Vol. XXIV. pp. 616—621.

Pp. 4-5. For Aryan immigration into the Dekkan, see D. R. Bhandarkar, *Carmichael Lectures*, 1918, p. 2 & ff.

Pp. 18-19. As regards the identification of the Rāsṭikas, Petenikas and Aparântas, see D. R. Bhandarkar, *Asoka*, pp. 32-33, and *Ind. Ant.*, 1919, p. 80, n. 4 ; also V. A. Smith, *Early History of India* (Edn. revised by S. M. Edwardes), p. 193 & f.

P. 23. The inscriptions of Asoka found at Supârâ and on the northern frontier of Mysore were not "stray edicts". At Supârâ the whole set of his Fourteen Rock Edicts must have been engraved, of which only a fragment of Edict VIII has now been preserved. As regards his inscriptions on the frontier of Mysore, they are three separate copies of his Minor Rock Edicts and speak of a prince of the blood royal as being placed in charge of that frontier province (D. R. Bhandarkar, *Asoka*, pp. 254-255, p. 258 & pp. 26—28). Since the *Early History of the Deccan* was published, another recension has been discovered at Maski in Nizam's territory.

P. 24. For a revised transcript and interpretation of the Nânâghâṭ inscriptions, see Bühler *Arch. Surv. West. Ind.*, Vol. V. p. 60 & ff. For the history deducible from them, see D. R. Bhandarkar, *Ind. Ant.*, 1918, pp. 71-72.

P. 26 & ff. For the revised transcripts and interpretations of the Nasik cave inscriptions, see E. Senart, *Ep. Ind.*, Vol. VIII. p. 59 & ff.

P. 32. n. 17. For D. R. Bhandarkar who agrees in this conclusion, see *Jour. Bo. As. Soc.*, Vol. XXIII. pp. 69—71 and *Ind. Ant.*, 1918, pp. 152-153. For a different view, see R. D. Banerji, *Jour. R. As. Soc.*, 1917, p. 279 & ff. and H. C. Ray Chaudhuri, *Political History of Ancient India*, pp. 311—313.

Pp. 33-34. The correct form of the name Sakasena is Siri-Sâta,—D. R. Bhandarkar, *Ind. Ant.*, 1918, pp. 155-156. For another inscription of Gautamī Yajña-śrī-Śâtakarṇi, see G. Bühler, *Ep. Ind.*, Vol. I. p. 95 f., and N. G. Majumdar, *Jour. Beng. As. Soc.* (NS.), Vol. XVI. p. 328 & Pl. Two more Śâtavâhana inscriptions have been since published, one by Sten Konow, *Zeit. Deut. Morg. Ges.*, Vol. LXII. p. 592 and the other by V. S. Sukthankar, *Ep. Ind.*, Vol. XIV. p. 155.

Pp. 34-35. For the different views about the family of the princes who issued the coins found at Kolhāpur, see *Ind. Ant.*, 1920, p. 31 & ff.

P. 36 & n. 23. For the correct reading and interpretation of the coin, see E. J. Rapson, *Jour. R. As. Soc.*, 1905, p. 797 & ff.

P. 42 & ff. For the Kshatrapa rule in the Dekkan and the restoration of the Śâtavâhana empire set forth in Section VI., read also D. R. Bhandarkar's *Dekkan of the Śâtavâhana* in *Ind. Ant.*, 1918, pp. 69-78 and 149-156 ; and H. C. Ray Chaudhuri's *Political History of Ancient India*, p. 305 & ff.

P. 49 & n. 8. As regards Śâtakarṇi of the Girnar Inscription (*Ep. Ind.*, Vol. VIII. pp. 44, l. 12), see the various views set forth in *Jour. Bo. As. Soc.*, Vol. XXIII. p. 66 & ff.

P. 51 & ff. As to the Purāṇa texts relating to the Andhrabhṛitya dynasty, see F. E. Pargiter's *Dynasties of the Kali Age*, p. 35 & ff. For comments on the texts, see V. A. Smith and S. M. Edwardes' *Early History of India*, p. 230 & ff.

P. 64. In respect of the time when Śâlivâhana-Śaka came into vogue, see J. F. Fleet, *Ind. Ant.*, Vol. XII. p. 214 ff.

P. 68. For another view of the authorship and date of the Saptaśatî, see A. Weber's *Ueber das Saptaçatakam des Hāla*, pp. 2—4.

P. 70 & ff. For a further account of the religious, social and economic condition of Mahârâshṭra, see D. R. Bhandarkar, *Ind. Ant.*, 1919, p. 77 & ff.

Pp. 77—81. One powerful dynasty, that ruled over Mahârâshṭra between the extinction of the Andhrabhṛityas and the rise of the Chālukyas, is Kaṭachchūri, known later as Kalachuri. Three copper-plate grants of this family are known : (1) the Ābhōṇā Plates of Śaṅkaragaṇa dated K. 347 and published by K. B. Pathak, *Ep. Ind.*, Vol. IX. pp. 297-298 ; (2) the Vaḍnêr Plates of Buddharâja, dated K. 360 and published by Y. R. Gupte *Ibid.*, Vol. XII. p. 33 ff ; and (3) the Sarsavṇî Plates of the same king, dated K. 361 and published by F. Kielhorn, *Ibid.*, Vol. VI. pp. 297-299. It is this Buddharâja who was defeated by the Western Châlukya prince Maṅgalarâja (Maṅgalêśa) and is referred to in pp. 84-85 of the *Early History of the Dekkan.* The capital of this dynasty, however, was Mâhishmatî (*Ind. Ant.*, 1911, p. 20 ; *Arch. Surv. Ind., An. Rep.*, 1913-14, p. 214).

Pp. 82—104. For the epigraphic records connected with the Early Chālukyas of Badāmī, see Nos. 1—52 of F. Kielhorn's *List of Inscriptions of Southern India* (*Ep. Ind.*, Vol. VII. Appendix). Some of the inscriptions of this dynasty published thereafter are :

(1) Lakshmeshwar (Dhārwār Dist., Bombay Presidency) Pillar Inscription of the *Yuvarāja* Vikramāditya granting some constitution to the

burgesses of Perigere. Ed. by L. D. Barnett, *Ep. Ind.*, Vol. XIV. p. 190.

(2) Ś. 609.—Jejurī (Poona Dist., Bombay Presidency) Plates of Vinayāditya (9th regnal year). Ed. by D. R. Bhandarkar, *Ep. Ind.* Vol. XIX. p. 63.

(3) Ś. 617.—Pāṭoḍā (Punjab) Plates of Vinayāditya (14th regnal year). Noticed by D. R. Bhandarkar, *Ind. Ant.*, 1911, p. 240.

(4) Ś. 625.—Rāygaḍ (Kolaba Dist., Bombay Presidency) Plates of Vijayāditya (8th regnal year). Ed. by K. B. Pathak, *Ep. Ind.*, Vol. X. p. 15.

(5) Ś. 672.—Kendūr (Poona Dist., Bombay Presidency) Plates of Kīrtivarman (II.) (6th regnal year). Ed. by K. B. Pathak, *Ep. Ind.*, Vol. IX. p. 202.

P. 96. For a more detailed history of the Arab invasion see p. 20 & ff. of *the Gurjara-Pratihāras* by R. C. Majumdar, in *Jour. Dept. Letters* (Cal. Univ.), Vol. X.

P. 106 ff. For epigraphic records connected with the Rāshṭrakūṭas of Mānyakheṭa, see Nos. 53—107 of F. Kielhorn's *List of Inscriptions of Southern India*. Some of the inscriptions published thereafter are :

(1) Ś. 690.—Taḷegaon (Poona Dist., Bombay Presidency) Plates of Kṛishṇarāja (I.). Noticed by D. R. Bhandarkar, PRAS. WC., 1913, p. 54. Ed. by Sten Konow, *Ep. Ind.*, Vol. XIII. p. 279.

Mentions his son Prabhutuṅga Govinda (II.).

(2) Ś. 694.—Bhāṇḍak (Chanda Dist., C. P.) Plates of Kṛishṇarāja (I.). Ed. by V. S. Sukthankar, *Ep. Ind.*, Vol. XIV. p. 123.

(3) Ś. 697.—Pimparī (West Khandesh Dist., Bombay Presidency). Plates of Dhārāvarsha-Dhruvarāja. Ed. by K. B. Pathak, *Ep. Ind.*, Vol. X. p. 85.

(4) Ś. 701.—Dhulia (East Khandesh Dist., Bombay Presidency) spurious (?) Plates of Suvarṇavarsha Pratāpaśīla Karkarāja, son of Dhruvarāja,

younger brother of Prabhūtavarsha (-Govinda II.) to whose reign it refers itself.

(5) Ś. 715.—Daulatabad (Nizam's State) Plates of Samarāvaloka Śaṅkaragaṇa, son of Nanna, who was brother of Kṛishṇarāja (I) and son of Karkarāja. Charter issued with the consent of Kalivallabha-Narendradeva (Dhruva-Nirupama). Ed. by D. R. Bhandarkar, *Ep. Ind.*, Vol. IX. p. 195.

(6) Ś. 793.—Sanjān (Thana Dist., Bombay Presidency) Inscription of Amoghavarsha (I.). Ed. by D. R. Bhandarkar, *Ep. Ind.*, Vol. XVIII. p. 243 & ff.

(7) Ś. 818.—Kuṇimellihaḷḷi (Dhārwār Dist., Bombay Presidency). Inscription of the time of Mahāsāmantādhipati Karṇa-vallaha who seems to be the Rāshṭrakūṭa Kṛishṇa II.-Akālavarsha. Ed. by L. D. Barnett, *Ep. Ind.*, Vol. XVI. p. 277 ff.

(8) Ś. 851.—Kaḷas (Dhārwār Dist., Bombay Presidency) Inscription of the time of the Rashṭrakūṭa king Govinda IV. Ed. by L. D. Barnett, *Ep. Ind.*, Vol. XIII. p. 326 ff.

(9) Ś. 868.—Tuppaḍ-kurhatti (Dhārwār Dist., Bombay Presidency) Inscription of the time of the Rāshṭrakūṭa Akālavarsha-Kṛishṇa III. Ed. by L. D. Barnett, *Ep. Ind.*, Vol. XIV. p. 364 ff.

(10) Ś. 868.—Kyāsanūr (Dhārwār Dist., Bombay Presidency) Inscription of the time of king Kannara (the Rāshṭrakūṭa Kṛishṇa III.—Akālavarsha). Ed. by L. D. Barnett, *Ep. Ind.*, Vol. XVI. p. 280 ff.

(11) Kyāsanūr (Dhārwār Dist., Bombay Presidency) Inscription of the time of Kandaravallabha, *i.e.* Kannara or Kṛishṇa III. Ed. by L. D. Barnett, *Ep. Ind.*, Vol. XVI. p. 283.

(12) Ś. 884.—Devīhosūr (Dhārwār Dist., Bombay Presidency) Inscription of the time of Akālavarsha Kannara-deva (the Rāshṭrakūṭa Kṛishṇa III.). Ed. by L. D. Barnett, *Ep. Ind.*, Vol. XVI. p. 285-286.

(13) Kyāsanūr (Dhārwār Dist., Bombay Presi-

dency) Inscription of the time of Nityavarsha-Amoghavarsha who is the same as Nityavarsha-Khoṭṭiga. Ed. by L. D. Barnett, *Ep. Ind.*, Vol. XVI. p. 284-285.

P. 112 & n. 19. For a detailed discussion and historical importance of the passage from the Jaina Harivaṃśa, see J. F. Fleet, *Ep. Ind.*, Vol. VI. p. 195 and ff.

P. 136. For the epigraphic records connected with the Later Chālukyas of Kalyāṇī, see Nos. 140-274 of F. Kielhorn's *List of Inscriptions of Southern India.* Some of the inscriptions of this dynasty published thereafter are :

(1) Ś. 929.—Hoṭṭūr (Dhārwār Dist., Bombay Presidency) Inscription of the time of Akaḷaṅkacharita-Iṛivabeḍaṅga Chālukya Satyāśraya. Ed. by. L. D. Barnett, *Ep. Ind.*, Vol. XVI. p. 74 ff.

(2) Ś. 393.—Sudi (Dhārwār Dist., Bombay Presidency) Inscription of the time of Tribhuvanamalla-deva, *i.e.* Chālukya Vikramāditya V. Ed. by L. D. Barnett, *Ep. Ind.*, Vol. XV. p. 75-77.

(3) Ś. 933.—Ālūr (Dhārwār Dist., Bombay Presidency) Inscription of the time of Tribhuvanamalla-Vikramāditya V. Ed. by L. D. Barnett, *Ep. Ind.*, Vol. XVI. p. 27 ff.

(4) Ś. 950.—Kuḷēnūr (Dhārwār Dist., Bombay Presidency) Inscription of the time of Jagadekamalla-Jayasiṁha (II.). Ed. by L. D. Barnett, *Ep. Ind.*, Vol. XV. p. 329 ff.

(5) Ś. 963.—Śirūr (Dhārwār Dist., Bombay Presidency) Inscription of the time of Jagadekamalla *i.e.* Jayasiṁha II. Ed. by L. D. Barnett, *Ep. Ind.*, Vol. XV. pp. 334-335.

(6) Lakshmeshwar (Dhārwār Dist., Bombay Presidency) Inscription of the time of Jagadekamalla II. Ed. by L. D. Barnett, *Ep. Ind.*, Vol. XVI. p. 44 ff.

(7) Ś. 959.—Hoṭṭūr (Dhārwār Dist., Bombay Presidency) Inscription of the time of Jayasiṁha (II) Jagadekamalla. Ed. by L. D. Barnett, *Ep. Ind.*, Vol. XVI. p. 75 ff.

(8) Ś. 960.—Hulgūr (Dhārwār Dist., Bombay Presidency) Inscription of the time of Jagadekamalla (Jayasiṁha II.) and the Yādava Kanhara. Ed. by L.D. Barnett, *Ep. Ind.*, Vol. XVI. p. 332 ff.

(9) Yewūr (Gulbarga Dist., Hyderabad) Inscription of the time of the Western Chālukya king Jagadekamalla, *i.e.* Jayasiṁha II. Ed. by L. D. Barnett, *Ep. Ind.*, Vol. XII. p. 269.

(10) Miraj (Miraj State, Bombay Presidency) Inscription of the time of the Western Chālukya king Jayasiṁha II. Ed. by L. D. Barnett, *Ep. Ind.*, Vol. XII. p. 309 ff.

(11) Ś. 977.—Baṅkāpur (Dhārwār Dist., Bombay Presidency) Inscription of the time of Chālukya emperor Trailokyamalla-(Someśvara I.) and the Kadamba *Mahāmaṇḍaleśvara* Harikesari-deva. Ed. by L. D. Barnett, *Ep. Ind.*, Vol. XIII. p. 168 ff.

(12) Ś. 973.—Sudi (Dhārwār Dist., Bombay Presidency) Inscription of the time of Chālukya Trailokyamalla (Someśvara I). Ed. by L. D. Barnett, *Ep. Ind.*, Vol. XV. pp. 77-80.

(13) Ś. 976.—Sudi (Dhārwār Dist., Bombay Presidency) Inscription of the time of the Chālukya Trailokyamalla (Someśvara I.). Ed. by L. D. Barnett, *Ep. Ind.*, Vol. XV. pp. 80-83.

(14) Ś. 980.—Sudi (Dhārwār Dist., Bombay Presidency) Inscription of the time of Someśvara I. Ed. by L. D. Barnett, *Ep. Ind.*, Vol. XV. pp. 83-85.

(15) Ś. 981.—Sudi (Dhārwār Dist., Bombay Presidency) Inscription of the time of the Chālukya Trailokyamalla Someśvara I. Ed. by L. D. Barnett, *Ep. Ind.*, Vol. XV. pp. 85-94.

(16) Ś. 975.—Muḷgund (Dhārwār Dist., Bombay

Presidency) Inscription of the time of Trailokyamalla *i.e.* Someśvara I. Ed. by L. D. Barnett, *Ep. Ind.*, Vol. XVI. p. 53 ff.

(17) Ś. 974.—Nīralgi (Dhārwār Dist., Bombay Presidency) Inscription of the time of Trailokyamalla-Āhavamalla i.e. Sōmēśvara I. Ed. by L. D. Barnett, *Ep. Ind.*, Vol. XVI. p. 66 ff.

(18) Ś. 988.—Hoṭṭūr (Dhārwār Dist., Bombay Presidency) Inscription of the time of Trailokyamalla-Āhavamalla (Someśvara I.) and Mahāmaṇḍaleśvara Jemarasa. Ed. by L. D. Barnett, *Ep. Ind.*, Vol. XVI. p. 82.

(19) Tiḷvaḷḷi (Dhārwār Dist., Bombay Presidency) Inscription of the time of Trailokyamalla (Someśvara I.). Ed. by L. D. Barnett, *Ep. Ind.*, Vol. XVI. pp. 337-338.

(20) Ś. 966 and 1067.—Hūli (Beḷgaum Dist., Bombay Presidency) Inscription of the time of Āhavamalla (Someśvara I.) and Jagadekamalla (II.). Ed. by L. D. Barnett, *Ep. Ind.*, Vol. XVIII. pp. 172-3.

(21) Ś. 991 and 997.—Sudi (Dhārwār Dist., Bombay Presidency) Inscription of the time of Bhuvanaikamalla (Someśvara II.). Ed. by L. D. Barnett, *Ep. Ind.*, Vol. XV. pp. 94-96.

(22) Ś. 996.—Sudi (Dhārwār Dist., Bombay Presidency) Inscription of the time of Bhuvanaikamalla (Someśvara II.). Ed. by L. D. Barnett, *Ep. Ind.*, Vol. XV. pp. 96-100.

(23) Ś. 993 and 994.—Gāwarwāḍ (Dhārwār Dist., Bombay Presidency) Inscription of the time of Bhuvanaikamalla, i.e. Someśvara II. and Mahāmaṇḍaleśvara Lakshmarasa (Lakshma or Lakshmaṇa). Ed. by L. D. Barnett, *Ep. Ind.*, Vol. XV. p. 337 ff.

(24) Ś. 993 and 994.—Aṇṇīgeri (Dhārwār Dist., Inscription of the time of Someśvara II. Ed. by L. D. Barnett, *Ep. Ind.*, Vol. XV. pp. 347-348.

(25) Ś. 996-97.—Nīralgi (Dhārwār Dist., Bombay Presidency) Inscription of the time of the Chālukya king Bhuvanaikamalla (Someśvara II.). Ed. by L. D. Barnett, *Ep. Ind.*, Vol. XVI. p. 68 ff.

(26) Niḍaguṇḍi (Dhārwār Dist., Bombay Presidency) Inscription of the time of Western Chālukya king Tribhuvanamalla—(Vikramāditya VI) and the Kadamba prince Tailapa II. Ed. by L. D. Barnett, *Ep. Ind.*, Vol. XIV. p. 12.

(27) Iṭṭagi (Dhārwār Dist., Bombay Presidency) Inscription of the time of (Western Chālukya) Vikramāditya VI. Ed. by L. D. Barnett, *Ep. Ind.*, Vol. XIII. p. 36 ff.

(28) Narendra (Dhārwār Dist., Bombay Presidency) Inscription of the time of Chālukya king Vikramāditya VI. and the Kadamba *Mahāmaṇḍaleśvara* Jayakeśin II. Ed. by L. D. Barnett, *Ep. Ind.*, Vol. XIII. p. 298 ff.

(29) Mutgi (Bijāpur Dist., Bombay Presidency) Inscription of the time of (Western Chālukya) Tribhuvanamalla (i.e. Vikramāditya VI.). Ed. by L. D. Barnett, *Ep. Ind.*, Vol. XV. p. 25 ff.

(30) Ś. 1006.—Sudi (Dhārwār Dist., Bombay Presidency) Inscription of the time of Tribhuvanamalla-vallabha (Vikramāditya VI.). Ed. by L. D. Barnett, *Ep. Ind.*, Vol. XV. pp. 100-103.

(31) Ś. 1006.—Sudi (Dhārwār Dist., Bombay Presidency) Inscription of the time of Tribhuvanamalla-vallabha (Vikramāditya VI.). Ed. by L. D. Barnett, *Ep. Ind.*, Vol. XV. pp. 103-105.

(32) Sudi (Dhārwār Dist., Bombay Presidency) Inscription of the time of Vikramāditya VI. Ed. by L. D. Barnett, *Ep. Ind.*, Vol. XV. pp. 105 ff.

Of the 38th year of his reign.

(33) Gadag (Dhārwār Dist., Bombay Presidency) Inscription of the time of the Chālukya Vikramāditya

VI. Ed. by L. D. Barnett, *Ep. Ind.*, Vol. XV. p. 348 ff.

Of the 23rd year of his reign.

(34) Lakshmeshwar (Dhārwār Dist., Bombay Presidency) Inscription of the time of Tribhuvanamalla i.e. Vikramāditya VI. Ed. by L. D. Barnett, *Ep. Ind.*, Vol. XVI. pp. 31 ff.

Of the 27th year of his reign.

(35) Lakshmeshwar (Dhārwār Dist., Bombay Presidency) Inscription of the time of Vikramāditya VI. and his feudatory Kadamba Taila III. Ed. by L. D. Barnett, *Ep. Ind.*, Vol. XVI. p. 35 ff.

(36) Lakshmeshwar (Dhārwār Dist., Bombay Presidency) Inscription of the time of Tribhuvanamalla or Vikramāditya VI. Ed. by L. D. Barnett, *Ep. Ind.*, Vol. XVI. p. 58 ff.

(37) Ś. 999.—Hulgūr (Dhārwār Dist., Bombay Presidency) Inscription of the time of Tribhuvanamalla Vikramāditya VI. Ed. by L. D. Barnett, *Ep. Ind.*, Vol. XVI. p. 329 ff.

(38) Hūli (Beḷgaum Dist., Bombay Presidency) Inscription of the time of Tribhuvanamalla (Vikramāditya VI.). Ed. by L. D. Barnett, *Ep. Ind.*, Vol. XVIII. p. 178 ff.

Of the 7th year of his reign.

(39) Ś. 1019.—Hūli (Beḷgaum Dist., Bombay Presidency) Inscription of the time of Tribhuvanamalla (Vikramāditya VI). Ed. by L. D. Barnett, *Ep. Ind.*, Vol. XVIII. p. 182 ff.

(40) Hūli (Beḷgaum Dist., Bombay Presidency) Inscription of the time of Tribhuvanamalla (Vikramāditya VI.). Ed. by L. D. Barnett, *Ep. Ind.*, Vol. XVIII. p. 189.

Of the 29th year of his reign.

(41) Ś. 1029.—Hūli (Beḷgaum Dist., Bombay Presidency) Inscription of the time of Tribhuvana-

malladeva i.e. Vikramāditya VI. Ed. by L. D. Barnett, *Ep. Ind.*, Vol. XVIII. p. 196.

(42) Hūli (Beḷgaum Dist., Bombay Presidency) Inscription of the time of Vikramāditya VI. Ed. by L. D. Barnett, *Ep. Ind.*, Vol. XVIII. pp. 199-201.

Of the 32nd year of his reign.

(43) Hūli (Beḷgaum Dist., Bombay Presidency) Inscription of the time of Tribhuvanamalladeva (Vikramāditya VI.). Ed. by L. D. Barnett, *Ep. Ind.*, Vol. XVIII. pp. 201-205.

(44) Nīlgunda (Bellary Dist., Madras Presidency) Inscription of the time of Western Chālukya king Tribhuvanamalla-Vikramāditya VI. Ed. by L. D. Barnett, *Ep. Ind.*, Vol. XII. pp. 150-155.

(45) Yēwūr (Gulbarga Dist., Hyderabad) Inscription of the time of Western Chālukya king Vikramāditya VI. Ed. by L. D. Barnett, *Ep. Ind.*, Vol. XII. p. 274 ff.

(46) Yēwūr (Gulbarga Dist., Hyderabad) Inscription of the time of the Western Chālukya king Tribhuvanamalla-Vikramāditya VI. Ed. by L. D. Barnett, *Ep. Ind.*, Vol. XII. p. 329 ff.

(47) Yēwūr (Gulbarga Dist., Hyderabad) Inscription of the time of the Western Chālukya king Tribhuvanamalla-Vikramāditya VI. Ed. by L. D. Barnett, *Ep. Ind.*, Vol. XII. p. 332.

(48) Yēwūr (Gulbarga Dist., Hyderabad) Inscription of the time of Vikramāditya VI. Ed. by L. D. Barnett, *Ep. Ind.*, Vol. XII. p. 334.

(49) Ś. 1095 and 1103.—Kurgod (Bellary Dist., Madras Presidency) Inscription of the Western Chālukya Someśvara [IV] Tribhuvanamalla. Ed. by L. D. Barnett, *Ep. Ind.*, Vol. XIV. p. 265 ff.

P. 160 & ff. For the epigraphic records connected with the Kalachuris of Kalyāṇa, see Nos. 275-300 of F. Kielhorn's *List of Inscriptions of Southern India*. Some of the inscriptions of this dynasty published thereafter are:

THE KALACHURIS.

(1) Hūli (Beḷgaum Dist., Bombay Presidency) Inscription of the time of Kalachurya king Tribhuvanamalladeva (Bijjala). Ed. by L. D. Barnett, *Ep. Ind.*, Vol. XVIII. pp. 208-212.

(2) Ś. 1084.—Hūli (Beḷgaum Dist., Bombay Presidency) Inscription of the time of king Bijjala. Ed. by L. D. Barnett, *Ep. Ind.*, Vol. XVIII. p. 212 ff.

(3) Yēwūr (Gulbarga Dist., Hyderabad) Inscription of the time of the Kalachurya king Rāyamurāri-Sovideva. Ed. by L. D. Barnett, *Ep. Ind.*, Vol. XII. p. 336.

(4) Iṭṭagi (Dhārwār Dist., Bombay Presidency) Inscription of the time of the Kalachurya king Saṅkamadeva. Ed. by L. D. Barnett, *Ep. Ind.*, Vol. XIII. p. 59 ff.

(5) Sudi (Dhārwār Dist., Bombay Presidency) Inscription of the time of the Kalachurya Saṅkama. Ed. by L. D. Barnett, *Ep. Ind.*, Vol. XV. p. 109 ff.

(6) Yēwūr (Gulbarga Dist., Hyderabad) Inscription of the time of the Kalachurya king Saṅkamadeva. Ed. by L. D. Barnett, *Ep. Ind.*, Vol. XII. pp. 338-339.

(7) Mutgi (Bāgewādi taluk of Bijāpur) Inscription of the time of Kalachurya Bhillama. Ed. by L. D. Barnett, *Ep. Ind.*, Vol. XV. p. 32 ff.

P. 205 & n. 60. Jñānadeva was a descendant (*suta*) in the pupil's line, that is, really a disciple of Nivṛittinātha. At the conclusion of his work he says that Nivṛittinātha was a pupil of Gahinīnātha and that the latter was a pupil of Gorakshanātha who himself was a pupil of Matsyendranātha. If Jñānadeva's date was Śaka 1212 (=1290 A.D.), Gorakshanātha has to be placed about the beginning of the 13th century A.D.